THE ENGLISH GENTLEMAN

BY THE SAME AUTHOR

As Philip Woodruff

NOVELS
Call the Next Witness
The Wild Sweet Witch
The Island of Chamba

SHORT STORIES
Whatever Dies

FOR CHILDREN
The Sword of Northumbria
Hernshaw Castle

HISTORICAL NOVEL
Colonel of Dragoons

HISTORY
The Men Who Ruled India:
  Volume 1 The Founders
  Volume 2 The Guardians

As Philip Mason

ABOUT RACE
An Essay on Racial Tension
Christianity and Race

The Birth of a Dilemma:
  The Conquest and Settlement
  of Rhodesia
Year of Decision:
  Rhodesia and Nyasaland 1960
Common Sense about Race
Prospero's Magic:
  Thoughts on Class and Race
Patterns of Dominance
Race Relations
Man, Race and Darwin (editor)
India and Ceylon:
  Unity and Diversity (editor)

HISTORY
A Matter of Honour:
  An Account of the Indian Army

BIOGRAPHY
Kipling: The Glass, the Shadow
  and the Fire

RELIGION
The Dove in Harness

AUTOBIOGRAPHY
A Shaft of Sunlight

HISTORICAL NOVEL
Skinner of Skinner's Horse

THE ENGLISH GENTLEMAN

The Rise and Fall of an Ideal

Philip Mason

William Morrow and Company, Inc
New York 1982

First published in Great Britain in 1982
by André Deutsch Limited
105 Great Russell Street,
London WC1B 3LJ

First published in the USA in 1982 by
William Morrow and Company, Inc.
105 Madison Avenue, New York, New York 10016

Produced, edited and designed by
Shuckburgh Reynolds Limited
8 Northumberland Place, London W2 5BS

Designer: Tim Higgins
Picture research: Anne-Marie Ehrlich

Library of Congress Catalog Card Number: 82-47651
ISBN: 0-688-01400-3

Typesetting by SX Composing Limited, Rayleigh, Essex
Printed and bound in Spain by Printer Industria Grafica, Barcelona
DLB 5078-1982

First Edition

1 2 3 4 5 6 7 8 9 10

For Mark and Verity

CONTENTS

Acknowledgments 8

Introduction 9

1 Behaving Like a Gentleman 15

2 The Heritage of the Past 21

3 The Gentleman in Chaucer 34

4 The Courtier 50

5 Court and Country 61

6 Elegance and Principle 70

7 The Gentleman as Sportsman 81

8 Colonel Newcome 106

9 The Voice of the Mob 119

10 A Romantic Realist 131

11 Almost a Religion 144

12 Factories for Gentlemen 161

13 Evan Harrington 175

14 Christian and Gentleman 181

15 Through Polish Eyes 188

16 The Edwardians 196

17 Over Half the Globe 207

18 A High Ideal 217

19 *Epilogue:* The Gentleman Today 227

Notes on Books 233

Index 237

ACKNOWLEDGEMENTS

Numerals refer to page numbers (abbreviations: L: left; R: right; T: top; B: bottom).

Grateful acknowledgement is made to the following for illustrations reproduced in this book:

Arthur Ackermann & Son 156–7
BBC Hulton Picture Library 151, 167, 171T, 171B, 183, 186, 198, 200, 208, 211, 212T, 213T, 214, 220
Bibliothèque Nationale, Paris 41
British Library/Ray Gardner 24, 31T, 32, 42, 43BL, 51BL, 51BR, 72TL, 72TR, 72B, 73, 107, 109, 111L, 111R, 112L, 112R, 113, 173, 202R
British Museum 89B
Cavalry Club 160
Constable & Co 30TL, 30TR, 30B
E.T.Archive 43BR, 44, 47T, 47B, 149, 212B
E.T.Archive/Tate Gallery 46
E.T.Archive/Eton College 159
Eton College 156
Giraudon 43T, 51T
Robert Harding/British Library 45

London Library/Eileen Tweedy 75L, 75R, 78L, 78R, 79, 100, 101, 102, 103L, 103R, 123, 126, 129, 133, 134, 138, 139, 141, 146, 164L, 164R, 165T, 165B, 166, 176, 179TL, 179TR, 179B
Mander and Mitcheson 202L
Mansell Collection 23, 31B, 53, 63, 65R, 86, 89T, 93, 94, 97, 150, 153T, 153B, 154T, 154B, 155T, 155B, 168, 172T, 172B, 197, 199B, 204, 205, 209T, 209B, 213B, 215, back jacket
National Gallery, London 28
National Portrait Gallery 58TL, 58TR, 58B, 158
Salvation Army 199T
Sotheby's Belgravia 48
Sotheby Parke Bernet 65L
Tate Gallery front jacket
Victoria and Albert Museum 66, 68, 95

INTRODUCTION

IN THE YEARS between the death of Queen Victoria and the outbreak of war in 1914, England seemed to most foreign observers hopelessly divided and to some on the brink of revolution. There was extreme wealth and luxury on the one hand and widespread poverty on the other; Ireland was on the point of civil war; strikes were upsetting the daily life of the comfortable and filling the newspapers. There was bitter controversy about votes for women and militant suffragettes; about the future of the House of Lords; about death duties designed to end the hereditary ownership of land.

But in August 1914 domestic quarrels disappeared and the nation was united as never before. Why was this? No doubt there were many reasons but one was the surprising degree to which the English people still accepted inequality as a necessary part of life and on the whole admired those who ruled them. England was still an oligarchy and most of the ruling class would have been described as "gentlemen". What was meant by this word is not at all easy to explain. It had different meanings in different mouths and the same person would use it in different senses. But it did stand for an ideal of conduct that was widely admired and this was one of the ties that unified the nation.

One reason why the idea of the gentleman was so widely accepted was that no one was quite sure who was a gentleman and who was not. There was no closed caste and a great many people used the term in such a way that it did not exclude themselves – or at least what they hoped their sons might become. There was thus a wide range of professional people and of those who would now be called white collar workers who identified themselves with the upper classes in the sense that they hoped to join their ranks. The typical middle-class Englishman was a snob; he loved a lord. He did not think he could become a lord but he did think his son might become a gentleman. He would very likely have put himself in a slightly higher social bracket than a detached observer might have thought fitting and for that reason he felt he was on the same *side* as the ruling classes. But there was also something quite different, a vast body of costermongers, jockeys, soldiers, flower-girls, newspaper boys, domestic servants, with no thought of rising in the world themselves, who admired the qualities they believed gentlemen possessed. According to Marx, they ought to have been full of rancour and immersed in the class war, but a great many of them were not. They cheered whenever they saw the Earl of Lonsdale, the embodiment of ostentatious unearned wealth.

At the beginning of this century, then, the concept of the gentleman was an element in the unity of the nation. This was partly because of its vagueness and ambiguity, but partly also because in the reign of Queen Victoria there had been an ideal of conduct which was generally thought to be proper for a gentleman, and which really was in many ways admirable.

The purpose of this book is to consider the various meanings people have attached to this word at different periods, and to observe some of the effects it has had on their behaviour. It is therefore less what the gentleman actually did than what it was thought proper for him to do that concerns me and it is more from literature than from life that I shall draw examples.

Since at least the time of Chaucer, there has been a distinction between the social meaning of the word and the moral; social rank and the behaviour proper to that rank don't always coincide, and no one was more aware of this than Chaucer. But his characters were not always so clear in their minds as he was. It is from this confusion that there arises a subtle counterpoint between what is thought proper and what actually happens that is the essence of comedy.

There is nothing simple about this interplay of meanings and relationships and it is further complicated by taking place against the backcloth of a paradox that at first sight is rather surprising. Until the French Revolution, English people took it for granted that social inequality was a fact of life, but in practice they often behaved as though all men were sons of Adam. After the French Revolution – when a nation founded on sharp social distinction proclaimed equality as its motto – the reverse was the case; the English upper classes became more and more uneasily aware that they were only human but in practice more and more inclined to behave as though the lower classes were not.

I first became aware of this paradox some years ago when I was trying to get the feeling of life in the reign of Queen Anne. I spent some time reading a collection of popular songs called: *D'Urfey's Pills to Purge Melancholy*. Among these were some verses about a young man in love with a girl he called Aminta. One night at an inn he slept in the next bedroom to Aminta and her maid Molly; the partition was thin and he could hear all that they said. Aminta and Molly were sharing the same bed and they argued about who should first use the chamber-pot. It is a trivial song, its coarseness unredeemed by wit, but it stuck in my memory because it suggested a society so very different from the Edwardian England in which I was brought up. Two hundred years after Queen Anne it would have been much less common for a lady to travel with a maid, but, if she did, she would certainly not have shared a bed with her, much less a chamber pot. Aminta and Molly knew that they were both human and performed the same physical functions. Nonetheless, they believed that in some undefined way they were *different* and Aminta was so sure about the difference that she did not bother to assert it. But Aminta's successor two hundred years later was not so sure. Equality was in the air; she had to assert her superiority by every means available.

Changes in opinion in such matters as this are gradual. Even in Paris, things did not change overnight. Philosophers had been talking about liberty and equality for a century before 1789; what happened in Paris did not immediately change attitudes in the remoter provinces and affected behaviour in England even more slowly and even then by reaction rather than directly. Still, broadly speaking, 1789 was the date when equality was loudly proclaimed in France; from that moment on, the upper classes in England could not forget it; they were on the defensive. They insisted more and more on social distinctions while step by step they conceded votes to wider and wider circles and abandoned such bastions of privilege as the Combination Acts and the Corn Laws. Both measures had defended the squires and the farmers; their repeal began the transfer of power to the towns, to industry and ultimately to the industrial labourer.

The movement of power was slow but on the whole consistent. The tide was running the same way throughout the whole period from 1789 to 1914. But on the surface of the water, in social behaviour, there was a counter-current, a movement the other way, as though the wind blew against the tide, an insistence on social difference that became more and more extreme as step by step the privileged gave way in the battle for power. Social difference was never so great as at the time of the Liberal government of 1906. To many of the upper and middle classes the measures of that government, and in particular Lloyd George's budgets, seemed to mark the end of an age – as indeed they did – and the beginning of an end to inequality and privilege. But the taste of the day showed an astonishing nostalgia for aristocratic rule. In provincial theatres and in popular novels, the heroes of romantic comedy, of bedroom farce and of stark adventure, were all likely to be young men of independent means and of no profession, often the younger sons of peers. The line runs from Rudolf Rassendyll of *The Prisoner of Zenda* and Sir Percy Blakeney of *The Scarlet Pimpernel* to Lord Peter Wimsey the amateur detective. These were popular heroes. Many a boy, as he laid his head on the pillow at bedtime, dozed off in a fantasy in which he played such a part as one of theirs. England seemed to be a nation of people who wanted to be gentlemen.

In France, it had once been quite clear what that word "gentleman" meant. About one person in seven of the population was "noble". It was a

legal status that carried legal privileges. But the French found the existence
of a separate privileged class intolerable and cut off the heads of its more
obstinate members. In England, there was never any such clear-cut distinction and by the nineteenth century the term "gentleman" had become
extraordinarily elastic; it meant very different things to different people. To
some it meant "anyone as good as I am or better". To others it still meant
some association with the ownership of land. But to everyone it also meant a
standard of conduct, a standard to which the best born did not always rise
and which even the humblest might sometimes display. The moral term, like
the social, did not always mean the same thing to everyone who used it and
yet somehow it did stand for something. And that one English word was used
in many other languages to express something peculiarly English.

"Gentleman" is not a fashionable word today. Indeed, it can hardly be
used without apology and is sometimes used with a sneer. Yet for most of the
19th century and until the Second World War, it provided the English with
a second religion, one less demanding than Christianity. It influenced their
politics. It influenced their system of education; it made them endow new
public schools and raise the status of old grammar schools. It inspired the
lesser landed gentry as well as the professional and middle classes to make
great sacrifices to give their children an upbringing of which the object was
to make them ladies and gentlemen, even if only a few also became scholars.

It was in the 19th century that the concept came to be so all-embracing
and so demanding and took on with much greater strength its moral overtones. But it had a much older pedigree, running back to Chaucer and
before. The Victorians did not invent it, but they found it useful and developed
it – not consciously, but rather as a sea-anemone will adopt a new source of
food and adapt its digestive system to deal with it. The Victorians, though
they were hardly aware of it, needed an imperial class, men who were
accustomed to give orders and to see they were obeyed, and to do this with
the minimum use of force, and with a consideration for the governed that
would inspire a minimum of resentment.

The Victorians needed this imperial class for the Empire but also at home.
Their need was for men resembling those pictured by Plato as the ideal
guardians of the state. But Plato's guardians would have been altogether too
virtuous and too inhuman. They would have aroused jealousy and dislike.
The Victorian gentleman-ruler had to include other elements, the sporting
and pugnacious, for one thing, which attracted the affection of the ordinary
people. But he also needed something that would distinguish him from the
mob. This the Victorians found ready-made in Chaucer's concept of *gentillesse*, a constellation of moral qualities which ought to go with gentle birth –
but doesn't always. Among these were courtesy to women, and, more than
courtesy, some idealization of women; also, generosity, openheartedness,
magnanimity. The Victorians added the requirement that the gentleman

must be *responsible*; he must fulfil his obligations and live up to his own standards. He should accept and exercise leadership.

The Victorians inherited the idea of the gentleman. They added to it, they developed it; they set up factories for gentlemen in their public schools. There must also be ladies as brides for the imperial class, so they set up public schools for ladies as well. Since boys were taught to be gentlemen and girls to be ladies at separate, and carefully segregated, establishments, and since the needs of the imperial class demanded that men should not marry until they were at least thirty, it is not surprising that the rest of the world sometimes thought that the English were a little odd about sex.

It was a remarkable achievement of the Victorian upper classes, not only to avoid revolution for a century and a quarter and to head a united nation in 1914, but also to rule a world-wide empire with a minimum use of force. It was done by refreshing their ranks by continual recruitment, creaming off the able and discontented from merchants, clerks and even artisans and at the same time persuading themselves, as well as the rest of the world, that there were things no gentleman would do and that there was a special moral excellence about what they did do. The whole edifice stood on this foundation, the concept of the gentleman.

It was the more remarkable because few of them understood how it was done. And it was based on a paradox they did not understand. Molly and Aminta were getting further and further apart, understanding each other less and less, pretending not to share the same physical characteristics, but politicians were talking about democracy and equality. Hardly anyone would have openly argued that there was some deep inherent difference between people who belonged to different classes, yet many people behaved as though there was; what is more, as though contact with a lower class might convey moral pollution. In the reign of Queen Anne, everyone had believed there was a difference but they had taken it for granted and disregarded it.

In the Victorian period, there was a good deal of discussion of what made a gentleman, and four distinct types emerged. There was the officer and gentleman; there was the scholar and gentleman; there was the Christian gentleman. There was also the gentleman sportsman. Any definition tends to emphasise one and ignore the others. None of them quite explains the gentleman's hold on popular imagination and they usually ignore the counterpoint between the social and the moral.

I have tried to put together some illustrations of the way people have thought and written about this subject, a series of vignettes. I repeat; the book is a series of illustrations. It is not a comprehensive treatise. It would be possible to write a far more laborious work that included much more but was much less readable. The desire to be a gentleman seems to me to run through and illuminate English history from the time of Chaucer until the First

World War, after which it began to die, at least as a social force. It would be impossible, in a single volume of a reasonable size, to deal thoroughly with every aspect of the subject and to cover every period. And that would not be the kind of book I want to write. My purpose is to stimulate and entertain rather than to instruct; to suggest lines of thought rather than to reach conclusions.

I shall not therefore regard it as reasonable criticism if I am told that I have not referred to this author or that. Of course I know that I have left out hundreds. I have usually drawn on those of whom I have most knowledge and whom everybody else knows too. A writer who made a name for himself in his life-time must be taken to represent to some extent the views of his readers and that is one reason why Dickens cannot be left out.

There are several reasons for choosing the examples from literature rather than from life. The first is that a good deal of the behaviour of a gentleman is unconscious and, even if he knows that it is because he is a gentleman that he is acting as he does, he is forbidden to say so. Memoirs and autobiographies therefore don't always present the direct illustrations I need, while in a novel the author can comment and tell one why a character behaves as he does. Again, this is a book about an idea and a novelist must express ideas which awaken a response in his readers. He is representative. Again, an event or a saying in a novel may make a point better than pages of explanation. But the main reason is quite simple and altogether personal. This book was written for pleasure, my own pleasure and, I hope, that of any readers who may have similar tastes. And I find I read more 19th-century novels than memoirs. Characters in Trollope are utterly alive to me, more real and more alive than almost any public figure.

The use of novels as illustrations has sometimes involved me in giving an account of the context, because no reader can be expected to remember exactly the circumstances of a book he may not have read recently.

As I began work on this book, I came on a sentence in the introduction to G. K. Chesterton's *The Victorian Age in Literature*. He wrote: "It is rather reassuring than otherwise to realize that I am now doing something that nobody could do properly." That is exactly how I feel. There is hardly a book in the whole range of English literature or a character in English history who has not something to say somewhere about the idea of the gentleman. All one can hope is to throw some light into a few corners. I have chosen the examples that my memory throws up and every reader will think of other examples and perhaps of other aspects. But I hope that will not lessen the interest; for myself, I have immensely enjoyed work which has been a reason for reading old favourites again and also for exploring some areas of which I knew little. I can only hope that some of that enjoyment may reach some others.

1
BEHAVING LIKE A GENTLEMAN

Fulfilling Obligations

IN 1872, in the very heart of Queen Victoria's reign, there was published *Middlemarch*, a novel that explores the life of a small English country town and the families in the neighbourhood. It is perhaps an odd choice to illustrate the concept of the gentleman, because the whole novel is a protest, delicately and indirectly expressed, never exaggerated, against convention, against the enslavement of the human spirit to the love of property and to social distinctions felt to be artificial. The people the author most admires come from the very middle of the middle class – Caleb Garth, who manages other people's farms and advises them on building and drainage schemes and Susan Garth, his schoolmistress wife. And the author is a woman and a rebel against conventional marriage. But the evidence of a hostile witness may carry more weight than the eager testimony of a friend, and George Eliot is much too good an observer to let her satiric purpose spoil her drawing. She shows very clearly how important this concept was to the mid-Victorians and how imperceptibly people slid in conversation from using the term to mark social rank to indicating a standard of moral behaviour.[1] Let us listen for a moment to Sir James Chettam.

"I do wish people would behave like gentlemen," said the good baronet, feeling that this was a simple and comprehensive programme for social well-being.

But although he said "people", Sir James Chettam was thinking of one particular person, his close neighbour and his wife's uncle, Mr Brooke of Tipton. Now Mr Brooke was, in one sense of the word, as good a gentleman as Sir James; the Brookes were second only to the Chettams among the landed proprietors in the villages near Middlemarch. Search backward in their pedigree and "you would not find any yard-measuring or parcel-tying forefathers – anything lower than an admiral or a clergyman". Sir James would never have questioned Mr Brooke's right to describe himself as a gentleman in a legal document. But Mr Brooke was not behaving as Sir James thought a gentleman should.

Sir James "did not usually find it easy to give his reasons; it seemed to him strange that people should not know them without being told". He would certainly have hesitated to put into words the first of Mr Brooke's short-comings. He wanted to stand for Parliament and there was nothing in itself wrong in that; it was a perfectly proper ambition for a country gentleman – provided that he stood well with the county and had consistent opinions which everyone could understand. Sir James might even have forgiven him for standing as a Whig if he had fulfilled that proviso. But he did not.

He was held to have contracted a too rambling habit of mind. Mr. Brooke's con-clusions were as difficult to predict as the weather; it was only safe to say that he would act with benevolent intentions, and that he would spend as little money as possible in carrying them out.

On this count alone, it seemed likely that he would make a fool of himself by his Parliamentary venture. What made this more certain was that he failed to come up to Sir James's standards of behaviour in another respect, much more easily expressed in words. He was a bad landlord. He had taken into his own hands the management of his farms and he was both negligent and mean. The gates of the fields were dropping off the hinges and the rain dripped through farm-house roofs.

Here, then, in one phrase from one Victorian novel, lie some hints about the ideal of "the gentleman". He should live with a due sense of his position among his fellows, with some attention to his reputation, to all that is meant by honour, expecting neither more nor less than he deserved. He must have, in other words, some idea of who he is. He must behave with consistency and with a central integrity. Above all, he must fulfil his obligations to those who have obligations to him. Those were some aspects only of a composite ideal, a pattern of human excellence which was to influence not only the literature of the 19th century in England but the way that boys and girls were brought up, the relation between town and country, between rich and poor, between men and women.

Clearly, the word "gentleman" was used in two senses. It might be a social label, indicating some degree of distinction above the lowest rung of society. Even within that sense, and even within that one period, it carried very wide variations when used by different people, while the meaning attached to it changed as the century wore on. But there was a second meaning, also carrying many different shades of significance in different mouths and at different times, but always suggesting certain standards of behaviour.

In this second sense, it is almost as though there had grown up within the national consciousness a rival to the official religion of the country. It was as though a considerable part of the population, including many of its leaders, had said:

"Yes, of course we are Christians; that is our religion and we go to church

regularly. But as a code of conduct we need something not quite so demanding, something which does not ask us to give away one coat if we have two,
which will indeed permit us to have several coats, an evening tail-coat for
balls and a morning tail-coat for weddings, as well as a dinner-jacket and
hunting pink and a number of tweed suits in various shades. Let us be allowed
those coats, and a butler and a five-course dinner, but then we need some
standard of behaviour which will tell us when we have overstepped the line.
It would be embarrassing, to an Englishman, to say a man has failed to
behave as a Christian, perhaps because in that respect we have all failed.
But one can say without blushing that a man has failed to behave as a
gentleman."

Consideration for a Woman

SIR JAMES CHETTAM was a gentleman in both senses of the word, by social
position and by behaviour – even though on the second count his qualification was somewhat negative. He did nothing that a gentleman should not
do. But he was very clear in his mind about what was not suitable behaviour
and he expressed himself on the subject before long more damningly and even
more justly in condemnation of another of his neighbours.

Mr Casaubon was the squire as well as the Rector of nearby Lowick; he
had been presented to the living by his uncle, from whom he had later
inherited the whole property. He had a substantial income and having
moved into the Manor he kept a curate in the parsonage house to do the work
of the parish, while he devoted himself to his great work, the *Key to all
Mythologies*. It was laborious work; he collected volume upon volume of
notes. He was nearing fifty and no one had supposed he would marry; the
blood of cuttle-fish ran in his veins, said a neighbour. But Mr Casaubon
made up his mind that he needed a wife who could be a devoted, obedient
and adoring helper in his work – and he thought he had found one in Miss
Brooke, the niece of Mr Brooke of Tipton. She was only nineteen and as
innocent as she was beautiful and headstrong. Dorothea Brooke became
infatuated with the idea of devoting her life to the noble cause of sharing the
life-work of a learned man. It would be like marrying Pascal, she thought.

Alas! Dorothea became gradually aware that her husband's great work
would never be written. Mr Casaubon was one of those assiduous collectors
of notes who fears to embark on the actual writing, partly because he is
afraid of the judgment of others but also because he is doubtful of his own
ability. He was, in short, a bookish pedant, frightened of life; and as this came
home to Dorothea, on him there slowly dawned the realization that instead
of an unquestioning devotee he had married a woman who thought for
herself.

Casaubon began to fear that Dorothea shared his own distrust of his powers, a distrust he dared not acknowledge. He began to be jealous of her independence of outlook. He was already jealous, on much the same grounds, of Will Ladislaw, a young and penniless cousin whom he had felt it his duty to educate. Will, too, knew that the great work would never be written. It was bitter to Mr Casaubon that the two people nearest him had both seen through the pretence by which he lived. And he knew that both were interested in matters outside his own vision. There arose in him "a sort of jealousy which needs very little fire; it is hardly a passion but a blight bred in the cloudy damp despondency of uneasy egoism". The reader feels that a load is lifted when Casaubon is found dead in the yew walk. But shortly before his death he had added a codicil to his will; he had previously left all his property to his wife without condition; now he made a provision that the bequest should be cancelled if Dorothea should marry Will Ladislaw.

Sir James was outraged. "There never was a meaner, mor ungentlemanly, action. . . . The world will suppose that she gave him some reason and that is what makes it so abominable – coupling her name with this young fellow's." And, a little later, on Mr Brooke remarking that Ladislaw was a gentleman, Sir James said in irritation: "I am glad to hear it. . . . I am sure Casaubon was not." He was not thinking of social standing.

That makes one more essential element in the character of the gentleman in Queen Victoria's reign. He must be scrupulous to avoid compromising a lady. By the end of the century, this feeling was so strong that in a military mess it was forbidden even to mention the name of any lady. Yet not much more than two centuries before *Middlemarch*, things had been all the other way. Every young gentleman was *expected* to be a lover and every true lover would blazon abroad the name of his mistress. In the romances with which Don Quixote was so besotted, the young hero would carve the praise of his beloved on rocks and compel perfect strangers to acknowledge her merits. And Orlando, smitten with Rosalind, must write verses on her name and hang them on every bough.

All this had changed. The Victorian young man might be bursting with the desire to tell everyone about his love but it was the act of a cad to mention her name, and "mistress" no longer meant the chaste queen of his heart but someone with the latchkey to a flat and some claim on a man's purse. Something frank and generous had become furtive. How did this change come about?

Personal Integrity

BEFORE LEAVING *Middlemarch*, there are two more brief scenes to record. Will Ladislaw was left penniless by Casaubon's will. But it so happened (by a complicated series of coincidences which need not concern us) that there was a rich banker in Middlemarch, Mr Bulstrode, whose fortune was founded on money which had belonged to Will's grandmother. She had meant to leave it to Will's mother, who had run away from home, because she felt the family's wealth had been discreditably acquired. Bulstrode knew she was alive but concealed the fact, married the grandmother and got her fortune for himself. So he had a guilty secret. He was a devout man and his conscience was disturbed. He offered Will an allowance – enough to keep him afloat until he could earn money as an artist.

Will was a man of mercurial temper and he flared up.

"My unblemished honour," he said, "is important to me. It is important to me to have no stain on my birth and connexions. And now I find there is a stain which I can't help. My mother felt it and tried to keep as clear of it as she could, and so will I. You shall keep your ill-gotten money. . . . It ought to lie with a man's self that he is a gentleman. Good-night, sir."

No doubt the fact that he was penniless made Will the more touchy. But he was putting his finger on an aspect of "being a gentleman" with which Sir James would have agreed. Honour is essential to a gentleman, and for him honour means not only good name in the eyes of the world but respect for himself – integrity, wholeness, self-sufficiency. Money Will felt he ought to despise; it couldn't be essential, because he hadn't any and he felt himself a gentleman. The perfect gentleman doesn't count the change – but that of course is usually because he *has* money and doesn't need to. Will had none but he was confident of an intangible quality more important than money.

Shortly after Will had scornfully refused his money, Bulstrode went as a matter of course to a meeting about a question of public concern, the kind of thing in which he had long taken a lead in the town. He did not know that rumours about his guilty secret were abroad and, when he rose to give his opinion, one of his leading opponents, the town clerk, at once stood up in protest. There are acts, he said, which the law cannot visit; perhaps Mr Bulstrode had not been guilty of such acts, but scandalous allegations had been made against him and the speaker called on him either to deny those allegations or to withdraw from positions which could only have been allowed him "as a gentleman among gentlemen".

Hardly anyone at that meeting would have been counted a gentleman by Sir James Chettam. Most of them had "yard-measuring or parcel-tying forefathers"; Mr Brooke, in his electioneering days, had asked them to dinner but not their wives or daughters, who would hardly have been suitable company for his nieces. But they had a standard of conduct to appeal to – and for Bulstrode, who was still unable to utter a direct lie and deny the rumours, the challenge was so shattering that he had to be helped from the room.

The two meanings then were interlocking. If you failed to observe the moral standards you might be excluded from the social class. Both meanings were complex and included many aspects; both were elastic and did not mean the same to everyone. This brief look at one Victorian novel has provided examples of men who failed to live up to what was felt proper for a gentleman, who must live consistently and intelligibly, with self-respect, performing his dues; who must show respect and consideration for women; must be independent and upright, of unblemished reputation. There are many more elements in the character of the Victorian gentleman to be brought to light, some of which, such as courage, he shared with other ideal types in other parts of the world. But where did he come from? The Victorians inherited a concept which they modified. What was his pedigree? *Middlemarch* has given us a preliminary impression. Let us unravel some strains in his history before we look at other aspects of the gentleman in his full bloom.

2
THE HERITAGE
OF THE PAST

Plato's Guardians

A RULING CLASS has usually established itself by force at some stage of its past and it is therefore not surprising that it should admire such qualities as courage and skill at arms. Its members have usually added other virtues which they have classed as "noble" and which they felt were especially *theirs*. Greeks, Rajputs, Maoris, have felt that courage, generosity and hospitality were qualities a king, a chief or a leader should display. But their ideas about behaviour to women have been very different from the Victorians and while some thought it perfectly proper for a chief or leader to recite the virtues of his ancestors and the achievements of himself, to the Victorian gentleman boasting was the mark of an outsider.

We are trying to tease out some strands in the Victorian idea of the gentleman and have already made a broad distinction between the social implications of the word and the moral. But the meanings interact and in what the Victorians inherited from the past there is not only an element going back to the Norman conquest and the feudal tenure of land but ideas common to many other peoples and going still further back into the past.

One strong influence was the Greek. Greek and Latin were the backbone of Victorian education and the Greek view of life was a model for many of the Victorians. And Plato has described at length the ideal guardians, the men he would choose to defend the state in war when they are young and from whom, when they are older, he would choose the wisest to act as magistrates, rulers and law-givers. They must be swift and strong, brave and high-spirited, dangerous to their enemies but gentle to their friends. They must be trained in body and mind, taught not only to handle their weapons and control troops in the field but to admire what is beautiful and to display in everything they do a sense of harmony and proportion. This training in a sense of proportion will make them virtuous and ensure that they do not try to overturn the state and become a danger to it.

Plato went on later to ideas that many Greeks would have found surprising, but, so far, he was stating what would have been widely accepted by most Athenians; the ideal for a man of good birth and education was that he should be beautiful and good, keeping a balance between body and mind and between what Plato calls the high-spirited elements in man, such as courage and ambition, and on the other hand the desire for knowledge and the admiration of beauty.

To this the Romans, in the high days of the Republic, added a stern admiration for duty and something they called *gravitas*, dignity, seriousness, the rejection of the trivial. They also felt it proper for a well-born Roman to despise personal power and to return, after holding high office, to a simple life on his country estate – a feeling that was also important to the English. The Roman combination of soldier and senator as well as the Greek harmony of athlete, scholar and artist contributed to the ideal of noble behaviour common at one time to most of Europe. The English picture of a gentleman came to differ in various ways from the European, but that strand from Greece and Rome was common to both and one of the strongest in the English ideal.

The English ideal grew away from the continental partly because of the social structure, and it is time to glance at that. But first I must be permitted a digression. It is the upper class who have written down the language. Until recently, they have taken it for granted that inequality is inevitable in human affairs. They have generally tried to console themselves for the burden of their comforts by believing that they have a monopoly of good behaviour. They *deserve* to be comfortable – they feel – because of their virtues and exertions. Words like churl and villain, which once denoted a social status, have come to carry offensive meanings, while "gentleman" has still a ring of commendation. No doubt churls *were* usually more churlish and less generous than gentlemen; they had less to be generous with. Even in French, *gentil*, which once meant nobly born, now means "considerate to others" or "civilized", while *vilain* means cheap or thoroughly bad. In conversation in Urdu, the common language of Northern India, the Arabic word *sharif*, which originally meant "noble" or "exalted" and was used of the head of a clan or of the Holy Qu'ran, has come to mean almost exactly what the French mean by *gentil*. But perhaps if the churls and villains had written the books, "gentle" and *gentil* might have meant "cruel" or "callous", indifferent to the sufferings of the poor, while "villainous" might have meant "faithful to one's friends".

There is a postscript to that digression. I asked an Afrikaner if there was a word in Afrikaans which would convey the meaning of the English expression "behaving like a gentleman". He reflected. "No," he said. "We should have to use the English word." But he thought again. "I'm bound to say," he went on, "that we should be far more likely to say: 'behaving like a white man'."

The custom of appropriating to one's own group the qualities one admires is not dead.

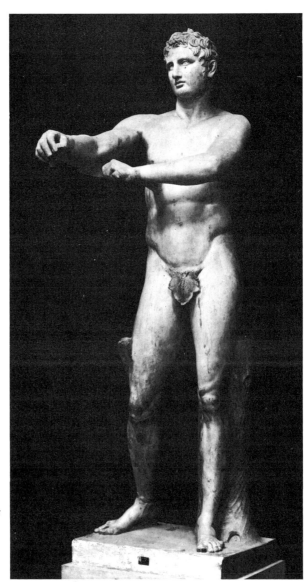

Apoxyomenos, by Lisippos. The Greek word for a gentleman was καλος κἀγαθός which means literally and exactly "beautiful and good". As in English public schools, cleverness need not come into the recipe.

The Degree or Mystery of a Gentleman

No DOUBT the people of England nine hundred years ago were conscious of differences we cannot see, local differences from county to county, social grades we do not perceive. Allowance has to be made for all we have lost in the haze of distance but broad outlines can be discerned and, from the Norman Conquest until the Black Death in 1348, England seems to have been socially far more like France than was ever to be the case again.

England in those three centuries was still mainly rural, and in the country, in spite of local variations, there was at first a clear distinction between

Comment nr̃e seig̃r par son ange enuoia les trois fleurs de lis dor en vn escu de asur au roy clou

gentle and simple.[2] As in France, to be "noble" or "gentle" meant to be a man whose father was known to all the neighbourhood as one who held land with a liability to bear arms. That was the condition on which he held his fief. If the word gentleman was used at all, it applied to everyone from the rank of squire up to the king and everyone in the chain had duties to those above and below him. Loyalty to the feudal superior therefore was the first of social virtues. It was the cement that held society together and since it was loyalty to a person, a breathing, visible man or occasionally a woman, it carried a strong emotional appeal. It was traitors to their lords whom Dante put in the lowest circle of Hell; Judas shared the deepest infamy with the assassins of Julius Caesar.

This was true on both sides of the Channel. The great difference lay in the system of succession and inheritance. In England before the Conquest, the general practice was to divide between brothers, but the Conquest changed that, with most important consequences. It was a military conquest and the Norman Duke was a feudal leader. No one knew better than he that a vassal who was too strong might be a danger to a feudal lord. He would have no such duke in England as he had been in France. But he was just as clear that the strength of a feudal leader lay in the strength of his immediate vassals. It was the man who held land who put soldiers in the field and neither the military command nor the land must be divided. It became the general law in England that the eldest son succeeded to the inheritance.

This was immensely important for the way English society developed. In the highest ranks of the feudal hierarchy, there might be a surplus of wealth or influence to provide for a younger son without dividing the fief, but this would naturally be less and less the case as you went down the scale. The younger sons of a man holding a single manor would usually have to look for means of support somewhere else. England was thinly populated, having, before the Black Death, less than two million inhabitants compared with more than twenty-two million subjects of the King of France. There was plenty of opportunity for a vigorous man.

The Black Death in 1348-9 took perhaps a third of the population and sharply accentuated the processes already at work. People at all levels moved about. It was hard to keep men tied to the land when there were so few hands available to plough and get in the harvest; higher wages were being offered somewhere else and men left their villages and tried to do better elsewhere;

"How Our Lord by his angel sent the three fleurs-de-lys of gold on a shield of blue to King Clovis" (the Bedford Hours, c 1423). King Clovis in fact was born in 466 AD and it is only in 1147 that the kings of France are first mentioned as bearing a coat sprinkled with fleurs-de-lys; and the *three* fleurs-de-lys were adopted by Charles v in 1376. No matter: it was convenient to suppose that marks of rank and birth came from heaven.

society everywhere became more fluid. When Chaucer was a boy, there were few serfs left in the fields; almost everyone was free and in the country there was already a rural middle class of yeomen, a term that included not only freeholders farming their own land, like Chaucer's franklin, but a growing class of tenant farmers who had capital and employed other men. Add to them the younger sons of the manor who were making their own living as wholesale merchants or lawyers or shipowners and you have by Chaucer's time a society already richly varied, with many grades and distinctions that are far from clear cut.

The Conquest, and the fact that it was military, also meant that there was a strong Crown. Before the end of his reign the Conqueror imposed a new development on the feudalism he had brought with him. At the Moot of Salisbury in 1087 he took an oath of direct allegiance from "all the land-sitting men that were in England". The vassal now held his fief from the King as well as from his immediate lord and he was made to understand that he must pay taxes to the King. The King of England never made with his nobles such a bargain as was made in France, where the nobles agreed to give up their own right to levy taxes in return for personal exemption. In France the process of strengthening the Crown was consistently one of depriving the nobility of power and compensating them by privilege, so that they were more and more separated from the rest of the community. And since all the offspring of a noble were noble too, there was a hard line separating this privileged and irresponsible order from everyone else. It was ended only by the Revolution.

In England, on the other hand, there soon arose a distinction between the small class who were noble, being peers of Parliament, and the much larger, and far less well defined, class of gentlemen. After the Black Death, and all the social confusion that followed, it was enacted in 1413 that in legal proceedings a man must state not only his domicile but his "degree or mystery". A younger son would therefore describe himself as "gentleman"; it was perhaps all he could say. No less an authority than Sir George Sitwell tells us that the first to give "gentleman" as his degree or mystery in a legal document was one Robert Erdeswyke of Stafford, "gentilman", who had served among the men-at-arms at Agincourt and was "charged at the Staffordshire Assizes with housebreaking, wounding with intent to kill and procuring the murder of one Thomas Page, who was cut to pieces while on his knees begging for his life".

But it was not only younger sons of the manor who would follow the illustrious example of Thomas Erdeswyke and describe themselves as belonging to this rank. There was recruitment from below as well and by 1570 the standards required were recorded by William Harrison in his *Description of England*. The ordinary meaning of the word, he thinks, was one whose ancestor came from Normandy with William the Conqueror and, by implication, had been given a manor with the obligation of military service. But in addition

whosoever studieth the laws of the realm, whoso abideth in the university, giving his mind to his book, or professeth physic and the liberal sciences, or beside [does] his service in the room of a captain in the wars, or [by] good counsel given at home, whereby his commonwealth is benefited, can live without manual labour and thereto is able and will bear the port, charge and countenance of a gentleman, he shall for money have a coat of arms bestowed upon him by heralds . . . and shall be called master, which is the title that men give to esquires and gentlemen, and be reputed for a gentleman ever after. . . .

He adds, obviously thinking of the French exemption from taxes, that the great advantage of this is that it costs the King nothing.

The Religion of Courtly Love

THOSE WHO were en-gentled as described by Harrison must have had some difficulty in adjusting their behaviour to their new degree; no doubt they were well aware that they were not regarded in the same light as the son of the manor. As Trevelyan writes, "his easy-going obsequious countrymen will touch their caps to him and call him 'Master' – though behind his back they will say they remember his father, honest man, riding to market astride his sacks of corn".

One difficulty that faced the self-made gentleman throughout the centuries was that there was an aristocratic standard of behaviour to women which was not the same as the plebeian. It was in this that the new gentleman of Victorian times would sometimes betray himself; "a touch of the hairy heel", his critics would say to each other, contrasting the cart-horse with the race-horse. In Chaucer's time, the attitude of a true gentleman was not by any means that of Sir James Chettam, but it was quite different from a peasant's. Chaucer makes a clear distinction between social position and true *gentillesse*, and an important part of *gentillesse* is behaviour to women. He was deeply influenced in this by the tradition of courtly love, which was strong in the French and Italian authors who so often provided him with his plots as well as his rhyme-schemes. And this was to colour the idea of the gentleman for centuries.

Courtly love was a tradition, a convention, in a sense almost a religion, although a religion known to fall something short of the truth. Only Dante managed to weld it into one with his deepest religious beliefs; other writers, for all their tears and sighs, have always a slight air of welcoming and enjoying something that they know to be a diversion. Nonetheless, it constituted a revolution that affected the literature of Europe, and the attitudes of men to women, at least in the upper classes, for six centuries. "Compared with this revolution," wrote C. S. Lewis – in a considerable overstatement – "the Renaissance is a mere ripple on the surface of literature."[3]

The essence of the cult was that its devotee vowed himself to the service, to the praises, to the adoration, of a high-born lady. She was the wife of someone else, often of his own feudal lord. Lancelot's love for Guinever, the wife of his King, is the example that everyone knows. The lover must do great deeds to prove his own worth and to glorify his lady's name; he makes no secret of his love. He must love her only and must show himself in every way worthy of her excellence. C. S. Lewis quotes a writer (Andreas Capellanus in his *De Arte Honeste Amandi*) who says the lover can only hope to win the lady if he proves his devotion both by deeds and eloquent words. He must be utterly faithful to her; the service of the god of love is "a kind of

The hero who rescues a lovely lady from a loathsome monster is a theme that goes back more than two thousand years to the myth of Perseus and Andromeda; it is a symbol perhaps of the difference between love and lust. In Ucello's 15th-century version, St George is hardly the perfect gentleman since he seems to have only just left an infants' school and shows surprise at his success. But the lady, who looks as though she were taking the dragon for a run before bed-time, is clearly a perfect lady: she displays no awareness of any plans that either the saint or the dragon might have for her future.

chastity" and he must be "virtuous, a good Catholic, clean of speech, witty, hospitable, ready to return good for evil, above all courteous, and to all ladies". "There is no good thing in the world and no courtesy which is not derived from love as from its fountain."

The lady is remote, on a pedestal; she can do no wrong – except cruelty to the lover, for it is not virtue but cruelty that keeps her remote. He tries to win her by the virtues proper to a gentleman; no one can truly be a disciple of the god of love unless he is noble in spirit and, by implication, by birth too. Indeed, to be quite prosaic, no ploughman or merchant could find the time to be a true worshipper at the shrine of courtly love. It is an aristocratic diversion to adore a remote princess. Perhaps in part it is the result of being sent away from home to serve as a page at the court of some great lord – or in Victorian times to boarding-school. A peasant brought up in a one-roomed hut with his mother and sisters knows very well that women have digestive systems and are human. Think of Sancho Panza, when he discovers that the peerless lady Dulcinea del Toboso – of whom he has heard so much as the lady who merits to be empress of the vast universe – is none other than his neighbour Aldonsa, daughter of Lorenzo: "Ta ta . . ." quoth Sancho, "I know her very well and I dare say that she can throw an iron bar as well as any the strongest lad in our parish. I vow, by the giver, that 'tis a wench of the mark, tall and stout, so sturdy withal, that she will bring her chin out of the mire in despite of any knight-errant . . . that shall honour her as his lady."[4]

That of course is deliberate mockery of the religion of courtly love, but it does underline the point that a peasant looks on a woman quite differently from a courtier. His view is based on the division of labour in the homestead. He knows that a woman is useful in the house and in the fields; she is a worker and if she were unfaithful her infidelity would be not only an attack upon his honour but a threat to his property and comfort. It is not surprising that courtly love is a religion for the aristocrat, who believed that it was "the seed of all those noble usages which distinguish the gentle from the villein; only the courteous can love but it is their love that makes them courteous . . ."

This tradition arose in the baronial courts of Provence. You must picture a lord and his lady surrounded by a court in which men predominate – landless knights hoping for employment in war, courtiers hoping for diplomatic missions, poets and painters and pages. They romanticised their allegiance to the lord and, if she were witty and beautiful, transferred it to his lady. She became, in the language of love, their *sovereign* lady; it was (says Lewis again) a feudalization of love.

There are obvious contradictions in all this. Loyalty was the supreme feudal virtue and to commit adultery with the wife of a feudal superior was surely the deepest disloyalty; witness the penalty inflicted on the squire who confessed under torture to his guilt with Margaret of Burgundy, Queen of

LEFT "There dwelt in the next village a young handsome wench with whom Don Quixote was sometime in love although she never knew nor took notice thereof . . ." Here is Aldonsa Lorenzo feeding her geese, as Sancho saw her (an illustration by Jean Bosschère, 1922).
RIGHT But in Don Quixote's eyes, Aldonsa became the peerless Dulcinea of Toboso . . .
BELOW The vision of the peerless Dulcinea floated always before Don Quixote's eyes . . .

ABOVE Terrible disasters sometimes befall the man who follows a
dream lady (illustration by Henry Alken, 1832) . . .
BELOW The end of another adventure (Gustave Doré). The whole
story of Don Quixote is a mockery of courtly love.

The other side of the medal: the ideal knight might pretend to sigh for some cruel and unattainable lady – but Sir Geoffrey Luttrell is handed his helmet and shield by his wife and daughter-in-law (the Luttrell Psalter, *c* 1340).

Navarre, daughter-in-law of Philip the Fair of France; he was broken on the wheel, castrated, flayed alive and beheaded. Such adultery would also be extremely difficult to keep secret; lords and ladies were surrounded by squires, pages and servants and at such small courts any privacy would be rare; someone was bound to know what was going on . . . small courts are great places for jealousy and gossip and under torture no one can be trusted. It seems to me that although the poets of courtly love proclaimed that bodily enjoyment was the true end of love, they cannot very often have achieved it. And since they sing about their love so loudly and openly, it seems likely that the lady's husband and everyone else regarded it simply as a literary convention which would never lead to anything more.

Nonetheless, the troubadour tradition ran on, an influence on both life and letters, until our own times. In love poetry it is a changing stream but recognizably from the same spring, through the courtly love poets such as Wyatt and Surrey, through Shakespeare himself – though he sometimes mocks it – to Keats and Tennyson. It is strong in Victorian and Edwardian popular literature, in the unattainable ladies to whom the heroes of the romantic novels of my boyhood vowed themselves. Think for a moment, and simply as one example, of Rudolf Rassendyll, who, on the strength of a family likeness, was crowned King of Ruritania to conceal the fact that the true king had been kidnapped. The true king was engaged to marry a princess who became for Rassendyll the one woman of his heart – but he must not touch her because it would be the act of a cad. It would be to take advantage of a position he had accepted for one day as a kind of trust on the absent king's behalf. So he and his Flavia must say good-bye and he must go away to make room for the real king. But once a year Rudolf, a private English gentleman, exchanged a red rose with Flavia, the Queen of Ruritania, and a message of three words: "Rudolf – Flavia – always!"

In life, the waters of the stream are not so easy to trace. There was an effect on formal manners and also on attitudes towards marriage and love. After the troubadours, ladies, as women and irrespective of rank, were given formal precedence over men. It became a mark of good breeding to rise when a lady entered the room and to speak of women with respect. No doubt Christian devotion to the Mother of God played a part in this, but we do not hear of it before the troubadours. Even the most cynical old roué of the 18th century knew that he must bow and flatter and defer to the opinion of ladies.

In life, of course the peasant's view of marriage and sex and property continued side by side with the poetic view. Nor was it confined to peasants. The marriages of young people – kings, nobles, or squires – were still arranged by their elders to cement an alliance, to round off an estate or to pay the debts of fathers. There were periods when to be witty meant to be cynical about the virtue of women. Nonetheless, the readers of poetry and plays and later of novels absorbed a great deal of extravagant praise of female beauty and virtue and ideal womanhood. They came to believe in love at first sight and in enduring passion. Many a young lady came to suppose that only an elopement to Gretna Green could bring her real happiness. Think of Lydia Languish – in the prosaic 18th century – who would have nothing to say to Captain Absolute because her aunt and his father thought it would be an excellent match for them both. He had to pretend to be a penniless ensign and plot an elopement – with "so becoming a disguise! So amiable a ladder of ropes! . . . How often have I stole forth, in the coldest night in January and found him in the garden stuck like a dripping statue! Then he would kneel to me in the snow and sneeze and cough so pathetically. . . . Ah, Julia, that was something like being in love!" Even her confidante Julia, who is nothing like so silly, says: "The mutual tear that steals down the cheek of parting lovers is a compact that no smile shall live there till they meet again."

Many a young man wrote verses – if he had the talent – to a not impossible she – and pictured her in dreams if he had not. Before the troubadours, men had thought (wrote C. S. Lewis) of love as "merry sensuality or domestic comfort or sometimes as a kind of madness or obsession". And some continued to think of it as a kind of embellishment to life like good cooking. But after the troubadours it was expected of a young gentleman to be an ardent lover, devoted to the service of his lady. The tradition took different forms in France and in England. Here, as we shall see, popular heroes continued to worship remote princesses from afar and the spirit of the troubadours sent lonely men to the ends of the earth to prove their worth by planting the flag or shooting elephants.

3

THE GENTLEMAN
IN CHAUCER

The Gentle Lion

THE BEGINNINGS of the Gentleman's pedigree are displayed with astonishing clarity in Chaucer.[5] There, in the second half of the 14th century, are Chaucer's men and women, far more like people in Britain in the second half of the 20th century than one has any right to expect. The pilgrims who met at the Tabard are on the whole a middle-class body; they include no earls or barons and only one field-labourer, the parson's brother; they range from a knight with wide experience in war – in modern terms a regular army officer who has reached the rank of, say, colonel – through merchant, lawyer, doctor, rich farmer and various ecclesiastics to a miller and a carpenter. Just as to-day an auctioneer selling a dog-kennel addresses his bidders as "gentlemen", the host at the Tabard speaks to the company as "lordings"; the prioress clearly wants to be thought more of a lady than she is and the franklin – a rich farmer in whose house it "snowed with meat and drink" – is eager that everyone should know what trouble he is taking to educate his son as a gentleman.

These social pretensions, these subtly differentiated grades, are the familiar background of the Victorian and Edwardian novel. But, in the reign of Richard II, Chaucer's pilgrims sit down to eat together at the host's table and join in telling stories. If army officer, parson, carpenter and handy-man had assembled by chance before a journey in the reign of Edward VII they would have wanted separate tables. This was not because in Chaucer's time men thought they were equal but for exactly the opposite reason; they were equal in the eyes of God, but in this world they knew very well that they were far from equal. They took it for granted that in England in 1387 things were arranged in an order of precedence. Each man had a degree or mystery, and although he might move up from one degree to another, the grades themselves did not change. The great fish-ladder round social barriers was the Church; men of the humblest origin might rise to be Cardinal or even Pope. But they had climbed round the waterfall from one pool to the next; the waterfall was still there. After the French Revolution, people were by no means sure that there would be another world and it was openly proclaimed that there ought to be equality here and now. The rich were far more uneasy about their privileges; therefore they stressed every difference they could and were much more reluctant to acknowledge their common humanity.

Molly and Aminta have made that point already (page 10). But while gentle and simple sat down to dinner together, they had very different tastes. When the host suggests that the summoner should tell them a tale "of mirth or japes" the gentry protest. "Nay! Let him tell us of no ribaldry!" they cry. The tales they tell are matched to their degree or mystery. The knight tells a tale of deeds of arms and fidelity in love; it is entirely in the tradition of courtly love and when it is finished, everyone said it was a noble story – but especially the gentlefolk. There is an implication here, I think, that everyone thought it *proper* to praise the story of Palamon and Arcite, but the miller, who was drunk already, cannot have thought much of it.

The miller's story, which follows immediately on the knight's, is by no means in the tradition of the troubadours. Nor is the carpenter's, which comes next. These tales are earthy and immediate. The miller (who, once he has started, seems to have forgotten his drunkenness) begins with a convincing picture of an entrancingly pretty and lively girl of eighteen; she is married to a stupid old codger but there are no sighs and tears about her; she goes to bed with the attractive student lodger Nicholas and enjoys herself. But the parish clerk, the amorous Absalon, had long been eying Alison; if she had been a mouse and he a cat, she'd have been pounced upon. He comes to serenade her while she is in bed with Nicholas – and there is nothing in the least idealized about the way she bounces out of bed and convinces him of her contempt. She promises him a kiss but sticks her bottom out of the window instead of her face and goes back to giggle about it with Nicholas.

Chaucer apologises for this "churl's story" as he calls it, and advises readers who don't like this kind of thing to turn the page; there is plenty for those who are more refined. The stories he allots to his characters show how he grades them; the miller, the carpenter and the summoner tell stories of which the central point is not far from the level of the seaside comic postcard. The knight, the lawyer, the clerk and the franklin tell tales of true love. Other stories in varying degrees are anti-clerical or cynical or traditional; roughly, the better the social position of the teller, the closer he sticks to the tradition of courtly love. Degree, a society ordered in social levels, is something Chaucer takes for granted.

This comes out even more clearly when he turns from actual men and women to fables about birds and beasts. *The Parliament of Fowls* ends with an assembly of all kinds of birds; they meet every year to choose their mates on St Valentine's Day. Nature, a noble empress full of grace, told the birds to arrange themselves according to their degree. The highest placed, the nobles or gentry, were the birds of prey; below them in order sat the eaters of seeds, the eaters of worms and last and lowest the waterfowl, who live in the mud. On her wrist Nature, like any earthly queen, had a hunting bird, in her case an eagle, a female, or rather – since one must show proper respect – a lady. Since she was the most "gentil", the choice would begin with her. Who would bid for her?

Three lordly eagles express their love, stating their claims in the language of the troubadours. The lady eagle blushed at this, fresh as a new red rose, but said nothing and Nature asked the Parliament to express an opinion. For the nobles, the birds of prey, the peregrine gave judgment, concluding that the lady should choose. Here the goose breaks in on behalf of the water-birds; this is a lot of fuss about nothing and all the others want to get on and choose their mates; let her choose quick and as for the defeated lovers, let them choose another. And the duck, with a quack, adds that there are more stars in heaven than a pair. The gentry are shocked at such vulgarity and the peregrine says on their behalf:

> Out of the dunghill came that word full right . . .
> Thy kind is of so low a wretchedness
> That what love is thou canst not see nor guess.

The cuckoo, speaking for the worm-eaters, comes in with much the same opinion as the goose and the duck, but with even more impatience to let the others get on with their choice. Eventually, Nature, the Queen, decides that the lady shall choose for herself and she – still in the troubadour tradition – asks for a year's delay to make up her mind. The rest of the birds take their mates quickly and disperse.

It would be silly to make too much of a fable, but to me this underlines the fact that for Chaucer and his audience it was an accepted convention that true love, and proper behaviour to women, were something understood only by those who were "gentil". It would be misleading to modernize this word as "gentle"; it means "having the qualities proper to a gentleman" – which does not get us much further – the emphasis being sometimes on birth, sometimes on upbringing, sometimes on consideration for others. Sometimes it is used as almost interchangeable with the word "free" and means "forgiving, generous, confident in one's own integrity". Nevill Coghill, who has so admirably translated Chaucer into modern English, sometimes uses "great-hearted" for this quality. And here another fable brings the point out. It occurs in the Prologue to *The Legend of Good Women*.

"For lo, the gentil kynd of the leoun," wrote Chaucer, which can be slightly modernized with very little change:

> But see the noble nature of the lion!
> For when a fly offendeth him or biteth
> He with his tail away the fly y-smiteth
> All easily, for of his genterye,
> He deigneth not to wreak him on a fly
> As doth a cur or any lesser beast . .

"Not of Our Elders . . ."

CHAUCER's perfect gentleman of course is the knight, who ever since he first rode out had loved chivalry, truth and honour, freedom and courtesy. There is a long list of his battles and sieges and campaigns, but although he had achieved such distinction by his courage and skill in war, in his bearing he was "as meek as is a mayde". "He never yet no villeinye ne sayde", which Coghill turns into: "He never yet a boorish thing had said . . ." There follows the most famous line in Chaucer, the one line almost everyone knows, but one very misleading if turned directly into modern English:

> He was a verray parfit gentil knight.

Coghill admits to great difficulty over this line and is clearly not satisfied with the best he can do – but it is quite easy to make a paraphrase: "he was a true and perfect knight, perfect in all the qualities a gentleman should have, courage and courteous behaviour and magnanimity".

And to this picture should be added the squire's, the perfect *young* gentleman. He is the knight's son and has already seen military service "in Flanders and Artois and Picardy". He was a lover, as the troubadours would have him be, and all he did was in hope to win his lady's grace.

> Singing he was, or fluting all the day
> He was as fresh as is the month of May . . .
> He could make songs and poems and recite,
> Knew how to joust and dance, to draw and write.
> He loved so hotly that till dawn grew pale
> He slept as little as a nightingale . . .

That is Coghill again and gets the spirit exactly.

Both the knight and the squire were "gentil" in every sense, by birth as well as by training and disposition. But Chaucer has no doubt that good birth by itself does not always mean true courtesy and all that he means by "gentillesse". He makes the point explicitly in *The Parson's Tale*, which is really not a tale at all but a prose sermon and which is perhaps not often read. But the parson is very precise: it is folly, he says, to be proud of "gentrye"; often the "gentrye" of the body, that is, good birth, takes away from the "gentrye" of the soul. We are all of one father and mother and of one nature. The signs of "gentillesse" are eschewing of vice and ribaldry and following virtue, courtesy and cleanness, and being "liberal", that is generous, but generous within reason, not to the point of extravagance and folly. The wife of Bath also makes the point that gentry by birth do not always behave as gentry should. Ten people can tell you something of the wife of Bath for one who knows anything of the parson, but she is so vital, so earthy and extrovert that it is a pleasure to dwell on her. And she brings out the point about courtly love admirably.

She was the sort of person who today would live in a comfortable house on the outskirts of a large town. She would dress to catch the eye and go to the hairdresser twice a week; she would go on cruises. Five husbands she had had and was looking round for a sixth; they had left her well off, and she was a shrewd woman at business. In the 1920s, one can see the wife of Bath in expensive furs and a big car; today she would wear tight red trousers. Scarlet was her favourite colour; she wore scarlet hose on the pilgrimage and boasted of a scarlet dress with which she had done great execution. She took a leading place in her suburban parish and would be furious if any woman went to the altar steps before her. Not that she professed to be holy; she lived her life in this world and meant to enjoy every minute; she liked food and drink and fun in bed and company and laughter; she was free of speech. A bawdy old baggage, the young men would call her behind her back. No woman ever stepped that was more militant a she – but not in the manner of the 20th-century champions of women's liberation. To be a sex-object was her aim and her weapon; she used her sexuality both as an enticement and as a threat and boasted of it. It was her glory.

There is not the least hint of the tradition of courtly love either in Chaucer's description of her in the Prologue or in the long discourse, about herself and her husbands and her views on life, to which she treats the company before she starts to tell her tale. She was a materialist about sex, which to her was bodily pleasure and a means to power and wealth. She would have had little time for sighs and tears and seven years of faithful service without reward. But it is to that tradition she turns for the background of her story, just as her modern counterpart might have turned to the conventional romantic story in the popular woman's magazine of her day. Chaucer, as he wrote the tale, cannot for a moment have forgotten who was supposed to be telling it. Her own voice constantly breaks through the traditional setting, but the central assumption of the story is that every lady at court had somewhere in the offing a faithful lover vainly sighing for her favours and eager to serve her.

Her tale is set in the court of King Arthur. A knight from the court happened one day upon a maid walking alone by the river and in spite of all she could say or do took her maidenhead by force. She complained to the king, and the knight was tried and condemned to death. But he was a pretty boy and the queen and her ladies begged for his life. At last the king gave in and he was brought before a feminine court, the queen and her ladies sitting as a judicial body. They would pardon him, they said, but on one condition. He must find the right answer to a question: "What do women most desire?" They would give him a year and a day to look for the answer but if he could not find it, the original sentence would be carried out and he must die by the axe.

All the ladies of the court were agreed on the answer to the riddle – but of course, in the convention of courtly love, it would not do to stay where he was and try to wheedle it out of one of *them*. It would not have been "gentil", or, as we might say, not cricket. He must wander away and ask women all over the world. But no two of them agreed and a year later he was back without an answer, due to forfeit his head next day.

As he rode towards this melancholy appointment, he saw a company of ladies dancing in a wood and with a sudden spurt of hope he turned to ask them his question. But they vanished and he found only one old hag, ugly, dirty and ragged. This should surely have put him on his guard, but he had not our knowledge of fairy tales; he seems to have been a very unsophisticated young man. Hoping for nothing, he wearily told her his story. She told him she could give him the answer – but he must promise to do whatever she should ask him. The poor fool agreed. Next day, before the queen and her ladies, he announced in ringing tones that what women wanted most was to have the same sovereignty over their husbands as they had over their lovers. In all the court there was no wife, widow or maid to say no to that – but in the midst of the tumult of congratulation up started the old hag and demanded – as you and I guessed long ago – his hand in marriage. He could not deny his promise and the court held that he must give what she asked or lose the benefit she had brought him by her answer – in other words, his head.

Most reluctantly, he married her and still more reluctantly went to bed with her. But he did not behave courteously. Instead of turning to her with affection, he *wallowed* in the bed, turning this way and that. "His wife lay still and wore a quiet smile." "Is this the way," she asks him, "that knights of King Arthur's court usually behave on their wedding night?" "What do you expect?" he asks petulantly. Surely she knows that she is not only old but ugly and poor and of humble birth? And here she turns on him and reads him a tremendous lecture. She could, if she liked, and if he were a little more courteous to her, put everything right – but did he not know that true "gentillesse" lay in behaving like a gentleman? It does not come from ancestors but of virtuous and noble life. It is a free gift, a matter of grace:

> Christ wills we claim of him our "gentillesse"
> Not of our elders, for their old richesse.

And she tells him that a man may come of the noblest family in the realm but if he himself is not courteous, if he does nothing on his own account that is "gentil":

> He is not gentil, be he duke or earl,
> For villein's sinful deeds do make a churl.

And after a good deal more of this, she asks him if he would like her to stay as she is, and have a loving wife but no fear of being cuckolded – or would he like her young and lovely and take the risk? "As you like," he says, perhaps a trifle wearily, and she perceives that she has the mastery of him and – lo and behold! – she is young and lovely and says she will be loving and faithful as well – so that his heart was bathed in a bath of bliss. And the wife of Bath, on behalf of all women, ends with this pious reflection:

> . . . and Jesus Christ us send
> Husbands, meek, young and fresh a-bed,
> And give us grace to master those we wed.

Generosity

THE WIFE OF BATH was not exactly a lady. Venus and Mars were the influence in her life and in her own account of her behaviour to her husbands she shows herself violent, masterful, and far from considerate. One stand-up, knock-down fight she records but also months of cruel nagging, meant to exasperate a man and get the better of him. She really cannot be regarded as an authority on "gentillesse". But she was telling a story she had heard from someone else. (It is to be found, as a matter of fact, in Gower's *Confessio Amantis*.) It was the kind of story that Chaucer's audience expected to hear; there is evidence that Chaucer read some of his poems aloud to the court of Richard II. They *expected* to be told that "gentillesse" was not just a matter of birth; this was the orthodox doctrine of the religion of chivalry and courtly love. So the old hag preached her sermon – with a few little touches added by the Wife. She no doubt would have thought it was stretching courtesy rather far to expect that fresh young bachelor to turn with enthusiasm to his hideous bride.

But though the Wife well understood the virtue of courtesy, at least in men, she did not say much about being 'free" or generous. The franklin's tale turns entirely on being "free". It begins with a variation on the theme of courtly love that is entirely suitable in his mouth. Chaucer calls the franklin a vavasour, which means the next in the feudal chain below a baron. A franklin, say the books, was "not noble", but as a freeholder of his land, and one who had been member of Parliament for the shire and a justice of the peace, he was poised tip-toe on the brink of formal recognition as "gentle". It is not surprising that he wanted to make courtly love respectable, bourgeois, comfortable, middle-class. His heroine, whose name is Dorigen, had a faithful lover, entirely according to convention, a knight who served her for many years and did many noble deeds. She broke with convention by marrying him in the end. He swore that he would serve her as lover, not exercise sovereignty as her lord – and they entered upon an ideal marriage:

> Thus doth she take her servant as her lord,
> Servant in love and lord in wedded life;
> He has his love as sovereign and as wife,
> A subject to his sovereign far above
> Since he has both his lady and his love.

The Heritage of the Past

Episodes from the life of Sir Galahad, from *Le Roman du Bon Chevalier Tristan*, one of the sources for Malory's *Morte d'Arthur*. Galahad receives the order of knighthood, wins his sword and takes part in a royal tourney. Galahad, the embodiment of purity, was the only knight of Arthur's court fit to undertake the supreme adventure, the quest of the Holy Grail. He was the perfection of chivalry, the ideal knight and gentleman.

Effegent vnt
lexvue vuvle
Seftoient pres
ala carose

Et vne dame leur chantoit
Oui lieffe appellee eftoit
Bien feut chanter et plaisanoit
Plue one mille et migroteme̅t
Son bel refrain miℓ bien lui fist
Car ℓ chanter mernelℓes fist

Elle auoit la voir clere et sanne
Laquelle neftoit pres vilanne
Et tre bien se sauoit ℓ baiser
feur du pic et remoiser
Les gens la renoient milℓ chere
pource quelle eftoit la premiere
De beℓℓe face et plaiuere
Courtoise eftoit et non pas fiere
De loyeuse fur garme
Et aussi ℓ solae fomme

The first part of the *Roman de la Rose* was written in French about 1240 AD by Guillaume de Loris on the theme of courtly love. The scene is set in a dream garden; the hero falls in love with an unattainable Rose which symbolises his lady's love. The poem was translated by Chaucer as *The Romaunt of the Rose*. It was a time when men emulated birds in the splendour of their courting plumage.

RIGHT The unicorn was an emblem of speed, valour and purity. It could defeat an elephant in battle, but became meek in the presence of a lady. The only way to catch a unicorn was to persuade a fair maid to sit waiting in a forest, when it would come and lay its dangerous spiked head meekly in her lap.

BELOW, LEFT A lover pleads his love to a lady and reproaches her for cruelty. But courtly love was a kind of game, and perhaps he does not really expect to win her.

BELOW, RIGHT Sir Edward Dymoke was Champion of England at the coronation of Edward IV, Mary and Elizabeth I. It was his duty to ride into Westminster Hall and throw down his gauntlet as a challenge to anyone who disputed the succession to the throne. The right to this office came to the Dymokes with the manor of Scrivelsby from the family of Marmion, hereditary champions to the dukes of Normandy. So he was undoubtedly a gentleman in the original sense, but there is no record of whether he possessed true *gentillesse* in Chaucer's sense.

The Gentleman in Chaucer

OPPOSITE, RIGHT Chaucer's knight –

"... a most distinguished man
Who from the day on which he first
    began
To ride abroad has followed chivalry
Truth, honour, generous thought and
    courtesy..."

ABOVE, LEFT The knight was Chaucer's
perfect gentleman, and his son, the squire,
was the perfect *young* gentleman:

"He was embroidered like a meadow
    bright
And full of freshest flowers, red and
    white.
Singing he was or fluting all the day;
He was as fresh as is the month of May."

BELOW, LEFT The franklin was a rich
farmer, not a tenant-farmer but a
freeholder. He was not "noble" or "gentle"
in the original sense of the word, but had

been Member of Parliament for the shire
and was a Justice of the Peace, and so
poised tiptoe on the brink of formal
recognition as "gentle". In his house "it
positively snowed with meat and drink".

BELOW, RIGHT The Wife of Bath.
Everyone has met someone like the Wife of
Bath, merry and bossy, fond of food and
drink and bright clothes, gossip and men
and flirting. She ended her story with the
pious reflection:

"... and Jesus Christ us send
Husbands meek young and fresh abed
And give us grace to master those we
    wed."

BELOW The ladies watch from balconies,
the knights fight below to prove their
fidelity in love, their courage, their skill at
arms. It was a game, part of the courtier's
game of chivalry and courtly love, the
background to many of Chaucer's tales.

Court and Country

ABOVE Dr Johnson described himself as "a
retired and uncourtly scholar", and in this
painting by E. M. Ward is shown waiting
upon Lord Chesterfield in the hope of
patronage. But he received no
encouragement when he was poor and
unknown; and when he was famous he
sharply rejected Lord Chesterfield's praise.
He said he had thought Chesterfield a lord
among wits – but found he was only a wit
among lords.

OPPOSITE, ABOVE Edward Stratford, 2nd
earl of Aldborough, was at one time in the
House of Commons for Taunton and later
in the Irish Parliament before the Act of
Union in 1801. But like many public
figures in the 18th century he liked to
spend much of his time in the country, and
in this painting by Francis Wheatley he is
seen at Waddesdon Manor on his
favourite horse Pomposo.

OPPOSITE, BELOW "Bobbin about to the
Fiddle" (1817). A family party rehearsing
for a visit to Margate. This family falls far
short of Lord Chesterfield's standards of
polish, but they want to appear more
polished than they are and, like Lord
Chesterfield, turn to a French instructor –
even though this is only two years after
Waterloo.

BOBBIN about to the FIDDLE — a Familly Rehersal of Quadrille Dancing or Polishing for a trip to Margate

"He begetteth a son and behold there is nothing in his hand."
At least a hundred years after Lord Chesterfield, fathers were still putting
all their hopes in a son who refused to be modelled exactly on his father's
expectations. A Victorian story picture, by John Byam Shaw.

Thus they lived in mutual courtesy and great bliss. It is courtly love domesticated. But after a time he had to go away on a long voyage. Dorigen was left lonely and sad. Her husband's squire, faithful to tradition, now confessed his love; he was dying for her; he *would* die unless he enjoyed her. She told him it was impossible – she would be his only on the day when those rocks, out to sea, disappeared beneath the waves. He went sadly away but found a magician who *did* make the rocks disappear. Dorigen believed she was bound in honour to keep her word – and to avoid the dilemma was about to kill herself. But her husband came back in the nick of time, heard the story, and insisted that she must do as she had promised. Off she went, obediently. But the squire, overwhelmed by the knight's generosity, decided that *he* could be generous too. He sent her back unravished. And, to complete the circle, the magician waived his fee, which would have beggared the poor squire, with the words:

> . . . dear brother
> Each of you did "gentílly" to the other . . .
> And even a clerk can do a "gentil" deed
> As well as any of you, do me heed.

And the franklin concluded triumphantly:

> Lordings, I ask you, which now of these three
> Deserves to be remembered as most "free"?

Here Chaucer seems to use "gentil" and "free" almost interchangeably and both mean "generous" – a most important part of being a gentleman.

4
THE COURTIER

The Italian Courtier

IN CHAUCER'S TIME, then, it was already accepted that a gentleman did not always behave as a gentleman should; the moral and social meanings are distinguished. But an important part of his behaviour is courtesy to women and here the conventional doctrines of courtly love are supreme, while it is the general view that only a man with leisure can practise all the virtues and refinements required by this convention. Chaucer died in 1400. Let us go forward a century and a quarter, to 1528, when there was published in Italy a book which was to score an astonishing success. A recent translator into English gives a list of over 140 editions in various languages and it influenced behaviour in Italy, Spain, France, England and Germany for three centuries. This was *The Book of the Courtier* by Baldesar Castiglione.[6]

"Courtier" does not mean the same as "gentleman" but in Italy at that time the two ideals were not so far apart as the words suggest today. The court was the highroad for any man of ambition; the soldier, the diplomat, the administrator, had each to serve a prince and each must please him if he was to have useful and honorable employment. Chaucer had begun as a page in the household of Lionel of Clarence, a son of Edward I, and had later been a personal attendant on Edward III, who sent him abroad on various missions of a commercial kind and eventually made him controller of customs in the port of London. Castiglione himself commanded fifty men-at-arms at the court of Urbino; later he held a variety of diplomatic appointments, ending as Papal nuncio at the court of Madrid. Almost everyone anyone has heard of before the middle of the 17th century was in some degree a courtier. A man who sought distinction must have a patron.

A courtier then was simply a gentleman with ambition and the two ideals are very close together.

The first English translation of the *Courtier* appeared in 1561, shortly after Queen Elizabeth's accession to the throne, but it was well known in England before that and is referred to in a somewhat similar book, Sir Thomas Elyot's

This is Baldesar Castiglione
(in a portrait by Raphael),
courtier and diplomat, poet,
scholar and soldier – the author
of *The Book of the Courtier*. The
Emperor Charles V called him
"one of the finest gentlemen in
the world". He was speaking
Spanish, in which the word
"caballero", like the English
"gentleman", means a standard
of behaviour as well as a social
position.

BELOW LEFT *The Book of the
Courtier*, by Count Baldesar
Castiglione, was published in
Italy in 1528.

BELOW RIGHT *The Governor* by
Sir Thomas Elyot first appeared
in 1531, three years after *The
Courtier*, and was clearly popular
since it was published again in
1534; it led to the appointment
of the author as ambassador to
the Emperor Charles V. It was
not a translation of *The Courtier*,
but like *The Courtier* it owed
much to Plato.

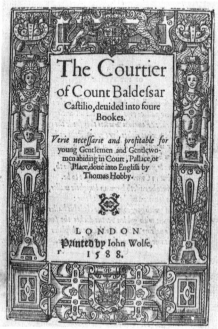

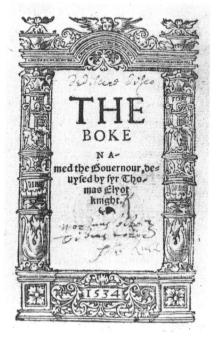

The Governor, published in 1531. There can be no doubt of its influence in England; it is part of the pedigree of the English gentleman.

Castiglione's book is an account of a discussion, supposed to have taken place at the court of the duke of Urbino, during four evenings between 1504 and 1508 when Castiglione was himself in the duke's service. The duke, Guidobaldo da Montefeltro, was an invalid and of a retiring disposition. It was his wife, Elisabetta Gonzaga, who was the centre of social life at his small but brilliant court and it was her custom, after supper, to collect round her a score or so of friends for relaxation before going to bed. Sometimes they danced or listened to music; often they talked and their conversation frequently took the form of "games" – conversations about an imaginary situation – usually arising from the convention of courtly love – and all that might come of it.

In Castiglione's book, they had met one evening as usual and began by discussing what "game" they should play. They decided in the end on quite a new topic. What makes the perfect courtier?

The duchess had deputed the presidency of the company to her friend Donna Emilia Pia, who commanded count Ludovico de Canossa to begin his account of the perfect courtier. His first point was that this paragon should be nobly born, a phrase to be understood in the continental sense, as one neither base nor bourgeois but the son of a gentleman. Such birth is like a bright lamp that illuminates his good qualities and stimulates him to virtue by the fear of shame and the hope of praise. Good qualities he must have – these are the endowment of nature – but whether they are bodily or mental, they must be developed to their fullest extent by training.

Here one of the listeners raised an objection: we all know men of noble birth who have vices and imperfections and men of obscure origin who are brave and virtuous. Of course; count Ludovico accepts the point without hesitation. But we are talking about perfection and the man of good birth has a long start; it is much easier for him to reach the goal; he is more likely to set himself the high target of excellence.

Having disposed of this, the count continues that the first quality the courtier must possess is the use of weapons and everything to do with the profession of arms. Stern to an enemy, he must be gentle to everyone else, modest, reserved, avoiding ostentation and insolent praise of himself. He should be well-built and athletic, open and frank of manner, prudent and firm. He must understand the rules of the duel and be skilled in horsemanship. He must be able to manage all kinds of weapons and to acquit himself well in dancing, hunting, swimming, leaping, tennis and vaulting. He should laugh and make jokes, tease his friends with good nature and always appear good-tempered and in control of himself.

Here a difficulty arises. Everything the perfect courtier does must be done with *grace* – that is to say, naturally and without apparent effort. But fencing

There is music, wine, fine buildings, polished conversation; it is the life of a courtier. How different from the peasants' toil!

and horsemanship need practice under the direction of skilled masters. How can all this hard work be concealed? A performance that is prosaic and laborious is distasteful; so too is an affected nonchalance. This grace that the courtier needs is, surely, a free gift from God and cannot be acquired by practice? The discussion glides away from the theological implication. A free gift can – and indeed must – be improved by practice. Perfection lies in achieving such a degree of mastery that everything seems easy and natural.

This applies to speaking and writing as well as to physical exercises. The speaker should be natural and unaffected, not only in speech but in writing, which is only another form of speech. Words of course must be properly arranged but they must seem to be spontaneous and the language must not be pedantic or unusual. Nothing will help the speaker if he does not know what he is talking about; the substance of what he has to say is all-important and he must be master of it. But however difficult his subject, he must try to make himself clear. He must use the language of everyday speech, but suited to people of taste and education; he is not to copy every phrase used by peasants and the ignorant. His speech must seem altogether unstudied, open and free.

The perfect courtier must be an honest and upright man, and the virtues he cultivates will include prudence and temperance. But since he must seek to please, to commend himself to his prince and to his companions, his mind will require ornament and the true adornment of the mind is the knowledge of literature. It is the hope of fame that is the reason for seeking perfection; fame is the spur to great and hazardous deeds and a man who is moved by lesser motives, such as desire for material gain, does not deserve the name of gentleman. And it is the written word that records great deeds and preserves their glory and fills men with the desire to win a like immortality. The man we are thinking of must therefore be well versed in Greek and Latin – though master of the vernacular too "so that he can talk to ladies". He must have read orators, poets and historians. He must write both verse and prose himself, so that he can understand the toil of writing and the niceties of style. But he should be reluctant to show anyone what he has written and must remember that he is a soldier who practises letters, not a poet who practises arms.

He must also be a musician, because music has a direct influence on the spirit and if practised regularly encourages virtue, just as physical exercise gives health to the body. Music is much more than a recreation and a relaxation. It has inspired men to courage and endurance and it makes long and arduous toil seem lighter, just as it soothes children to sleep. Reapers in the field and soldiers on the march respond to its influence and it seems to minister in some way to man's deepest needs. It is part of the harmony of nature. And, to conclude, our accomplished courtier must both draw and paint, because the world is a noble picture, designed by the hand of God. And with this ends the first day's discussion, and for my purpose the most significant part of the *Book of the Courtier*.

The Perfect Lady

A RECENT TRANSLATOR of Castiglione into English has remarked that "it is hard to think of any work more opposed to the spirit of the modern age. It is 'elitist'; it is competitive. It does not give much thought to social justice". But this is to judge one generation by the standards of another; in the 16th century everyone assumed that inequality was inevitable. Nonetheless, it is true that Castiglione's courtiers are very different from either Plato's guardians or the Victorian gentleman or Chaucer's knight. They resemble the guardians in many ways; they are altogether like them in admiring mental and bodily excellence, skill, beauty, training, balance of accomplishments. The insistence on music is very like Plato. But they are light-hearted, gay,

even frivolous. They seem to have little sense of obligation to those dependent on them. They show no sign of one aspect of Chaucer's *gentillesse*.
Chaucer's perfect knight is courteous to inferiors and what makes him
"gentil" is that he is generous, magnanimous to the defeated, to the poor, to
the unhappy. There is not much about these virtues in *The Courtier* and count
Ludovico's acknowledgement that nobility of character does not always go
with noble birth seems a trifle perfunctory. Moving to Urbino from the
road to Canterbury, we seem to have come into a world of sharper divisions
between the classes. It is a brilliant world, bright with varied colours; there
is something intensely attractive about the soldier-poet, skilled in music and
painting as well as fencing and dancing, learned in Greek and Latin but bold
in war, eager to savour every breath of life. Yet in spite of all this brilliance,
this excitement, this intense concern with music and art and the graces of
life, this feeling that all knowledge can be mastered, something has been lost.
Compared with Chaucer's, Castiglione's world is less kindly and less human.
His people are no more concerned about the village down the hill below the
castle than Plato was about the slaves who made the good life possible for
the Athenian citizen. But it is not easy to be sure whether the difference is
mainly between the ages in which they lived or between Italy and England.

Later, the discussion turned on the behaviour of the perfect lady and was
made controversial by the lord Gaspar Pallavicino, who contended that
women were only an inferior kind of men, "like unripe apples". He was only
21 and had perhaps recently been disappointed in love; at any rate, the
others made allowances for him. Or perhaps he made his points with such a
bantering air that no one took them seriously. At any rate, they were not
resented, though the lord Magnifico – a kind of friendly nickname for
Giuliano dei Medici – came nobly to the defence of women, who were, he
maintained, the same as men in essence, differing only in accidental qualities
which had to do with the bearing and rearing of children. He regarded the
qualities of women as complementary to those of men and, except in bodily
exercises and the use of weapons, the qualities required of a lady were the
same as those of a courtier. But she must be even more prudent than he,
particularly in anything that might in the least compromise her reputation
for modesty. While the man should always display some degree of sturdy
manliness, she must combine "a soft and dainty tenderness with an air of
womanly sweetness". Like the gentleman, the lady should avoid affectation,
move gracefully, be mannerly, intelligent, neither arrogant nor envious,
neither slanderous nor vain nor quarrelsome nor silly. She must be ready to
talk to any man, but she must be neither indelicate nor prudish, nor catty
about other women. She must have knowledge of literature, painting and
music and must of course know how to dance, but above all must have virtue,
so that she is honoured.

One assumption that would have surprised the Victorian English goes unchallenged. Women have stronger sexual desires than men – but every-one concedes that they are usually less inclined to give way to them. My lord Magnifico maintains that however hateful her husband may be the ideal court lady must yield to her lover nothing but her spirit. Of course, if she is unmarried and her admirer is a man she may love, then she may show signs of liking – but never appear wantonly to offer herself. He and she alike must move step by step, never making an advance from which it is not possible to withdraw, showing their feelings by use of the eyes, by silences, by sighs and glances, before proceeding to words.

On the last evening, which makes the fourth book of *The Courtier*, Ottavi-ano Fregoso, who later became doge of Genoa, gave the discussion a more philosophical turn. What is the purpose, he asks, of all this striving for per-fection? What is the courtier trying to achieve? Is it not a waste of time to spend so much effort on learning to dance and sing? Surely the courtier's real aim must be to win the esteem of his prince so that he can speak to him quite frankly and advise him to act with justice and liberality? The ideal courtier must become a statesman. This opens the way to a much wider discussion on the nature of virtue and the best methods of government, most of which is not to our purpose here. The conclusion is that the courtier of mature wisdom who advises a prince, from loving the soul of a woman, may rise to love the universal beauty which adorns all human bodies and thence to love the abstract idea of beauty which is Love itself.

This is Plato's doctrine of the love of ideal beauty, which is very different from the vivid belief in a life after death which all Chaucer's pilgrims shared. It is something possible for a man of learning and leisure – but what would Sancho Panza have made of it? "Ta ta," he would have said at this, as at the religion of courtly love.

The English Courtier

To the English in the reign of Queen Elizabeth, the Italian language, Italian letters, verse, painting, music, were rather as the Greek had been to the Roman. Things Italian stood for polish, subtlety, artistic success, but at the same time the Italians, except for Venice, were a divided people, decadent, not of much consequence in the world. Nonetheless, the ideal courtier was closely modelled on the Italian, and, as we have seen, Casti-glione was known in England from 1561. It was almost thirty years later that Spenser began to publish *The Faerie Queen*. The purpose of this great work was, he said, "to fashion a gentleman or noble person in vertuous or gentle discipline".

It would be no easy task to disentangle from the rich allegory of *The Faerie Queen* all that Spenser intended as being directed to this purpose. All I need say is that it was designed to consist of twelve books, each relating the adventures of one knight, personifying one of twelve virtues; the Sixth Book is the *Legend of Sir Calidore or of Courtesie,* and Sir Calidore is generally thought to represent Sir Philip Sidney. It was to Sidney that Spenser had dedicated *The Shepherd's Calendar,* the first long poem which had established his name; he had also drawn a picture of the ideal courtier, again identified as Sidney, in an early satire, *Mother Hubberd's Tale* and there is also *Astrophell,* a pastoral elegy on the death of Sir Philip Sidney.

It was not only Spenser who thought Sir Philip Sidney "the president of noblesse and chevalrie". His countrymen accepted him as the perfect courtier and throughout Europe his name stood high for learning, courtesy, wise counsel and a kind of romantic chivalrous devotion to his Queen, to his religion, to his honour and to his lady – once she was out of reach.

The court of Queen Elizabeth I of England was the perfect setting for an autumn flowering of the tradition of courtly love. Here courtiers could profess devotion to a lady who really was their sovereign – and a very exacting sovereign too – but who was also a star of the first magnitude, a jewel of the first water, astonishing by her power to capture the hearts of her people, by her intellectual ability, by her learning and magnificence – and yet a woman with all the qualities men have traditionally attributed to women. And she was out of reach. She lorded it over them, flying into rages, healing with a smile, leading them on, tantalising and provoking them. In that brilliant court the language of courtly love exceeded itself in hyperbole. And among the young men who professed devotion to Gloriana, Sidney was in one sense the first, the admired of all. Leicester might be accused of personal machinations and improper ambition, but not Sidney. His devotion to the queen was exactly right, expressing loyalty to a prince, admiration for a woman, a warm personal blend of both to her, Elizabeth, but making no claims, exciting no envy.

His sonnets to Stella were addressed to Penelope Devereux, whom it had once been intended he should marry. He cannot be said to have pressed his suit vigorously and it was only after her marriage to Lord Rich that the sonnets show much feeling.

Sidney became a legend before his death at the age of only 32. Yet this universal admiration was based not on achievement but on acclaim, a general acclaim not of what he did but of what he was. He left *Arcadia,* which he had not meant to publish, the series of sonnets to Stella, *A Defense of Poesie*; he had achieved some minor diplomatic triumphs. He had not done much, but to everyone he was the ideal for every courtier.

It is what people thought of him that concerns us and in particular what Spenser thought. In *Mother Hubberd's Tale,* as well as in *Astrophell,* he describes his hero, who thinks always of honour, speaks ill of none, will neither intrigue nor fawn nor flatter. He spends the day in horsemanship, practising with his weapons, study and music. All this is very like Castiglione and one

ABOVE LEFT Sir Philip
Sidney, described by
Spenser as "the president of
noblesse and chevalrie",
was regarded by his
countrymen as the perfect
courtier.

ABOVE RIGHT Robert
Dudley, earl of Leicester,
was handsome, tall, witty,
brave – everything a
courtier should be – except
that some said he would let
nothing stand in the way of
his ambition.

LEFT Robert Devereux,
earl of Essex, succeeded his
father when he was ten,
and his charm and wit soon
made him a favourite of the
Queen. But he was never
master of himself; he lost
his temper and turned his
back upon the Queen, who
slapped his face. Far from
the perfect courtier.

cannot doubt that Spenser knew the *Book of the Courtier*. To Spenser, Sidney was the perfect knight of the Renaissance, soldier, lover, poet, musician, scholar and courtier. It is in the legend of his life, not in Spenser's verse, that something is added. When he rode to the walls of Zutphen, Sidney met a companion who had no leg-armour and since he did not wish his courage to owe anything to the advantage armour gave him, he took off his own; it was this that led to his death by a bullet in his thigh. And, as he was carried to his death-bed — but the one thing everyone knows about Sidney is that he refused a cup of cold water because a dying soldier's need was greater than his. Everyone remembers it because it was the last touch that was needed to turn the perfect courtier into a perfect gentleman. And this of course was Christian not Platonic.

Sidney was a legend, an ideal. He does not seem quite true. Shakespeare's characters on the other hand are utterly real. Shakespeare did not question the Renaissance ideal. Hamlet is the Renaissance gentleman; Hamlet has

> The courtier's, soldier's, scholar's eye, tongue, sword,

just like Castiglione's ideal, but he is different because he is so intensely alive. There break out from his moody introspection sparks of something altogether his own. When Ophelia says sadly: "You are merry, my lord" and he throws back the bitter, offhand, answer: "O God, your only jig-maker"; when Polonius says he will treat the players according to their desert and Hamlet turns on him angrily: "God's bodikins, man, much better; use every man after his desert and who should 'scape whipping?" we are in the presence of a man who is like no one else in the world. He is a king's son; he happens also to be a gentleman.

Shakespeare had no doubts about that essential inequality in the human condition, which he called degree. He spoke his own opinion when he put into the mouth of Ulysses the famous speech on degree:

> The heavens themselves, the planets and this centre
> Observe degree, priority and place . . .
>
> O! when degree is shak'd
> Which is the ladder of all high designs,
> The enterprize is sick. How could communities
> Degrees in schools and brotherhood in cities. . .
> The primogeniture and due of birth
> Prerogative of age, crown, sceptres, laurels,
> But by degree, stand in authentic place?
> Take but degree away, untie that string,
> And hark! what discord follows!

He is sure too that there is something sacred about a crowned king, but that does not hinder him from seeing that the man holding the office may be a very feeble and imperfect man, nor that duties go with the office. His ideal king goes among his soldiers on the night before Agincourt because he knows their importance in the scheme of degree. Shakespeare never for a moment supposed that all courtiers were like Sidney or Hamlet; he shows us Osric, the "water-fly", vain, idle and silly, and plenty of wicked courtiers too. He knows too that there are plenty of country gentlemen as well as courtiers, and no doubt in every county of England there was many a country gentleman not very different from Justice Shallow, drowsing away the later years of his life with memories of what a devil he had been long ago as a student at one of the Inns of Court, going into the orchard after supper to eat a pippin of his own grafting, giving orders to his man of all work – orders about serving precepts and sowing red wheat and putting a new link to the bucket for the well, and perhaps too giving some ear to that man of all work when he puts in a good word for a man he knows to be a knave. Such country justices were nearer to their servants than to courtiers.

The age of Shakespeare shared with the age of Chaucer a concern for simple unlearned men that was unknown to Castiglione. All the same, something had been lost; the classes had begun to move apart. Elizabethan courtiers far more often than not showed a contempt for the common folk which they might also extend to country gentlemen like Justice Shallow, and the tenderness for the poor and the old that had been so widespread in Chaucer's time had gone. Most of the accomplished folk at court, I suspect, would have shared the feeling of Hippolyta rather than the Duke's at Bottom's play of Pyramus and Thisbe. Theseus, a true gentleman, is kind about this very unsophisticated performance. He speaks to Hippolyta in praise of the "fearful duty" and "tongue-tied simplicity" of the actors. But she will have none of it: "This is the silliest stuff that ever I heard," she says.

5
COURT AND COUNTRY

Lord Chesterfield and his Unfortunate Son

SHAKESPEARE HIMSELF went through the process described by Hollings and was en-gentled by a coat of arms. The Elizabethan was a great age for recruitment to the gentry from the ranks of craftsmen and merchants. But while birth was not essential, the emphasis, in considering what made a gentleman, was very much on accomplishments and manners. The influence of Castiglione was strong at Elizabeth's court and Chaucer's insistence that true *gentillesse* did not always go with social rank and included courtesy to the weak was less in evidence.

Nor did the 17th century in England add much to the concept of the gentleman, although it provided some noble examples of the combination of graceful accomplishment with courage and dignity. But in France there was a conscious attempt to define and put into practice a standard of conduct and taste that owes much to Castiglione and something to the tradition of the troubadours. This was the cult of *honnêteté*, a word that did not mean at all what an Englishman is inclined to expect, nor what it means in current French.[7]

The salon of Madame la marquise de Rambouillet was the nursery of that cult. She found the court of Henri IV coarse in language and manners; it was Gascon, rough, provincial. She invited her friends to meet at the hôtel de Rambouillet where they amused themselves, rather as the duchess of Urbino's friends had, by music, dancing and conversation. It was a place where men of letters and men of fashion met on equal terms and gradually established standards of taste, language and behaviour proper for "honnêtes gens", people like themselves, of high standards, refined, civilized people. They had lived through turbulent times and had seen civil war, chaos, insurrection; perhaps this was one reason why they admired purity of language, clear thought, clear form, polished phrases, work well constructed.

No one gave more thought to what made the essence of "honnêteté" than the Chevalier de Méré. He was, says Sainte-Beuve, who wrote of him two hundred years later, the Castiglione of his age, a man who had served with distinction in wars by land and sea, who strove for perfection in dancing, music, horsemanship, fencing and the use of language, whether in speech or writing.[8] But Sainte-Beuve adds: "I do not advise you to read him; he is tolerable only in short extracts." And he adds that de Méré laid open claim to something that is good only if one says nothing about it.

In his time, however, de Méré was accepted as the arbiter of elegance. He preached a doctrine of enlightened hedonism. The "honnête homme", he says, must observe "les bienséances", the *fitting* ways of doing things, and the essence of this is consideration for others. "To be happy with the least pain to oneself it is necessary that others should be happy too; *bienséance* is really no more than self-love well ordered," said one of his friends. Perfect leisure was the propitious climate for "honnêteté". It is only "fainéants", people with neither *métier* nor profession, who can develop cultivated minds and tender hearts, who do not look for high places before kings but seek only to bring joy to everyone. It is sordid to wish to please for some ulterior motive; the true *honnête homme* seeks to please simply for the sake of giving pleasure. "I know nothing under heaven to be put before honnêteté," cried de Méré; "it is the quintessence of all the virtues."

There is a note of sentimental enthusiasm here and something artificial about the whole cult. The aim was to give pleasure to others – but there is a strong implication that the "others" are "honnêtes gens" too – members of the cult. The term "honnête homme" in this sense faded out of the French language but, while it lasted, the cult provided a standard not entirely dependent on birth, and its memory was of influence both in France and in England. In particular, it made an important contribution to the strange experiment of the earl of Chesterfield, who set about making in flesh and blood a perfect living gentleman.

Lord Chesterfield had achieved some distinction as a diplomat and as the Lord Lieutenant of Ireland. He had the Garter before he was forty and had a reputation as a wit, as an orator and as a writer. But he withdrew from politics and in the later part of his life devoted himself almost entirely to the education of his son. Philip Stanhope was not his heir, being illegitimate, the offspring of an affair with a French lady, Elisabeth du Bouchet, whom he had met when he was Ambassador at the Hague. She was not noble; she had no fortune; Chesterfield himself was in debt and in 1732, when her baby was born, he was back in England, out of employment and out of love. They discussed marriage but appear to have agreed amicably that he should make a marriage of convenience. This he did with great success. He married Petronilla Melusina, the daughter of George i's German mistress, the duchess of Kendal, who was immensely rich. Petronilla continued to live with her mother, next door to Lord Chesterfield in Grosvenor Square; Elisabeth du Bouchet lived with her son in Marlborough Street. It was an odd arrangement, but he was now wealthy. Chesterfield paid the bills and looked after the boy; he had no child from his wife and came gradually to believe that his last and greatest work was to be Philip Stanhope – *his* creation, the perfect courtier, wit and gentleman.

Of course it is one of the recurring tragedies of human life. In every country, in every generation, self-centred men have supposed that their sons would grow up exactly like themselves and they have been disappointed. But in Lord Chesterfield's case, there is an added poignancy, because he expected so much, because he lavished on his son's education such reams and reams of detailed instruction, because he expressed himself so admirably and often with such good sense and yet was so obstinately blind to his son's circumstances and feelings.

Philip Stanhope had no right to his name, which he bore by his father's courtesy; he had no fortune of his own, nothing but what his father allowed him. But he could not complain of neglect. His father's concern for his education began at a very early age; letters, both in French and English, arrived at Marlborough Street and soon his governess must see that they were answered punctually and neatly. The letters – on special occasions they were in Latin – continued when the governess had been replaced by a tutor. They continued at Westminster School, where Philip spent the years from ten to fourteen. Westminster had a reputation for Greek and Latin, and four years "at a great school", Lord Chesterfield considered,

Grosvenor Square in the late 18th century. The country was close to the town from the point of view of a bird – but miles away in spirit.

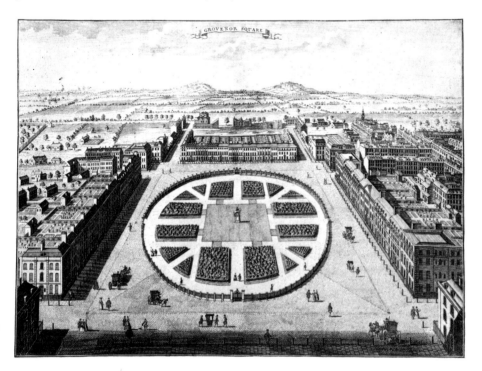

would teach a boy "to shift for himself and to bustle in the world". Such a boy, he thought, "acquires a worldly sagacity at fourteen, which a domestic education would not give him at twenty". At fourteen Philip left West-minster and was sent on a prolonged tour of the continent with a tutor.

The letters followed him at frequent intervals and he was expected to reply at length, with his reflections on the people he had met, the political situation, the condition of the army, the progress of communications and industry. He was being trained to become a member of Parliament and also a diplomat, but above all to be an "honnête homme".

Lord Chesterfield put the essence of his views in one sentence in a very early letter to his son.[9] "As learning, honour and virtue are absolutely necessary to gain you the esteem and admiration of mankind, politeness and good-breeding are equally necessary to make you welcome and agreeable in conversation and common life." As to learning, he was to be master of Greek and Latin and fully acquainted with the great writers of antiquity; he must be fluent not only in English and in French, the tongue of his mother, but also in German and Italian; he ought to know well "history and geography, ancient and modern; philosophy, rational logic, rhetoric; and the constitutions and civil and military state of every country in Europe". "Take nothing for granted," continued Lord Chesterfield, "on the bare authority of the author, but weigh and consider in your own mind the probability of the facts and the justness of the reflections." But he must never fall into the errors of pride or pedantry. "Wear your learning, like your watch, in a private pocket; and do not pull it out merely to show you have one."

As to virtue, Lord Chesterfield became explicit only towards the end of what he called his son's apprenticeship. By virtue, he meant good behaviour in respect of "vices of the heart, lying, fraud, envy, malice and detraction". "I do not extend [the term] to the little frailties of youth, flowing from high spirits and warm blood." It might, certainly, have been embarrassing, both to Philip and himself, if he had. "Distinguish carefully between the pleasures of a man of fashion and the vices of a scoundrel," he continued. "In Paris an *arrangement*, which is in plain English a gallantry, is as necessary a part of a woman of fashion's establishment as her house, table and coach. A young fellow must be a very awkward one to be reduced to, or of a very singular taste to prefer, drabs and danger to a commerce (in the course of the world not disgraceful) with a woman of health, education and rank." "I will by no means pay," he went on, rubbing the point in, "for whores and their never failing consequences, surgeons." No doubt it was this passage that led Dr Johnson to say he taught the morals of a whore and the manners of a dancing-master. Johnson, of course, was about as far removed from Chesterfield's ideal as a man could well be.

Chesterfield, however, considered that "the solid advantages of the

Lord Chesterfield devoted
many years to trying to
make his son the perfect
gentleman. Dr Johnson said
he taught the manners of a
dancing-master and the
morals of a whore – but the
essence of his teaching is
that the art of pleasing lies
in wanting to please.

Poor Philip Stanhope! His father tried to make
him the perfect gentleman, and reproached him for
lacking polish and ease of manner. But his father
was earl of Chesterfield and a knight of the Garter, while
Philip was illegitimate and had nothing of his own
but a taste for old books – and ease of manner
comes from confidence, not reproaches. In this carefully
posed portrait by John Russell, painter to George III,
he is shown in a theatrical costume.

mind and heart were wasted without the art of pleasing", and, like de
Méré, he thought that the secret of pleasing was *wanting* to please. "You
will please others as you are attentive and civil to them." "Study a man's
aversions and weaknesses and remember them and do not put him out by
forgetting that he may have an aversion to, let us say, cats or cheese."
"Flatter a man by complimenting him on his foibles, not on the subject in
which he knows himself to excel." "A real beauty" – for example – "should
be flattered on her intelligence." "Do as you would be done by is the surest
method of pleasing."

Detail from *The Duet* by Arthur Devis (1711–87). Here is a young couple gracefully observing *les bienséances*, a favourite word of Lord Chesterfield's for the accepted ways of pleasing by trying to please.

All this will be ruined unless it is done with apparent ease. "Perfect good-breeding is equally inconsistent with a stiff formality, an impertinent forwardness and an awkward bashfulness." That awkward bashfulness "is the characteristic mark of an English booby", who "will get his sword between his legs or drop his hat and his cane when he enters a room". A well-bred man "talks to kings without concern; he trifles with women of the first condition with familiarity, gaiety, but with respect; and converses with his equals . . . upon general common topics that are not quite frivolous". "A gentleman observes *les bienséances* with his footman, even with a beggar in the street; he considers them as objects of compassion not of insult; he speaks to neither *d'un ton brusque* but corrects the one coolly and refuses the other with humanity."

Poor Philip Stanhope! It never seems to have occurred to his father that brilliance and ease of manner come of confidence and that to tell a boy not to get his sword between his legs when he comes into a room is just the way to make him do it. It was all very well for the earl of Chesterfield to be sure he could win every heart if he tried – but a very different matter for a boy without name or fortune of his own. Philip could not pretend to his father's certainty that the world would like him and he had tastes, if nothing else, of his own; he preferred old bookshops to the salons of sophisticated ladies. He did not even wish to have what his father called the "brillant d'un galant homme". He was a sad disappointment. His father wrote to him, rather wistfully: "I want that all the world shall like you as well as I love you." But in the end, the best diplomatic post he could obtain for Philip was one with which years before he had threatened him as the ultimate in failure. "Do you want to be no more than the Resident at Ratisbon?" he had written, and that was just what Philip became. He died at the age of 38. His father then heard for the first time that he had been married nine years and had two little boys. Lord Chesterfield wrote kindly to the widow, under-took the education of the boys and started writing them letters in their turn – but not with his old confidence.

The Country Squire

MANY PEOPLE TODAY will find Lord Chesterfield odious. The cool reproof for his footman, his humane refusal of the beggar, are a long way from Chaucer's *gentillesse*, and he is just as far from the troubadours. Women, he thought, were only "children of a larger growth", and "a man of sense only trifles with them, plays with them, humours and flatters them as he does with a sprightly forward child". The best of the Victorians might well have concluded that he was not quite a gentleman himself.

On the other hand, compared with de Méré and his friends, it strikes an English reader that he had a sense of public duty. Of course it had been the deliberate policy of the French crown that the nobles should have no power of their own. It was by depriving them of power that the unity of the king-dom and the strength of the crown had been established. In England, that had been achieved under the Tudors, and more recently the crown in its turn had been tamed. It was the great nobles who ruled the nation and the lesser gentry, the squires, who ruled the countryside. As far as nine-tenths of the people were concerned, it was the magistrates who were the govern-ment, responsible for the king's peace and for everything that concerned them. And the magistrates were the squires. All over England people had before them, walking about, visible, flesh-and-blood gentlemen who ruled them, sometimes harshly, but on the whole by standards which – except in the matter of poaching – they accepted themselves.

But while more public-spirited than his French counterpart, he was not coarse, as many of the squires were. What he believed in was the *enlightened* pursuit of pleasure. It was folly to aim at being what was called "a man of pleasure . . . drinking, gaming and swearing do not make for true pleasure

Sir Henry Morshead felling his timber to settle his gambling debts (by Thomas Rowlandson, 1816). All through the 18th century and into the 19th great families were being ruined by reckless gambling losses and new families taking their places – thus adding to the uncertainty as to who was a gentleman!

and are disgusting to a man of sense". And again: "sottish drinking, indiscriminate gluttony, driving coaches, rustic sports such as fox-chases and horse-chases, are in my opinion infinitely below the honest and industrious professions of a tailor and a shoemaker". "The longest life is too short for knowledge, consequently every moment is precious." Here he was very different from most of his countrymen, standing emphatically for the court, as opposed to the country, and for the French influence in English life.

The contrast between court and country had never been more marked than after the return of Charles II from exile in 1660. The plays of the Restoration are full of polished London gentlemen with French manners who laugh at boorish squires up from the country with names like Sir Tunbelly Clumsey,[10] who talk with provincial accents and get drunk. They smell and show their feelings and do not know how to behave. "You think you're in the country, where great lubberly brothers slabber and kiss one another when they meet, like a call of serjeants – 'tis not the fashion here . . ." says Witwoud in *The Way of the World* to his brother Sir Wilful Witwoud, meeting him after long absence.

The literature of the 18th century teems with portraits of country squires: amiable and lovable, if eccentric and sometimes rather silly, like Sir Roger de Coverley; boisterous, drunken, brutal yet affectionate like Squire

Western; quirkish, choleric, hypochondriac and determined to conceal good actions, like Matthew Bramble;[11] one could go on for ever. They could hardly be more different from the fine courtiers, the Mirabells and Lord Foppingtons, of the Restoration stage nor from Lord Chesterfield. Yet the two traditions, of the squire and the courtier, do merge in the English gentlemen of the Victorian age.

Two points only need to be underlined. Until the French Revolution everyone took for granted what Shakespeare called "degree", the fact of social difference. Squire Western "did indeed consider a parity of fortune and circumstances as necessary an ingredient in marriage as difference of sexes . . . and had no more apprehension of his daughter's falling in love with a poor man than with any animal of a different species . . ." But the barriers were not clear cut. It was not always easy to tell who was who. "Nay," said the landlady (again in *Tom Jones*), "if I thought he was a gentleman's son, thof he was a bye-blow, I should behave to him in another manner, for many of these bye-blows come to be great men, and, as my first husband used to say, never affront any customer that's a gentleman." Moll Flanders, looking round for a husband, remarked that "she was not averse to a tradesman, but then I would have a tradesman, forsooth, that has something of a gentleman, too, that . . . he might become a sword and look as like a gentleman as another man . . ." "'Tis something of a relief," she sighed on another occasion, "even to be undone by a man of honour rather than by a scoundrel;" and what she means by a man of honour is a man with a touch of style, who could pass for a gentleman, as she could pass for a lady.

Certain of inequality, even though not always quite clear who was who, the English of the 18th century lived in close physical proximity with their servants and made them confidants of the most intimate secrets. In the reign of Queen Anne, great ladies at table would joke with their footmen, but as the century wore on they came by little and little to insist on greater social distance. The easy familiarities of the Waitwells and Mincings of the Restoration comedies – who know just what the young master has had to pawn and to what strange expedients her ladyship has to resort for her complexion – are replaced by Lord Chesterfield's cool correction of his footman; and when Boswell embarks on his Continental tour, his servant finds it necessary to reproach him for talking to him in a tone that is too familiar. He has not, his servant fears, "les manières d'un Seigneur. Il a le coeur trop ouvert . . ."

That insistence on aloofness may stand to underline the growing stiffness of class barriers, which crept over the century as slowly, as intermittently but as inexorably as stiffness in the joints of an aging man.

6

ELEGANCE
AND PRINCIPLE

A Gentleman's Daughter

About thirty years ago, Miss Maria Ward of Huntingdon, with only seven thousand pounds, had the good luck to captivate Sir Thomas Bertram of Mansfield Park in the County of Northampton, and to be thereby raised to the rank of a baronet's lady, with all the comforts and consequence of a handsome house and a large income.

IF YOU HAD never read a word of Miss Austen's novels before and were to begin with *Mansfield Park*, you might be pardoned for missing some of the implications of that opening sentence. But those who know her will picture a change of expression as she wrote it – a movement at the corner of the mouth, something less than a smile, a tremor not unlike the dimple on the surface of a Hampshire trout stream which betrays the strength of the current below, a gleam of demure satisfaction at hitting on just those words. She was beginning a novel in which she meant to illustrate how "captivation" might degenerate into a torpid benevolence, as Lady Bertram's own marriage did; how disastrous it might be to marry – as Lady Bertram's elder daughter married – with only "comforts and consequence" in view; how truly appalling on the other hand might be the result of marrying, as Lady Bertram's younger sister did, "to disoblige her family". Miss Austen meant also to show how charming manners may conceal a lack of principle and how a selfless love may endure without hope. She was setting out, in short, to write "only a novel" – "only a work in which . . . the most thorough knowledge of human nature, the happiest delineation of its varieties, the liveliest effusions of wit and humour, are conveyed to the world in the best chosen language".

Of course, it is as novels that Miss Austen's books should be read. It would indeed be a strange inhuman creature who did not become involved in the affairs of her characters. But they are social history too. They are minute and exact sketches – worked, as she wrote in a letter to a nephew, with a fine brush on a little bit of ivory two inches wide – of the way her people thought about marriage, property, social differences, and the kind of behaviour which was proper for ladies and gentlemen. It is hard to find a single word for this behaviour; it included "elegance", "gentility", an air and a manner, but also good taste, sound principles, fidelity, consideration for others, much of what Chaucer would have called "gentillesse" and the Chevalier de Méré "honnêteté". She observed, she recorded, she laughed.

Her books were published in the early years of the 19th century and she died in 1817, but Miss Austen belongs in spirit to the 18th century. She writes from the point of view of a lady of the lesser gentry at the end of that century and, embedded in her novels, are pictures which illustrate to perfection the ideas which that century bequeathed to the Victorians as to the proper behaviour of a gentleman. But it would be a lifeless and quite unreal analysis to extract her thoughts on that subject from the flesh and blood of her novels. Her thoughts on love and marriage are inseparably blended with her thoughts on good taste, on elegance, on comfort and on principle, and her reflections on one reveal her views on the other. She must be looked on in the round. And besides – it is always a pleasure to recall her.[12]

Take, for instance, Charlotte Lucas, musing on her engagement to Mr Collins – who only two days before had proposed to Elizabeth Bennet and had been refused.

"Mr Collins, to be sure," thought Charlotte, "was neither sensible nor agreeable: his society was irksome, and his attachment to her must be imaginary. But still he would be her husband. Without thinking highly either of men or matrimony, marriage had always been her object: it was the only honourable provision for well-educated young women of small fortune, and, however uncertain of giving happiness, must be their pleasantest preservative from want. This preservative she had now obtained; and at the age of twenty-seven, without having ever been handsome, she felt all the good luck of it."

She was, all the same, uneasy. She knew that Elizabeth Bennet – her closest friend – would think less well of her. She was right. To Elizabeth:

Charlotte the wife of Mr Collins was a most humiliating picture. And to the pang of a friend disgracing herself, and sunk in her esteem, was added the distressing conviction that it was impossible for that friend to be tolerably happy in the lot she had chosen.

It was not long after this that Mr Darcy made his first proposal of marriage to Elizabeth. He told her that he had struggled in vain against his strong feelings; it was a most unsuitable match, for on her mother's side she had connections in trade, while, he, with many acres, a wide park and a splendid mansion, was allied with the noblest families in the land. But he had struggled in vain; he surrendered and laid his heart at her feet. To his astonishment, she refused him and added, after some exchanges:

ABOVE LEFT When Elizabeth Bennet first saw Mr Darcy, she thought he was insufferably proud and stand-offish. He was rich and well-connected; everyone flattered him and he was bored by flattery – and showed it.

ABOVE RIGHT If Mr Darcy was haughty, Sir William Lucas was both pompous and obsequious.

LEFT Elizabeth never flattered Mr Darcy, and when she began to be impertinent he so far improved that she began to feel she would have him.

OPPOSITE Lady Catherine de Bourgh insists that Elizabeth Bennet must not marry Mr Darcy because her uncle is "in trade". But, although she does not say so, Elizabeth has already rejected him; his behaviour does not come up to her standard of what is "gentlemanlike".

"You are mistaken, Mr Darcy, if you suppose that the mode of your declaration affected me in any other way than as it spared me the concern which I might have felt in refusing you, had you behaved in a more gentlemanlike manner."

He had failed in the same department of courtesy as the young knight in the wife of Bath's tale. He had emphasized his grandeur and her deficiencies. It was not "gentlemanlike". It was not magnanimous.

Much later, after various misunderstandings had been cleared up, she began to feel she might forgive him, but hardly dared to hope for the opportunity until the intervention of his aunt Lady Catherine de Bourgh. Lady Catherine had heard the rumour of an engagement and came to put an end to any such idea. Was Miss Bennet engaged to Mr Darcy? Would she undertake to repudiate any such proposal? Miss Bennet must decline to answer such questions. Surely Miss Bennet could see that such an alliance would "ruin him in the eyes of all his friends and make him the contempt of the world"! Surely she could see the unwisdom of trying to abandon the sphere in which she had been brought up!

"In marrying your nephew," replied Elizabeth, "I should not consider myself as quitting that sphere. He is a gentleman; I am a gentleman's daughter; so far we are equal."

"True, you are a gentleman's daughter. But what was your mother? Who are your uncles and aunts?"

Lady Catherine is finally routed by the spirited remark:

"Allow me to say, Lady Catherine, that the arguments with which you have supported this extraordinary application have been as frivolous as the application was ill-judged."

Lady Catherine stormed away to impose her will on the young man, but her account of Miss Bennet's obstinacy was just what he needed to bring him a second time to her feet – and this time all was bliss. He had seen his error and all her impertinence was rewarded. After their marriage, Mr and Mrs Darcy were most intimate with Mr and Mrs Gardiner – that very uncle whose involvement in trade had been so alarming. But Mr Gardiner, brother of Elizabeth's mother, "was a sensible, gentlemanlike man, greatly superior to his sister, as well by nature as by education". Not of our elders cometh *gentillesse* – or, at least, not only of our elders.

Prudence and Sensibility

WITH ALL HER fire and courage, Elizabeth Bennet was never lacking in sense. Marianne Dashwood, on the other hand, made sensibility her guide. At seventeen she exclaimed:

"I am convinced that I shall never see a man whom I can truly love! I require so much!"

But, as you remember, such a man did appear in the form of Willoughby. He agreed with Marianne about poetry, about picturesque beauty and the infamy of second marriages. Willoughby was "exactly formed to engage Marianne's heart . . ." A good horseman, he danced well, he had good taste in drawing and music. In short, he was very like Castiglione's perfect courtier – but alas! he was lacking in *principle* and he was fickle. He is one of the line of fascinating young men which includes Wickham in *Pride and Prejudice*, Henry Crawford in *Mansfield Park*, Frank Churchill in *Emma* and Mr William Elliott in *Persuasion*. Each of them shows what Miss Austen would call a marked preference for one of her heroines, each fails in fidelity, in staying power, in steadiness.

The troubadours are not altogether forgotten; romantic love is everything for Marianne and still something for Miss Austen, though to be regarded with humour, with realism and with prudence. A prudent young lady, though in spite of herself her affections may be aroused by a young man greatly her superior, will never reveal it. And her sense of propriety, her perception of what is genteel and elegant, will preserve her from any attachment to a young man markedly inferior.

Superior, you may ask, in what? Inferior in what? No one had a sharper sense of *degree* than Jane Austen but the scale by which she measured is of very complex construction. Consider the reflections of Emma – "handsome, clever and rich" – when she gets home after Mr Elton, inflamed by Mr Weston's good wine, had proposed to herself instead of to her little friend Harriet Smith, for whom she had intended him:

... that he should talk of encouragement ... suppose himself her equal in connection or mind! – look down upon her friend, so well understanding the gradation of rank below him, and be so blind to what rose above, as to fancy himself showing no presumption in addressing her! – it was most provoking.

It was not, you notice, only a matter of wealth and "connection" but of "mind", by which she meant elegance, good taste, and consideration for

Willoughby was just the man to win Marianne's heart – young, handsome, enthusiastic about music and poetry, a fine horseman – but Marianne was poor and when a girl with money appeared ... !

"The officers of the ——shire were in general a very ... gentlemanlike set ... but Mr Wickham was far beyond them all in person, countenance, air and walk ..." But he proved untruthful and unreliable.

others. Emma was a heroine whom Miss Austen thought nobody would like very much but herself and her creator often teases her for her insistence on "degree". But all Miss Austen's heroines, not only Emma, would have agreed in condemning the society in which the unfortunate Fanny found herself when she went home after nine years at Mansfield Park in the household of Sir Thomas Bertram. Fanny had refused Henry Crawford – rich, charming, the admired of all. She alone had perceived his lack of *principle* – and everybody – even kind Edmund whom she secretly adored – thought she must be out of her senses to turn him down. Sir Thomas, also kind although awe-inspiring, thought that a girl who could refuse so advantageous an offer would be the better for seeing the result of an imprudent marriage. So he sent her home on a visit to her own mother, Lady Bertram's sister, who had married a Lieutenant of Marines, "without education, fortune or connections". She soon had "a large and still increasing family, a husband disabled for active service but not the less equal to liquor and company, and a very small income to supply their wants". After her long absence, Fanny was appalled at the noise and squalor of a small house in which nine children were growing up, and she soon began to long for the space, the quiet, the ordered decorum of Mansfield Park. There, she thought, "if tenderness could be ever supposed wanting, good sense and good breeding supplied its place . . ." Here in Portsmouth there was not only ceaseless tumult but company she found distasteful. "The men appeared to her all coarse, the women all pert, everybody underbred."

To be "pert" was one of the worst offences against "good breeding". Elizabeth's mother, Mrs Bennet, had been an embarrassment to her two elder daughters because of her lack of breeding, but she was not pert. She was silly; whenever an eligible young man looked at one of her daughters, she would jump to the conclusion that he was about to propose marriage and bustle away to one of her neighbours to crow over the conquest as though her married daughter had just paid the first visit in her elegant landaulette and pair.

Mrs Elton, however, was not so much silly as pert and vulgar. She made a poor impression from the start. "Her person was rather good; her face not unpretty; but neither feature, nor air nor voice, nor manner was elegant." She sought always for effect; she talked incessantly of her rich connections; she patronized and domineered. She even tried to patronize Emma. She was insufferably familiar. On top of all, she was ill-natured. The Eltons took the first chance they could of humiliating poor little Harriet Smith and Mrs Elton was the only person in Highbury to show malice when Mr Knightley and Emma became engaged.

Warmth and Fidelity

IT WAS GOOD NATURE and real kindness on the other hand that redeemed the vulgarity of Mrs Jennings. No one could deny that she was vulgar; she embarrassed both Elinor and Marianne by teasing them about the "beaux" for whom she supposed them to be sighing. But she thought they would like it; she was kind and motherly, even to Marianne, who was sometimes so deep in sensibility that she did not even try to be civil. One of Mrs Jennings' daughters was redeemed by the same good nature, but her other daughter, Lady Middleton, was very different. "Though perfectly well bred, she was reserved, cold, and had nothing to say for herself beyond the most common-place inquiry or remark."

It is easy then to see who failed to reach Miss Austen's standards. Those of whom she approved must pass her tests not only in good manners but in a taste for drawing, music and poetry. They must have a sense of humour and also be capable of enthusiasm. They must have been brought up to express themselves well and be what she called in a letter "conversable" – sociable and ready to talk. To all this they must add consideration for others. How stern Mr Knightley was with Emma when she fell from grace and was rude to Miss Bates! He gave her a sharp scolding, and she knew she had deserved it. "Never had she felt so agitated, mortified, grieved at any circumstance in her life." She had failed in that courtesy to the unfortunate that she knew was the essence of *gentillesse*. But she was sorry for what she had done. She went to call on Miss Bates next day.

The point that no amount of external polish can make up for a lack of warmth is made even more explicitly in *Persuasion*, the last of the six canonical novels. Anne Elliott had suffered a great deal from the "heartless elegance" of her father and her elder sister.

She prized the frank, the open-hearted, the eager character beyond all others. Warmth and enthusiasm did captivate her still. She felt that she could so much more depend upon the sincerity of those who sometimes looked or said a careless or a hasty thing, than of those whose presence of mind never varied, whose tongue never slipped.

This is a long way from Lord Chesterfield, whose "heartless elegance" had matched Sir Walter Elliott's.

Miss Austen was a novelist, and to her each situation and each person was unique. There are lovers in every novel she wrote but there is all the difference in the world between their feelings for each other. Contrast, for example, the supreme crisis in the affairs of Emma with that in Anne Elliott's. Up until this moment, Emma had thought of Mr Knightley as an uncle – young, much liked and much respected but basically an uncle; when she realised that another woman was in love with him "it darted

Of all Miss Austen's heroes, Captain Wentworth was most perfect – a successful officer in the Royal Navy, and faithful to the memory of Anne Elliott through all misunderstandings.

How different from the "heartless elegance" of Sir Walter Elliott were Captain Wentworth's naval friends! How much more honest and manly the pursuits of their leisure!

through her with the speed of an arrow, that **Mr Knightley** must marry nobody but herself". She is possessive, exclusive. But when Anne Elliott and Captain Wentworth – all misunderstandings at last cleared away – are suddenly given the chance to be alone, they seized it "with smiles reined in and spirits dancing". Nothing could express more exactly their equality in delight.

Every marriage, too, was different. It would be a pleasant digression to speculate on how Emma's marriage and Elizabeth Bennet's and Anne Elliott's would have turned out. But behind the differences, one can discern an ideal marriage, one that reconciled the old cult of courtly love – grown respectable like Dorigen's married love in the franklin's tale – with the kind of marriage that Sancho Panza would have understood, in which the material goods on either side could be counted up. In the same way, it is possible to generalize about the men she dislikes, who are either pompous and insensitive, like Mr Collins and Mr Elton, or elegant but haughty, like General Tilney and Sir Walter Elliott, or fickle and shallow, like Willoughby and Henry Crawford. The true hero has not only the air and manner of a gentleman – style and elegance – but must have *solid* qualities too. He must have warmth; he must be faithful and enduring in love; he must have staying power. He may be rather silent in general company; indeed, Mr

Darcy and Mr Knightley might appear rather taciturn and even occasionally grim. Only Henry Tilney and Captain Wentworth would immediately engage a young girl's fancy.

Charm was flashy and likely to be dangerous; solid worth was reticent about its own value. A reserve about the deeper feelings is the hinge on which the plot turns again and again; it is the heart both of *Persuasion* and of *Pride and Prejudice*. A proud silence, an austere reserve, were increasingly to be part of the right behaviour for a gentleman as the century wore on. It echoes Castiglione's point that in love no advance should be made from which retreat is not possible, but what to the Italian courtier was a game, to the English lady was deadly earnest. There ought to be reserve on the part of both sexes – very different indeed from the days when a young man felt he must carve his lady's name on every tree. Miss Austen's heroes and heroines would have thought it vulgar to parade so intimate a feeling. But a vulgar young lady like Miss Steele *wanted* to be teased about the Doctor and when Henry Tilney explained to Catherine that his brother's affair with Isabella would not last long he said: "The mess-room will drink Isabella Thorpe for a fortnight." There was still a long way to go before the tight-lipped regimental reticence of the late Victorians took hold.

Miss Austen was aware of every element of ambiguity in the word "gentleman", whether used as a marker of social position or implying a standard of conduct. There was a moment of embarrassment for Anne Elliott, early

"The mess-room will drink Isabella Thorpe for a fortnight". Such is the prophecy of Henry Tilney in *Northanger Abbey* which was published in 1818; but by the end of the century it was not the act of a gentleman to mention a woman's name in the mess.

in *Persuasion,* when her father's agent could not remember the name of "a gentleman who lived a few years back at Monkford". Nor could her father. But Anne knew very well who was meant; he was the brother of the young naval officer to whom she had once been engaged.

"You mean Mr Wentworth, I suppose?" said Anne.

"Wentworth? Oh, ay, Mr Wentworth, the curate of Monkford. You misled me by the term *gentleman.* I thought you were speaking of some man of property . . ." said Sir Walter. But in his daughter's judgment, both the Wentworths had a "gentillesse" she did not perceive in her father.

"The village down the hill", on the other hand, is not much more in evidence here than in Castiglione's scheme. For a man to be a good land-lord is part of his duty; for a lady, the poor are there to be visited. In the brief period when Henry Crawford is trying to win Fanny's approval, it is to please her that he hurries away to Norfolk to busy himself with looking after his tenants. When her father decides to let Kellynch Hall, Anne Elliott is concerned that the tenants should be people who will not neglect the villagers and before she leaves she goes to every house in the parish "as a sort of take-leave". Emma took Harriet once on a charitable visit to a poor sick family and as they left the cottage, she said to Harriet:

> "These are the sights, Harriet, to do one good. How trifling they make everything else appear! I feel now as if I could think of nothing but these poor creatures all the rest of the day . . ."

But a turn in the lane brought Mr Elton into sight and it was not long before Emma was pursuing her plot for marrying him to Harriet. Good breeding demanded politeness to Miss Bates and principle demanded kindness to the poor, but there was not much notion of common humanity. They were still a different species.

Nonetheless, the kind of man Miss Austen and her heroines admired may stand in the line from Chaucer and Castiglione, as a picture of the gentleman, not the only picture but one of the best which the 19th century inherited from the 18th and to which the Victorians added their own specific contributions.

7

THE GENTLEMAN
AS SPORTSMAN

The Corinthian Tradition

MISS AUSTEN'S WORLD is not only delicately drawn but viewed from a feminine angle. Her ideal of the gentleman makes one part of the inheritance of Victorian England, but it is far from being the whole.

Quite a different figure from Mr Darcy or Mr Knightley would have presented itself, if you mentioned the word gentleman, to many of Miss Austen's fellow-citizens. They would think of the Corinthian, the sportsman, or the blood. Courage, pugnacity, readiness to take a risk, disregard for money – often reckless extravagance, often a callous disregard for the feelings of other people – these were qualities of the eccentric sporting characters who flourished in the first half of the 19th century. Some of them were great nobles; some were wealthy squires. Most of them had a wide popular backing which continued through the century. Their behaviour was not always decorous but they were liked and admired; they did contribute something to the popular picture of the gentleman and to that readiness to accept class differences that dominated Queen Victoria's reign.

There were people who spoke of the Prince Regent as the "First Gentleman of Europe" – sometimes, no doubt, ironically, but if it had been always in mockery Thackeray would not have needed to launch that blistering attack which begins:

What is it to be a gentleman? Is it to be honest, to be gentle, to be generous, to be wise, and, possessing all these qualities, to exercise them in the most graceful outward manner? Ought a gentleman to be a loyal son, a true husband and honest father? Ought his life to be decent – his bills paid – his tastes to be high and elegant – his aims in life lofty and noble?

If to those questions the answer was yes, then, wrote Thackeray, the Prince was on every count no gentleman.[13] But even he had a following and this was perhaps because there persisted in the minds of Englishmen, right through the century and well into the next, an indulgence, sometimes an affection, for the rich, hard-riding spendthrift, preferably a master of foxhounds, or a race-horse owner, or an amateur of boxing, or all three.

The Prince Regent himself was hardly a sportsman, but he borrowed some of their glory; he shared the affectation of being knowledgeable about horses and the "noble art" of fisticuffs.

It was the custom in those days [wrote Thackeray, of the year 1810] with many gentlemen to dress as much like coachmen as possible: in top-boots, huge white coats with capes, Belcher neckerchiefs and the like adornments; and at the tables of bachelors of the very first fashion, you would meet with prize-fighters and jockeys and hear a great deal about the prize-ring, the cock-pit and the odds . . .[14]

Forty years later, in 1853, Surtees makes the same point:

Just then, up came a broad-brimmed hat, above a confused mass of greatcoats and coloured shawls.

"Holloa, Jack?" exclaimed Mr. Puffington, laying hold of a mother-of-pearl button, nearly as large as a tart-plate – "not off yet?"

"Just going," replied Jack with a touch of his hat, as he rolled on; adding, "Want aught down the road?"

"What coachman is that?" asked we.

"Coachman!" replied Puff with a snort; "That's Jack Linchpin – Honourable Jack Linchpin – son of Lord Splinterbars – best gentleman coachman in England."

It was not only noble lords who were guilty of this kind of affectation. John Thorpe, in *Northanger Abbey*, "seemed fearful of being too handsome unless he wore the dress of a groom, and too much like a gentleman unless he were easy where he ought to be civil and impudent where he might be allowed to be easy". Ben Allen and Bob Sawyer in *Pickwick* are in the same tradition. It still showed signs of life among Oxford undergraduates in the 1960s, although, when they frayed holes in their new jeans, it was in order to be thought, not "sporting" but "of the people".

Lawlessness too was part of the tradition. Thackeray, again of 1810, says:

. . . Bludyer, a brave and athletic man, (a friend of the writer's) would often give a loose to his spirits and mill a Charley or two. . . . The young bloods of those days thought it no harm to spend a night in the watch-house . . .

A "Charley" was a night-watchman, the predecessor of the "Bobby", and to "mill" of course was to fight with fists. Again forty years later, Surtees writes:

We were at the Finish together till six this morning – such fun! – bonneted a Charley, stole his rattle, and broke an early breakfastman's stall all to shivers.

And, at any rate until 1914, it was thought suitable to steal policemen's helmets on Boat Race Night, conduct falling far short of *gentillesse*.

But the cult of sport and the widespread admiration for the sporting hero can best be illustrated by sketching three famous figures, known – indeed reverenced – throughout England for their feats on the hunting-field and with their fists. They are Thomas Assheton Smith, George Osbaldeston, and the fifth earl of Lonsdale. Assheton Smith was born in 1776, Osbaldeston ten years later, and Lord Lonsdale in 1858, a year before Assheton Smith's death; Lonsdale died in 1944, so between them they covered a century and a half.

Le Premier Chasseur d'Angleterre

Fox-hunting became a cult, almost a religion, with high priests, genuine devotees, and a host of hypocritical followers whose devotion was only a matter of fashion. Assheton Smith, who was described by Napoleon as "le premier chasseur d'Angleterre", was one of the high priests, perhaps *the* high priest. His biographer, Sir John Eardley-Wilmot, Bt, begins his account of his hero's life with a eulogy on fox-hunting:

The manly amusement of fox hunting is entirely, and in its perfection, exclusively, British. Its pursuit gives hardihood, and nerve, and intrepidity to our youth, while it confirms and prolongs the strength and vigour of our manhood; it is the best corrective to those habits of luxury and those concomitants of wealth which would otherwise render our aristocracy effeminate and degenerate; it serves to retain the moral influence of the higher over the lower classes of society, promotes good fellowship among equals and is one of the strongest preservatives of that national spirit by which we are led to cherish, above all things, a life of active energy, independence, and freedom.[16]

The English have usually been able to persuade themselves that there is a serious moral purpose behind whatever they enjoy. As recently as the winter of 1940, Lord Leconfield, feeling that it was his duty to keep up the standard of horses and hounds, not to mention the national character, was hunting, with only his whipper-in and one other, when he rode to what he took to be the hulloo of someone who had viewed the fox. It proved to be only the cheer of a spectator at a village football match. He was outraged. "Have you people nothing better to do in wartime than play football?" he shouted.[15]

At the beginning of the 19th century, when this cult began to develop, fox-hunting had just passed through a revolution. The typical hounds of the 18th century had been slow and heavy; when one old hound "made long-drawn proclamation of the scent", each particular hound must "ratify and confirm it for himself". "Not a yard would they go without scent." The horses were slow and the men ponderous. The master of the Heavyside hunt in *Mr Romford's Hounds* rode at 19 stone. Neither master, huntsmen nor followers were in a hurry. They had time to enjoy meeting each other; they had time to enjoy the country scene, the structure of elm and oak etched in filigree against the sky, the sharp autumnal scent of rotting fern. When at last they set to work, they would recognize the note of each particular hound, revelling in the good work of old Conqueror and applauding the progress of young Ringwood. There was not much galloping; they would trot along a lane or canter ponderously over a meadow.

All that had changed before Assheton Smith became master of the Quorn. There the long reign of Mr Meynell had gradually transformed the picture of what a run should be. Now the object was to push a fast straight-running fox briskly out of covert into open country where he would follow a line of several miles towards the next refuge before he was killed. The pack were a team, trained to rally at once to a hound who spoke to scent; they must be level in looks and performance and must run "as though a table-cloth would cover them", with no stragglers. Once hounds and huntsman were away behind their fox, the field rode to be near hounds and be up at the finish. The more fashionable the pack, the more competitive the field. He must be a bold horseman, well-mounted on a near-thoroughbred horse, to see a death with the Quorn.

Leicestershire provided the best galloping country, with big fields of permanent grass and stiff fences which must be leaped by the keen riders, all eager to beat each other in what was almost a cross-country race. In a "provincial" hunt, there would be fewer keen riders and a larger contingent who would look for a gate or a gap instead of riding straight to hounds.

Thus a schism developed between those who rode to hunt and those who hunted to ride. The master of the Quorn had always to bear in mind some three hundred jealous riders, who, if a fox turned left or right, might overrun his line and spoil the hounds' performance. They were many of them dare-devil riders, little interested in the work of the hounds. At the other extreme, with a provincial pack, there would be survivors of the older fashion, men who did not want to break their necks and loved to watch slow careful hounds.

Assheton Smith was an unequalled rider, absolutely fearless and always with his hounds, which he usually hunted himself, but he had no sympathy for mere competitive riding. He rode to be with hounds and would let his hounds hunt their line themselves, never lifting them unless they were clearly at fault. He was brusque, sometimes downright rude, to anyone who pressed his hounds.

He was at school at Eton from the age of seven, for eleven years, and would say, characteristically, that he learned nothing there. But in fact he did acquire a life-long admiration for Horace, apart from cricketing, rowing and boxing. At Eton, he was chiefly remembered for "his famous battle with Jack Musters", still spoken of by Etonians, says his biographer, sixty years later. On that famous day at Eton, they pounded each other for more than an hour; Smith always said that Musters had ruined for ever any claim he might have had to good looks, but when it was over they were friends for life.

Musters was another hero of the Corinthian age, second only to Assheton Smith and Osbaldeston. Of Musters, Nimrod, the famous hunting writer, wrote: "There was a time when he could have leaped, hopped, ridden, fought, danced, played cricket, fished, swum, shot, played tennis and skated with any man in Europe" – a list of excellences that would have pleased neither Castiglione nor Lord Chesterfield.

Assheton Smith was "one of the best batsmen in England" but cricket was only a summer pastime. Hunting was his passion; he was a master of hounds for 48 years and hunted, sometimes four days a week and sometimes six, until he was 78. His ruling principle was that he must be with his hounds and if a fence was too big to leap he would still ride straight at it, trusting to get to the other side with a fall, which would do no serious harm either to him or his horse. "There is no place you cannot get over with a fall," was one of his sayings and he would add that every man who rode must *learn* to fall, relaxing the muscles so as to fall loosely and clinging to the reins so that he need waste no time catching his horse. He could ride horses that no one else could manage at all, having a very light hand on the rein, which he treated like silk (said Nimrod), but above all having a *way* with a horse, so that the most intractable brute would recognize him at once as a master and seem in his hands like a polished lady's hack. He once changed horses at the covertside, taking over an incorrigible puller he had never ridden before. The horse was in a very severe bit; Smith took off the curb-chain and put it in his pocket. "We shall never see you again," said its owner. But in his hands it was a lamb. He had a similar power with hounds. Long before he was in sight, his servants knew that he was coming by the behaviour of his hounds, and once he appeared no huntsman or whipper-in could hold them.

When the doctors suggested that his wife might benefit by a winter in Madeira, she and he alike felt that a winter abroad was unthinkable. It would be better to bring Madeira to England. So a conservatory was built, more than three hundred feet long and connected with the house by a broad covered walk of glass, another 900 feet in length and all warmed by hot water pipes. "I suppose the Squire means to hunt indoors when there's a frost," said a passing farmer.

But to his descendants of the 20th century as well as to his ancestors of the 18th, the strangest thing about Smith would have seemed his readiness to take on anyone with his fists. There was the coalheaver whose dray was obstructed by Smith's horse, which he had tied up outside a bank at Loughborough, but which had moved out across the street. The drayman gave the horse a flick with his whip – which of course was resented by a high-spirited

Thomas Goosey of the Beauvoir (painted here by John Ferneley) was almost as famous in hunting circles as one of the great Masters such as Assheton Smith and Osbaldeston. A professional huntsman had to be a judge of a horse and a hound, a fine horseman, skilled in the habits of foxes and wise in his dealings with farmers, gamekeepers and earthstoppers – not to mention members of the hunt.

and highly fed hunter. Smith was out of the bank in a minute. "Defend yourself," he said and the coalheaver was only too ready. He was the terror of the neighbourhood and 14 stone to Smith's 11; they went at it hammer and tongs. A crowd collected and the cheering brought the constables. They were separated, both having been severely punished, but the drayman on the whole having had the best of it. Next day, Smith sent the man five pounds with a message that he was the best man he had ever fought. "God bless his Honour," said the drayman, who had been afraid he might get into trouble. But he added that he had earned the money – "for his blows are like the kick of a horse".

His pugnacity continued until the end of his life. At the age of sixty-nine, he quite inexcusably knocked down a solicitor's clerk, twenty years old, who brought him a letter that Smith found both impertinent and dishonest. "Except for my father," he said once, "I am the worst tempered man in England." But it was a sudden quick temper for which he usually made swift amends. And there was equally sudden generosity. Once as he rode home after hunting, a violent downpour forced him to take shelter under a tree. From a nearby cottage of cob and thatch, a labourer came out to offer him fire and shelter. Next morning a carpenter and bricklayers turned up to build that man a better house. It was like the bounty of Haroun al-Raschid.

Assheton Smith was by no means the typical Corinthian. He did not bet; he drank very little; he held racing in contempt; he walked to church every Sunday. He was an excellent man of business and reorganized his slate quarries in North Wales so as vastly to increase their output. He was interested in the design of ships and boats and helped to pioneer a revolution in the lines of ships. He was for many years a member of Parliament and, although he seldom spoke in the House, he did a good deal behind the scenes and was conscientious in voting in important divisions. He would hunt his hounds near Andover in the morning and then drive post – that is in relays – in a light chariot with four horses, to Westminster, meeting his hounds next morning an hour later than usual, punctually at twelve o'clock. He was a friend of the duke of Wellington, whom he resembled in a certain forthright simplicity and in a strong sense of duty.

To read of Assheton Smith is to be staggered by the physical energy of a man who would sometimes ride thirty miles or more to a meet and back the same day, who would hunt all day and every day – and hunt, mark you, as huntsman – and yet had time for so much else. But he would not be remembered just for energy. He *was* remembered because of his pre-eminence as a horseman and a huntsman. Whenever any other man was praised, a genuflexion was made to the name of Assheton Smith. In 1840, when he revisited his old country of the Quorn, twenty-four years after he had given up the mastership, two thousand horsemen turned out to meet him and there were so many spectators in carriages and on foot that hunting was impossible.

Assheton Smith, like Osbaldeston and Lonsdale, was a *card*, a term that later in the century was to be used of a *character*, a man with sufficient confidence to do unconventional things and get away with them. Yet with all this self-confidence went that fierce readiness to show himself as good a man as anyone with his fists. Was this perhaps something to do with 1789 and the proclamation of liberty and equality on the other side of the Channel? Can it be that among Englishmen who drew wealth from the land there was a feeling, well below the conscious level, that to justify privilege a man should be able to show that he could take on anyone and show himself equal or better in the most physical way possible?

The Squire

GEORGE OSBALDESTON, generally known as The Squire, was nearer the accepted picture of a Corinthian than Assheton Smith; he betted and raced and never looked at the accounts of his estates. But he was not a hard drinker. Smith, towards the end of his life, remarked that he wished he had been matched in his prime against Osbaldeston at boxing, rowing, shooting and riding.[17] He thought, on reflection that he would have chosen the boxing first, since he might have so damaged his adversary as to have a better chance of winning the other contests. But as masters of fox hounds, it would have been hard to judge between them, Osbaldeston being the only man who could really be put in the same class with Smith. These two, wrote a well-known sporting journalist in 1861, were

... the two most brilliant stars which have ever arisen in our hunting hemisphere; in whom every requisite was combined – genius and talents of the highest order – energy and activity – quickness of decision – coolness in action. They placed confidence in their own capabilities, yet placed the greatest in their hounds. They knew thoroughly well when to let well alone – never interfering with the sagacity of the animals under their command.

But they were very different characters. Osbaldeston had the misfortune to be left with vast estates and without a father when only six years old. A fond mother not only spoiled him but vied with him in extravagance; she had already reduced his inheritance before he came of age. He ended in poverty. He says himself that he lost £200,000 by racing and betting and another £100,000 "by the misdeeds of agents". That is his view of the case; the truth is that he would neither take the trouble to look after his affairs nor deny himself anything he wanted nor say no to anyone who asked a favour.

At Eton he was constantly in trouble and constantly flogged. It was a brutal place. On one occasion, he played truant and was trying his hand for the first time at driving a gig with two horses tandem, a difficult art. The horses got away from him and bolted while coming down St Anne's Hill in Windsor Great Park. They hit a tree; the gig was smashed and the two occupants thrown out and badly shaken. Of course he was flogged; he remembered that he "was too stiff and sore to unbutton his small clothes to receive the birch" and another boy had to act as valet.

At Oxford he hunted three days a week and boasts that he was in a number of scrapes. He became a member of Parliament, but "I did not consider it an honour at all; I considered it a great bore". At the age of 24 he became for the first time a master of fox hounds and began to hunt the Burton country in Lincolnshire. He was to be a master for most of the rest of his life, usually hunting his own hounds and going out six days a week.

But it was his "matches" that made him famous. A "match" was almost always done for a bet. Matches were made on dog fights, on cock fights, on individual feats of endurance. They were not confined to the gentry; indeed, they were a link between the sporting gentry and the keepers of public-houses, gypsies, grooms, footmen and boxers. In 1816, one Baker, "a smuggler by profession", walked 1,010 miles in 21 days as a "match".

ABOVE George Osbaldeston (1787–1866), in a portrait attributed to Lambert Marshall. It is easy to see why Osbaldeston was called "the Squire". He was elected to Parliament but "thought it a great bore", and spent the rest of his life hunting and making "matches". He was unsurpassed as a horseman and a breeder of hounds.
BELOW The Quorn hounds in full cry, "the hunt at the height of its glory and the pace too good to enquire". Osbaldeston is leading.

The Squire made matches on everything, backing himself at pigeon-shooting, partridge-shooting, trotting, boxing, driving, tennis, cricket, billiards.

The best-known of his matches was his ride of 200 miles at Newmarket. Colonel Charritie bet George Osbaldeston a thousand guineas that he could not ride on horseback 200 miles in less than ten hours, all rests and changes included. He was allowed as many horses as he liked. He decided to ride fifty heats, each of four miles, using 28 horses, several of which did two heats, while one did four. It was a fine piece of organization and training; he rode eighty miles a day for some days beforehand and on the night before the match went to every stable, checking saddles and stirrup lengths. There was one halt of eight minutes in which he ate and drank as much as he could. He finished the two hundred miles in eight hours and 42 minutes, which means an average speed of more than 22 miles an hour, including stops.

On another occasion, when he was hunting from Northampton, he rode 17 miles to the hunt, had a good day's hunting, covering 25 miles, and 17 back to Northampton, where he changed and rode relays of hacks the 44 miles to Cambridge – 103 miles for the day. At Cambridge he went to a ball and danced all night, having just time to change back into hunting clothes, breakfast, and ride back another 40 miles to the meet next morning. This was done not for a bet but for pleasure.

Four years after the 200-mile ride occurred the famous duel with Lord George Bentinck. There are various accounts of this and no one can be quite sure of the details. But this much is clear. Lord Wilton made up a house party every year for races in his own grounds at Heaton Park near Manchester. The handicapper was always one of the house party and to the Squire and some of his friends it seemed that the members of the house party were kindly treated in the handicapping. Another man might have talked it over with Lord Wilton. Osbaldeston determined, characteristically, to take the law into his own hands. He bought in Ireland a good horse, called Rush, unknown in England. He gave Rush an early morning trial a week before the meeting at Heaton Park and, finding that he was going well and seeing that someone was watching, pulled up before the finish of his gallop. That was common practice and not discreditable. He ran Rush on the first day at Heaton Park, riding himself, and took care not to win. This he virtually admits in his memoirs. As a result, he was well handicapped for the big race next day and almost certain to win. There were bets against him at ten to one, but the odds quickly came down to two to one, and as the Squire rode to the start Lord George Bentinck offered him a bet of two hundred to one hundred, which he accepted. He won easily. Lord George did not pay for some months and Osbaldeston asked for the money. Lord George said it was damned robbery and he wondered he had the impudence to ask for it – but eventually paid. Osbaldeston resented the expression "damned robbery"; by the standards generally accepted in racing circles, he had done nothing out of the way. He forced Lord George into a duel, saying he would pull his nose at Tattersall's if he continued in his first refusal. The Squire could put twelve shots out of twelve into the ace of spades at twelve paces and to face him in a duel was regarded as certain death.

The night before the duel, an old friend, George Payne, who had been in the secret and had won money on Rush, but had refused to act as Osbaldeston's second, found him at the Portland Club, got him away from the card-table, and "walked him up and down outside for two hours, arguing with him to drop it". Osbaldeston at first was adamant. " 'He said it was a damned robbery and as sure as you stand there I will shoot the beggar dead tomorrow morning . . .' " At last Payne said to him: " 'You know Bentinck was right; it was a damned robbery; and if you kill Lord George to-morrow, there will not be a single gentleman in England who will ever speak to you again.' Osbaldeston looked at me and turned and left me without a word."

The details of the encounter are not clear but all accounts agree that Lord George fired and missed and Osbaldeston then deliberately missed him. George Payne's story shows that although he had been prepared to go along with Osbaldeston in keeping it dark that Rush was a good horse – and he must have known he had been pulled – he regarded it as a very different matter to bring Lord George to a duel and kill him. Osbaldeston was one of those self-centred men who find it difficult to see how their conduct appears to anyone else, and it took Payne's words to bring him to his senses. The duellists made it up afterwards, at Andover, in 1843, where the Squire won a race on Lord George's horse. He was not one to cherish malice but he could never admit that he had been in the wrong.

Nobody comes out of the story with his knightly armour altogether untarnished, but it does suggest that there was a sportsman's morality – below the level of a gentleman's – but still providing limits beyond which no one could go.

In sporting circles, it was regarded as acceptable to trick an opponent over a match, provided the letter of the contract was observed. Mr Paul Methuen once said that it was all very well for Osbaldeston to drive a coach with a team of his own chosen horses but he would not do so well with the horses a professional coachman had to put up with. A match was quickly made. Osbaldeston was to take the place of any professional coachman chosen by Methuen, Methuen loading the coach, the journey to be completed in the usual time. Methuen chose the stage from St Paul's Churchyard to Brentford, regularly driven by a coachman known as "Hell-fired Dick". Dick's first team out was notorious. "Some were blind, others jibbed and would not start." Osbaldeston made friends with the man who usually held their heads at starting and with his help got off well. But at the bottom of Ludgate Hill, Methuen rode up and said the bet was off because he had had help at starting. The Squire did not admit that this was in the contract, but he turned his horses, drove back and started again without anyone at their heads, a thing Hell-fired Dick never did. It is needless to say that he won in good time; we should not otherwise have heard the story. It was then found that Methuen had crammed the coach with the heaviest passengers he could find – eighteen Lifeguardsmen!

Osbaldeston also tells of a Mr Cruickshank who backed himself to kill pigeons released from a trap a hundred yards distant from the gun. But he had installed a device which induced the pigeons to fly over his head. After some shots, Mr Cruickshank's adversary appealed to the Squire, who was the umpire. "Do you consider the trap fair?" he asked. "Certainly not!" he replied, and the match was off – but no one thought any the worse of Mr Cruickshank for the attempt.

Osbaldeston lived then in a world in which everyone was trying to get the better of someone else, and usually for money. In this world of sport, he was constantly appealed to; his judgment was trusted. He was admired, almost reverenced. Near the time of his death, someone happened to say he had just seen "The Old Squire". A thoughtless or ignorant acquaintance asked: "The Squire of where?" "Why, the Squire of England!" was the indignant reply. And among fox-hunters and racing men and boxers and thousands of his countrymen he had achieved his one declared ambition: fame as a sportsman. He won fame because of his skill and endurance and unflinching courage but also because he was generous and would never say no to a challenge of any kind.

But was he a gentleman? Certainly, by the standard of the College of Heralds, he was; he inherited enormous landed estates, came of an old family, bore coat-armour. But in the moral sense his claim seems doubtful. He was too eager to win to suit either Castiglione or Lord Chesterfield; he had not a particle of de Méré's sensibility. He did not leave his readers or his hearers in much doubt of his successes. He wrote in his memoirs:

Kissing and telling is against all honour, is base ingratitude and most degrading to any man who pretends to the character of a gentleman. Therefore the lady's name must be omitted from the following narrative.

But the story follows – and a couple more.

Engagingly frank, perhaps, but not what Thackeray expected of a gentleman.

Almost an Emperor

IT WAS SAID of Hugh, fifth earl of Lonsdale, that he was "almost an Emperor but never quite a gentleman". His family, the Lowthers, were of very ancient lineage, having held lands at Lowther since before the Norman Conquest, avoiding sequestration and also any marked distinction, and adding to their stronghold in Cumbria considerable estates in Rutland and Leicestershire.[18] So with him there was even less doubt about the social qualification than with Osbaldeston. As to behaviour, the doubts arise for much the same reason. There was a blatancy, a loudness, in them both. The Old Squire was a great hero with Hugh Lowther and the two men resembled each other in temperament; impulsive, pugnacious, extravagant, neither could refuse a challenge, both would do almost anything to win, neither could keep quiet about a success.

Hugh Lowther was a younger son and the allowance his brother made him was never enough. He got into debt and London society did not regard him as at all the thing. Eventually he sold to moneylenders his right to the succession. His brother bought in the debt and created a trust, tying up the income for the benefit of the estate. When Hugh succeeded, at the age of 25, the trustees allowed him an income of a mere £100,000 a year and tried to protect the estate against his extravagance. He could seldom be persuaded to see them in any light but as enemies determined to keep him out of his own. To make things worse, he had no hope of a son. His wife was a fine horsewoman and insisted on riding in her first pregnancy. She had a bad fall and lost not only the child but any hope of another. From then onwards

Hugh Cecil Lowther, 5th earl of Lonsdale, and his wife Grace,
by Lynwood Palmer (1868–1941)

Hugh Lonsdale saw himself as "the Last of the Lowthers" – although he had a brother and a nephew to succeed him – and spent as though the world would come to an end with his death.

He was master in turn of the Quorn, the Pytchley and the Cottesmore – a pack to which he felt he had a hereditary right since his ancestor had founded it. His ancestor had walked the hounds between Rutland and Westmoreland at the beginning and end of each hunting season, but now they went by a special train. Hugh himself always travelled by a special train, in which one coach was sometimes allotted to his shooting dogs; he would be accompanied by an entourage of over a hundred, including a private orchestra with 25 members. It was the duty of a secretary to stay awake all night and give a £5 note to the station-master at every station where they stopped.

When Hugh, earl of Lonsdale, entertained Kaiser Wilhelm II of Germany, the roads from the railway station to Lowther Castle were lined by troopers of the Cumberland and Westmoreland Yeomanry and the hunt servants of the Quorn headed the long procession of carriages, blowing fanfares on their horns. The postillions and footmen on each carriage wore the magnificent Lonsdale livery of canary yellow jackets with dark blue facings, white beaver hats and white buckskin breeches. It was a royal occasion and everything had to be royal. One day during the visit, Lonsdale suggested after luncheon a stroll with a gun, in the course of which they happened to pass a wood of firs on the slope of a hill. He thought it might be worth putting a dog into the wood – and as the dog went in, a dozen concealed keepers

OPPOSITE The Quorn moving away from the meet. Even here, at perhaps the smartest and most exclusive hunt in the country, there were cyclists and people on foot eager to see all they could.
ABOVE Hunting the fox was a sport in which not only the top-hatted members of the hunt took part but local farmers in their bowlers, while all over the countryside people turned out on foot to watch and cheer. It was not only a sport but a spectacle and a cult. (A painting by Randolph Caldecott.)

emptied bags of live rabbits trapped the night before. The Kaiser picked up 67 rabbits.

"There's often a rabbit or two in that wood," said Lord Lonsdale.

In magnificence, Lonsdale was easily the master of Osbaldeston. The enormous cigar, the gardenia in his button-hole, his beautifully matched chestnut horses and his carriages panelled and picked out in yellow, the yellow liveries – all stamped him a master of showmanship. His cigar bill was £3,000 a year. He raised a private regiment of yeomanry in the Boer War and a battalion of infantry in the First World War. At the Derby the crowds cheered him as though he were the king. He was indeed almost an emperor.

As a sportsman, his interests were very nearly as wide as the Squire's. He was not a betting man but his matches were as numerous and perhaps even better known than the Squire's because in his day more people read newspapers. The first was his challenge – in his 21st year – to walk a hundred miles against an American, Mr Weston, who was in London at the time and highly spoken of as a pedestrian. The match took place on the evening of 17 June 1878, from Knightsbridge Barracks to the Ram Jam Inn, north of

Stamford on the Great North Road, almost exactly 100 miles. Hugh Lowther finished the course in 17 hours 21 minutes, making an average speed of a fraction over $5\frac{3}{4}$ miles an hour including stops; Mr Weston gave up when he knew he was beaten.

More famous still was his match against the earl of Shrewsbury; it was to be a twenty-mile drive in four stages, Dorking to Reigate; in the first stage each was to drive a one-horse buggy; in the second a two-horse trap; in the third a four-in-hand, and in the fourth each was to ride postilion with two horses and an open phaeton. In the end, Lord Shrewsbury did not come to scratch, having been dissuaded by his wife; Lonsdale carried out the drive against the clock, covering the twenty miles in 54 minutes $15\frac{1}{2}$ seconds – better than 20 miles an hour, including changes.

He was summoned to appear before the magistrates for furious driving and there was delighted controversy in the press, not only on the match itself, but on the behaviour of the contestants, Lonsdale of course being far the more popular. Shrewsbury considered that Lonsdale had "impugned his character as a sportsman" and there was talk of writs for libel. The writs came to nothing but the press continued to enjoy itself. A sporting paper announced that it had exclusive and authoritative information that rival political leaders, Lord Salisbury and Lord Hartington, had agreed on a similar match of four five-mile heats, hopping, crawling, rolling and finally walking on stilts.

Before he succeeded to the title, Hugh Lowther crossed the Atlantic for "a sparring match" with John L. Sullivan, the heavyweight champion of the world, who had toured the United States offering $1,000 to anyone who could knock him down. The money was never claimed. The meeting with Sullivan was conducted with a good deal of secrecy because it was illegal at that time, but Lord Lonsdale wrote an account of it later, describing how he fought Sullivan for five rounds and knocked him out in the sixth, himself suffering a broken ʻrib and a broken bone in his right hand. He took a keen interest in boxing all his life, founding the Lonsdale Belts as prizes for boxing and thus starting the system of classifying boxers according to weight. He played a big part in drawing up the Queensberry Rules and fought several battles in the law courts which helped to make boxing legal. He was President of the National Sporting Club and founded the International Horse Show. The Automobile Association still uses as its distinguishing mark the yellow of his livery. He became the best known man in England since the duke of Wellington.

His popularity with the masses was due partly to the fact that he behaved as they thought an earl ought to behave. He spent money on hunting, on race horses, on actresses, on magnificence. But he combined with his magnificence the common touch; he had, for example, early in his career established an early breakfast club for porters at Covent Garden and he had

Hugh, 5th earl of Lonsdale, "almost an emperor but not quite a gentleman". He was recklessly extravagant, but beloved by the crowds, who cheered him wherever he went. This portrait is by W. Howard Robinson.

always a liking for costers. There was a class for costermongers and their donkeys at the International Horse Show, and everyone was delighted when Lonsdale changed hats with a Pearly Queen and danced with her in the arena at Olympia on the last night of the show.

There was a humorous sympathy between the aristocrat who would not behave sedately and the criminal underworld. Once at a race meeting, a friend of Lonsdale's lost a valuable jewelled tiepin. He at once went to Lonsdale as the one man who might know how to get it back. Lonsdale found a shady character of his acquaintance who knew all the pickpockets and pointed out that the pin was well-known and no fence would touch it. Eventually he was told that if in ten minutes his friend would go to a certain gate and say "Cuckoo" to a clergyman he would see there he could have the pin back for £25. All went smoothly. Sir George got his pin. As he left the enclosure, a little boy ran after him.

"Sir George! Sir George! 'Ow much did you give that parson?"

Sir George told him.

"Cor!" said the boy. "And he only give me ten bob! And it was me what pinched it!"

In 1928, on the fiftieth anniversary of Lonsdale's wedding, people from all over the world subscribed to present him with a golden casket and a large sum of money – a quarter of a million pounds – for any purpose he liked. It was a tribute to his services to sport. There had never been anything like it – gifts from thousands and thousands, not only of his fellow-subjects, in Britain, in India, in the Dominions, but of Americans too – a mark of affection to a man who all his life had done with enormous gusto what he most enjoyed doing.

He had married before he succeeded to the title and wealth, in the face of opposition from both families, but since that unhappy fall, his wife had been often an invalid and could play little part in much of his life. She observed forgivingly behaviour that was often far from discreet. There were in-fatuations, occasional scandals. At Lowther there was a private staircase from his ground floor bedroom to a guest bedroom on the floor above; there were shooting-boxes on the moors to which he would suddenly ride at night. Nonetheless, he was, after his fashion, a good husband. The pair of them kept up, all their lives, affectionate nicknames from those first honeymoon days when there had never been any money. "Mr Tommy" and "Mrs Tommy" they had been to each other then, and every night, even when alone together in the vast dining room at Lowther, he would rise after dinner at one end of the long table and say:

"Mrs Tommy, I give you a toast. The King, Fox-hunting and the Ladies!" And when that had been drunk, she would rise and reply:

"Mr Tommy, I give you a toast. The King, Fox-hunting and the Gentlemen!"

In spite of the scandals and the pretty ladies, he was perhaps nearer being a gentleman in regard to his wife than his flamboyance would permit in most other respects.

A Rare Good 'Un

THE CROWDS who went to the Derby cheered Hugh, earl of Lonsdale, until they were hoarse, but there were always some raised eyebrows among his peers. There was another and quite different tradition in the sporting world. This other tradition may be illustrated from the engaging pages of R. S. Surtees, although not by direct example. Most of the people in Surtees are cads, bounders or snobs, pretending to be what they are *not*. From the point of view of this book, his novels are like photographic negatives, in which the positive highlights appear as dark masses. Only occasionally do we see a picture of a man Surtees admires – and he is always a man who does not pretend.

Of course, Surtees is a comic writer. His stories are meant to make us laugh – and so they do. He is best known for Jorrocks, but *Handley Cross* – the centre-piece of the Jorrocks saga – is not his best book. The adventures of Jorrocks – the fat cockney grocer who knocks his h's about but dreams of

hunting and becomes a master of foxhounds – are very loosely strung together and the subsidiary characters are less convincing than those in
Mr Sponge's Sporting Tour, *Mr Romford's Hounds* or *Ask Mamma*, in all of which
there is more of a plot. But in all the novels there are rich comic characters
and all depict the same kind of world.[19] Love of hunting excuses almost
everything except pretence. Jorrocks never pretends to be anything but a
grocer – "a Post Office Directory not a Peerage man" – for, as he said, "there
are but two sorts o' folks in the world . . . Peerage folks wot thinks it all right
and proper to do their tailors and Post Office Directory folks wot thinks it's
the greatest sin under the sun not to pay twenty shillings in the pound –
greatest sin under the sun except kissing and then telling". Jorrocks is never
a gentleman but he is always a sportsman. He is full of scorn for Mr
Marmaduke Muleygrubs, a retired staymaker who lives in a house he is
trying to turn into a castle, buys pictures of "ancestors" from dealers in
London and knows nothing of fox hunting. He is no more impressed by the
"Cut-em-Down Captains", cavalry officers who race each other across
country, glorying in the number of falls they get and caring nothing for
hounds. It is part of the joke about Jorrocks that he is very fat and will not
face a leap but he makes no pretence, even about that, and wins affection
because he really does love hunting.

Mr Sponge is another hero conceived in mockery who in the end wins an
unexpected liking. His antecedents are obscure, but he seems to have some
private means although nothing like enough for the kind of life he enjoys.

Mr. Sponge was a good-looking, rather vulgar-looking man. At a distance his height,
figure and carriage gave him something of a commanding appearance, but this was
rather marred by a jerky, twitchy, uneasy sort of air, that too plainly showed he was
not the natural, or what the lower orders call the *real* gentleman.

He took enormous trouble over his clothes, affecting "the severe order of
sporting costume". "Every article seemed to be made to defy the utmost
rigour of the elements." "His hat (Lincoln and Bennett) was hard and heavy.
It sounded upon an entrance hall table like a drum." His trousers were "a
perfect triumph of the art". "They looked more as if his legs had been
blown in them than as if such irreproachable garments were the work of
men's hands." With all these advantages, he had a rare knowledge of horses,
the courage and skill to ride them, and a passion for fox-hunting. It was a
pity that he had not the means to keep up a stable.

He overcame the difficulty by an arrangement with Mr Benjamin
Buckram, a shady horse-dealer – but horse-dealers in Surtees are always
shady – from whom he acquired a showy piebald hack, that had been in a
circus – and still stood up on its hind-legs if it heard a band – and two un-
deniable hunters, good-looking horses and good ones to go, that would
have been "worth a mint of money" if they had not both been extremely

self-willed in any but the most skilful hands. With these assets – and a groom who was all right when sober – Mr Sponge cast himself upon the waters at Laverick Wells. His object was to get some hunting and as soon as possible free board and lodging for himself and his horses – and, if opportunity offered, to sell one of the horses to the joint benefit of himself and Mr Buckram. This he soon succeeded in doing – and to a mug so egregious that, when he found he couldn't ride him, he was actually hornswoggled into paying Sponge a further sum for taking the horse back.

Meanwhile, rumour had put it round that Sponge was immensely rich and he was soon invited to stay at Jawleyford Court. It was one of those invitations in which no actual date is suggested, but which no one expects to be taken literally and accepted at once. But that is just what Sponge did. Open the door an inch and he would have his foot inside. Jawleyford had never supposed that Sponge would descend on him at once and bring his horses. But he had two marriageable daughters and Sponge was said to be very rich. He made the best of it and the first night he put on the most pretentious dinner he could. Mothers in Surtees are always scheming, and marriageable daughters usually not far behind; the Jawleyford girls were ready to be captivated, but Sponge was too keen on his hunting to spend the day whispering on a sofa. He would be off to the meet as soon as he had breakfasted. In the end, his groom gave him away – and once the servants

OPPOSITE Mr Sponge with the groom "who was all right when sober". Mr Sponge affected "the severe order of sporting costume", and always looked the part; but he was not "what the lower orders call a real gentleman".

RIGHT Mr Jawleyford addressing his tenants. He was Mr Sponge's first host – or should one say victim? – and is damned in Surtees' eyes because he did not take hunting seriously.

knew, the secret leaked upstairs. Jawleyford lowered the standard of entertainment. "The fare, the lights, the footmen, the everything, underwent grievous diminution." Sponge was moved out of the best state bedroom into a little dog-kennel of a room, known as the condemned cell, where the fire always smoked. He was obstinate to hints and impossible to get out of the house, until an offer came from Mr Puffington, who had made his money in starch and retired to the country. Mr Puffington too rumbled Mr Sponge in the end and once again he had to pretend that he didn't understand the hints about making an end to his visit.

But at this juncture there arrived Mr Jogglebury Crowdey of Puddingpote Bower, with another general invitation to come for a visit. Mr Crowdey was still under the impression that Sponge was rich and Mrs Crowdey wanted to get him as godfather for her latest infant, Gustavus James. Once again, Sponge snapped at an invitation not meant to be taken immediately; once again he turned up without warning. It was a step down in the social scale. Jogglebury Crowdey had inherited from an uncle a small country estate and was chairman of the board of poor law guardians, but he had no pretensions to style. He drove

. . . a queer-shaped jumped-together lack-lustre-looking vehicle, with a turnover seat behind, now in charge of a pepper-and-salt attired youth with a shabby hat, looped up by a thin silver cord to an acorn on the crown and baggy Berlin gloves, while Puddingpote Bower was the kind of house in which the visitor "dived straight into the passage", about which were "scattered children's hats and caps, hoops, tops, spades, and mutilated toys". However, the driver of the shandrydan, who was also the stable-boy, was hastily transformed into a footman, while Mary Ann, the maid of all work, became a parlour-maid and Mrs Crowdey, having retired to re-arrange the dinner, reappeared in "a close-fitting French grey silk, showing as well the fulness and whiteness of her exquisite bust as the beautiful formation of her arms". She was a good deal younger than Jogglebury, who became very jealous of Sponge's flattering admiration. But it would be a digression to dwell longer on Mr Sponge's adventures and to reveal Mr Jogglebury Crowdey's eccentric reason for pretending to hunt.

No one could pretend that Surtees' novels are literature of the highest order. His characters are cartoons, almost allegorical, illustrating as a rule one vice or one characteristic, and usually exaggerating it. Young ladies, if good, like Belinda Jorrocks, have beautifully rounded forms and silken eye lashes but not much more. The only woman who really comes alive is "the beautiful and tolerably virtuous Miss Lucy Glitters of the Astley's Royal Amphitheatre", who had learned to ride in a circus and is not only a superb horsewoman but will lead the men over any fence you show her. She is also "a good sort", good-natured and loyal to old friends. She is certainly a sportsman and almost a gentleman, although not quite a lady. She becomes Mrs Sponge, which is more than Sponge deserves.

Surtees is a satirist. Hardly anyone escapes his lash. The aristocracy do not; the Duke of Tergiversation puts politics before hunting and, crime of crimes, he came late to a meet of his own foxhounds, having kept the field

Mr Jogglebury Crowdey of Puddingpote Bower. Mr Sponge has to move on as one host after another rumbles him. Mr Crowdey is a step down in the social scale and his true reason for hunting is eccentric.

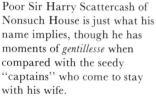

Poor Sir Harry Scattercash of Nonsuch House is just what his name implies, though he has moments of *gentillesse* when compared with the seedy "captains" who come to stay with his wife.

The Earl of Scamperdale had been Lord Hardup so long that he would spend no money on anything but hunting, and breakfasted on porridge made from the same meal he fed to his hounds. Here he is, with his friend Jack Spraggon, after his dinner of stewed tripe and onions, drinking gin and water and meditating on the sins of Mr Sponge.

waiting more than an hour. The Earl of Ladythorn, another noble master of hounds, is more interested in farmers' wives than foxes – although readers might forgive him a good deal for employing as huntsman such a butt for satire as Dicky Boggledyke. The Lord Viscount Lovetin is a shadowy figure and Sir Harry Scattercash what his name implies – a sad weak wastrel, though he has moments of *gentillesse*. Much the best picture of an aristocrat – although undeniably eccentric – is the Earl of Scamperdale, who had a "deal of rat-catching cunning" and – having served a long apprenticeship as Lord Hardup – "did not spend a halfpenny on anything but hunting". He lived in what used to be the steward's room, breakfasted on oatmeal porridge laced with dripping – the same oatmeal he gave his hounds – and had for dinner beefsteak and batter pudding or stewed tripe and onions, followed by gin and water. But he was a good man to ride across country and his hounds showed capital sport.

Surtees cannot have spent long on revising his text. The words pour out in rapid succession; he sees the man or the house he is talking about and his pictures have the rich convincing detail of a Hogarth print. We know just what everyone had for dinner and what the stingiest upstarts paid for their port. A graduated scale of gentility – or, in reverse, of vulgar pretentiousness – is what he provides. Many of the social gradations he portrays would in two more generations be obliterated by the single much sharper distinction of a public school accent. Mr Francis Romford bore the same name as another Mr Francis Romford whom everyone can look up in Burke's *Landed Gentry*. There they would find that Francis Romford, Esq was the owner of Abbey-field Park, patron of three livings, a Justice of the Peace and Deputy Lieu-tenant of the County. This coincidence enabled the wrong Mr Romford to set up as a master of hounds without a penny, entirely on credit. But, like Squire Western a century before him, he talked with a rich country accent and was quite ignorant of polite behaviour; by the end of the century he could not possibly have passed for the "right" Mr Romford.

The people you might meet hunting with Surtees range from the con-temptible Duke of Tergiversation and the eccentric Scamperdale through the pretentious humbug Jawleyford and various upstarts like Sir Moses Mainchance, Marmaduke Muleygrubs and Puffington to yeoman farmers like Imperial John, masters of harriers like Major Yammerton and farmers like Mr Springwheat, with his buxom wife – the sister of Mrs Jogglebury Crowdey and just as good looking. It is a long and varied procession but there are no hard and fast lines between them. They all sit down to the hunt breakfast together.

Occasionally there is a glimpse of the servants' point of view. "Call for Burgundy with your cheese and they will know you are a gentleman", was the advice Mrs Pringle gave her son. She meant the servants – and although destined to be Countess of Ladythorne, she had been a lady's maid herself. But we never hear the voice of the farm labourer.

Hardly anyone avoids the lash of the satirist. But let us end with one who does, to show the kind of man Surtees really admired.

Mr Stanley Sterling was a comfortable man and was waited upon by a woman. After that, we need scarcely say that he was a bachelor, for where is the lady who will submit to be tended by one of her own sex. . . ? . . . He lived at a pretty, old-fashioned, gable-ended, grey-roofed place, called Rosemount Grange: where there was always a spare stall for a horse and a hearty welcome for a friend. Moreover there was generally a good wild fox to be found in his cover . . . next morning.

Everything at Rosemount Grange is just as it should be; there is nutty sherry and clear ruby port; the cook does not attempt side-dishes but concentrates her talents on a few general favourites:

The ox-tail soup was beautifully clear and hot, the crimped cod and oyster-sauce excellent, while the boiled fowls and ruddy ham ran a close race with the four year-old leg of roast mutton in giving a relish to the "sweet or dry" [champagne]. Macaroni and mince-pies followed . . . and a bottle of Beaujolais circulated with the cheese . . .

It was a very simple dinner. The four bachelor guests then made themselves comfortable at a horse-shoe table before the fire, where two bottles of bright port wine circulated until it was time for tea and whist. Next day, that famous cover, into which no man with a gun was ever admitted, "abounding in blackthorn, gorse, broom and fern – presenting in every part dry and most unexceptionable lying –" proved indeed to hold a fox who gave them a splendid run and eventually found a sanctuary in a badger's burrow at Brockholes. Mr Stanley Sterling was well up on a five-year-old iron grey of his own breeding.

There were those who wanted the fox dug out and given to the hounds.

"He's a rare good 'un," exclaimed Mr Stanley Sterling, anxious for his preservation.

Mr Romford agreed and took his hounds home. Mr Sterling's verdict on the fox would have been Surtees' verdict on Mr Sterling – "a rare good 'un", just what he admired, sound, unpretentious, everything just right, a sportsman and a gentleman.

I shall argue that, in the 19th century, a nation nominally, but not wholeheartedly, Christian had set up an alternative code of ethics, the behaviour proper for a gentleman. England contained a subtly graded society, of which the upper and middle ranks had made of this code of behaviour almost a religion – a sub-Christian cult. Strangely enough, there was a considerable section of the working classes who accepted the cult too – sometimes jeeringly, sometimes affectionately. And, just as the cult of Apollo at one shrine would emphasise the god's patronage of music and at another his association with the sun, so their acceptance of the gentleman as leader was focussed on cricket, on hunting and on racing. A gentleman would captain the cricket team, though it might include better batsmen; hunting was for the well-mounted country gentry, though the farmers could follow and half the countryside would come to the meet. The gentry were the priests of their own cult.

8
COLONEL NEWCOME

The Book of Snobs

THE CORINTHIANS were a side-shoot from the main line of the gentleman's pedigree. True, they constantly reappeared, in varying forms, in successive centuries, and they were a part of the image of the gentleman as he took shape in the popular mind. But the Corinthian was often in danger of failing to be quite a gentleman because he was too blatant or too keen to win. Let us turn back to the true line.

In the middle of the 19th century, there is a portrait of a gentleman who is in direct descent from Chaucer's Knight and Sir Philip Sidney. Colonel Newcome is not an ideal figure such as the courtiers of Urbino tried to construct, nor is he such an abstraction as Lord Chesterfield dangled before the eyes of his unhappy son; he is a character in a novel but a living creature who loses his temper and is often unwise and who is sometimes a little absurd, even to those who love him most, but who for more than half a century provided a pattern of a gentleman's behaviour.

His creator, William Makepeace Thackeray, came, say the books of reference, of "yeoman stock" in the north of England. But for at least four generations, the Thackerays were gentry by occupation – as defined by the Elizabethan William Harrison – those who "abide in the university and give their minds to their book". His great-grandfather had been a King's Scholar at Eton, a fellow of King's College, Cambridge, Headmaster of Harrow and Archdeacon of Surrey. His father and grandfather were both in the civil service of the Honourable East India Company and William Makepeace, born at Calcutta in 1811, suffered the common fate of children from India, being sent home as a grass orphan when he was six years old.[20]

Thackeray is one of the earlier examples of what was to be a regular pattern of education – preparatory school, public school and university – and it may be that this upbringing had something to do with his protracted adolescence. He does not dwell on his experiences at school, although "Dr Swishtail's Academy" is his usual name for a prep school and "Slaughterhouse" his early variant on Charterhouse. But something needs explanation.

Not until *Vanity Fair*, which began to appear in 1847 when he was 36, does he settle down with any degree of comfort to tell a story without hiding behind pseudonymous editors such as Titmarsh and Fitzboodle or burlesque intermediaries, such as James Yellowplush the footman and Major Gahagan, who express themselves in facetious misspelt dialect that is painful to a modern reader. Even in *Vanity Fair*, his undoubted masterpiece, he is nervous about presenting Becky Sharp, his greatest creation, as she is, without comment. She had come to life in his hands and had run away with him but he is always in a twitter lest the reader should think he *approves* of Becky's behaviour – so he is constantly scolding her. This is surely a remnant of the selfconscious diffidence which spoilt his earlier work.

He was always concerned about gentility. After Surtees and the Corinthians, his novels take us back to the main stream of idealism about the behaviour of a gentleman, and also to the main stream of the English novel's interest, which is in the interplay of love with pounds, shillings and pence, of parental prudence with youthful infatuation, of class with character and conviction. But before we come to the novels and to Colonel Newcome, it is worth spending a few minutes on *The Book of Snobs*, a collection of pieces from *Punch* which appeared originally in a series called *The Snobs of England*. Heavily satirical, it shares Surtees' hatred of pretence and, like Surtees again, it illustrates what a gentleman should be by what he should not.

The word "snob" is said originally to have meant a cobbler or shoe-mender, and it was an easy step from this to apply it to manual workers in general. In Cambridge, for most of the century, it meant "town" as against "gown". It marked a position in the social hierarchy, as "churl" and "villain" and "gentleman" had once done. But, like those three words, it acquired a moral meaning too; it came to mean the way that a person of that rank in society might be expected to behave – of course, by the literate classes. Pushing, ostentatious, trying to make oneself rank higher than the circumstances warrant – that was an easy transition. The next was to some-

Britannia kisses the toe of a baron. The main point of Thackeray's *Book of Snobs* (reprinted as a book from articles in *Punch*) was that the British were a nation of snobs and always loved a lord. This and the other drawings from his books are by Thackeray himself.

thing a shade subtler and a snob became someone who attached an unreal importance to the accidents of birth, rank and wealth. In the last sense, Sir Walter Elliott of *Persuasion* was a snob of snobs, but he was not a snob in the original sense of the word or the second; he really was a baronet, and by descent.

Thackeray in his novels uses the word in all three senses, but in *The Book of Snobs* he usually inclines to the third. In his first article, he attempts a definition – not a very good one. A snob is "one who eats pease with a knife", that is, someone who "does the wrong thing in the wrong place in the wrong time, ignoring social convention". This is clearly the second meaning; a person who has got out of his place in society does not know the conventions. It would certainly not apply to Sir Walter Elliott. But in his second article, Thackeray moves on to the modern use of the word. "He who meanly admires mean things is a snob," he writes, and this clearly would include Sir Walter and his "heartless elegance". It is this line that he develops in more than thirty articles. "It is impossible," he writes, "in our condition of society not to be sometimes a snob. Our children are brought up to respect 'the Peerage' as the Englishman's second Bible." "The Court Circulars distort the brains of the fashionable just as the Chinese distort the feet of Mandarins' daughters." In all the middle-class squares and districts of London, there is "not one house in ten where 'the Peerage' does not lie on the drawing-room table".

How much happier everybody would be if they were less pretentious! He describes a dinner party at which footmen are hired for the occasion, puddings and ices are delivered from the confectioners and, in short, every effort is made to convince the guests that their hosts live at a much higher standard of ostentation than in fact they do. And he bursts out against "the infernal Snob Tyrant who governs us all, who says 'Thou shalt not love without a lady's maid; thou shalt not marry without a carriage and pair...'"

"Gentility," he writes in *Mr Brown's Letters to his Nephew* – a series that followed *The Book of Snobs* – "gentility is the death and destruction of social happiness among the middle classes in England," and he has a long passage on the benefits of being a man born into an assured station in life, beyond the middle age, and sufficiently sure of himself to pay no attention to what other people may think, such a man, in short, as Mr Stanley Sterling. But let us move on to the novels.

Three Officers

THE FIRST NOVEL is *Vanity Fair*, and it is the best in the sense of being the most readable and popular. It has dull passages, there is too much moralizing, but surely every reader's eye must brighten whenever wicked little Becky appears. Everything was against her in Vanity Fair; she was penniless, her

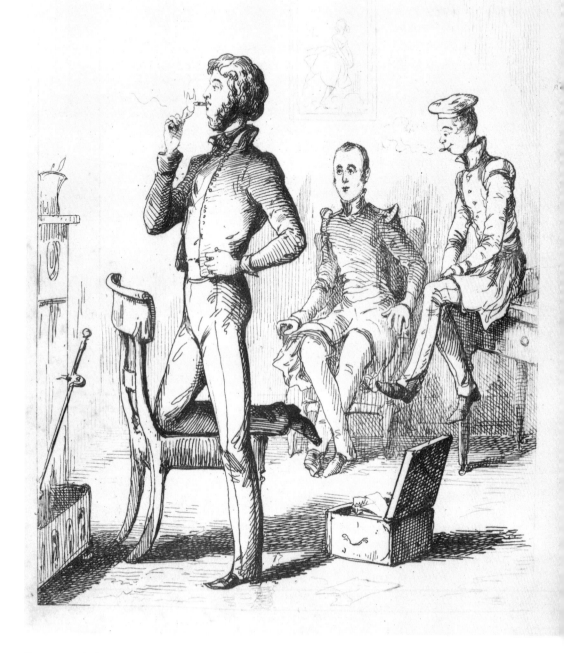

Everyone admired George Osborne, even his fellow subalterns. He was good at all games, he was rich, he had beautiful whiskers. But Becky saw through him and said he was "a selfish humbug, a low-bred Cockney dandy, a padded booby, who had neither wit nor manners nor heart".

father was a drawing master, her mother a French "opera-girl", but she won the admiration of almost every man she met – and, for a short time at least, of quite a number of those women whom she thought it worth her while to fascinate. Almost every male reader thinks he would have enjoyed her company – feeling confident that *he* would have been too wide awake to be taken in. She is not entirely a villain: "I think I could be a good woman if I had five thousand a year," she mused. And she is funny; when she set about captivating the dowager countess of Southdown, who was deeply *serious* about religion and also about health, she feigned not only unease of soul but some disturbance of body – and afterwards made a wonderful story for her dissolute acquaintance in London of how the countess came to her bedroom with a pile of pious pamphlets and a terrible black draught and of how she professed her gratitude and tried to send the countess away so that she could dispose of both in privacy – but the countess would not go till poor Becky had downed that nauseous mixture, to her great discomfort.

But we are concerned not with Becky but with the light the novel throws on the idea of the gentleman, and we have in fact three samples, all officers in the army, all falling well short of perfection, George Osborne, Rawdon Crawley and William Dobbin.

George Osborne had certainly been endowed with *style*. He:

... had an air at once swaggering and melancholy, languid and fierce. He looked like a man who had passions, secrets and private harrowing griefs and adventures. His voice was rich and deep. He would say it was a warm evening, or ask his partner to take an ice, with a tone as sad and confidential as if he were breaking her mother's death to her, or preluding a declaration of love.

It was no wonder that his luxuriant whiskers "curled themselves round the affections" of so many young ladies. But he was not only a drawing-room man; he had high spirits and plenty of courage. He had fought a duel; as he bounded downstairs for the march to Waterloo, where he was to meet his death:

... his pulse was throbbing and his cheeks flushed: the great game of war was going to be played, and he one of the players. What a fierce excitement of doubt, hope and pleasure! What tremendous hazards of loss or gain! What were all the games of chance he had ever played to this one? Into all contests requiring athletic skill and courage, the young man, from his boyhood upwards, had flung himself with all his might. The champion of his school and his regiment, the bravos of his companions had followed him everywhere; from the boys' cricket-match to the garrison-races, he had won a hundred of triumphs; and wherever he went, women and men had admired and envied him.

But such whiskers, so deep a voice, such universal success, might be no more than glossy vulgarity unless *style* was regulated by a good heart and a

ABOVE As to heart, George Osborne was hardly the perfect lover. From the start he took for granted the devotion of dear little Amelia . . .

. . . and within a few weeks of his marriage – and just before his death at Waterloo –

he asked Becky to run away with him (right). Becky is Thackeray's most brilliant creation, but he never dared be fair to her because he was afraid his readers would think he approved of what she did. She was clearly much more attractive than she appears in his drawings!

proper modesty. George's father, who had made his money as a merchant – and in tallow, not a very genteel commodity – was domineering, hardhearted and selfish. He had long ago ordered George to marry Amelia Sedley, and George had obediently entered into the understanding. But when Amelia's papa went bankrupt, old Osborne not only told his son to break off the engagement, but forbade him, in very opprobrious terms, to mention her name in his house.

"I am a gentleman, though I *am* your son, sir," George answered haughtily. "Any communications which you have to make to me, or any orders which you may please to give, I beg may be couched in that kind of language which I am accustomed to hear."

Old Osborne's behaviour had been atrocious; he was a very unprepossessing character, but one must feel some sympathy with his reply to that:

"My father didn't give me the education you have had, nor the advantages you have had, nor the money you have had. If I had kept the company *some folks* have had through *my means*, perhaps my son wouldn't have any reason to brag, sir, of his *superiority* and *West End airs*. . . . But it wasn't considered the part of a gentleman, in *my* time, for a man to insult his father."

Until that quarrel with his father, George had hardly given a thought to Amelia, who was breaking her heart for him. But, angry after the quarrel, he began to listen to the promptings of William Dobbin and at last rushed off, full of love and tenderness, to marry her – sure that his father would come round. But within a week of his marriage he was flirting with Becky, and, in a few months, on the eve of Waterloo, wrote her a letter begging her to leave her husband and run away with him. Becky saw through him; she had called him "Cupid" behind his back while she led him on, and in the last pages of the book tells his ever-mourning Amelia the truth about him:

"Couldn't forget *him*!" cried out Becky, "that selfish humbug, that low-bred Cockney dandy, that padded booby, who had neither wit nor manners nor heart!"

That was perhaps putting it rather high; he was not quite without heart. But essentially Becky was right.

Colonel Rawdon Crawley of the Life Guards was the genuine article, a heavy swell and an adept at living on nothing a year – until the bailiffs caught up with him.

Becky was much more than a match for Rawdon Crawley, and soon had him as her devoted servant. Not even the Wife of Bath could have asked for more!

William Dobbin was a plain plodding fellow with none of George Osborne's dash and swagger. But Becky, who knew the genuine article when she saw it, said he was one of the best gentlemen she had ever seen; and in the end he married dear little Amelia, whom he had always worshipped.

Rawdon Crawley was quite another pair of shoes. He was a baronet's son and an earl's grandson; he was in the Life Guards, instead of a marching regiment. He was a heavy swell. He thought George Osborne one of the greenest young fellows he had met for a long time and set about fleecing him, taking money from him at billiards and piquet, trading on the fact that young Osborne, with a self-made father, would like to be seen with Crawley of the Life Guards.

Rawdon was "delightfully wicked"; that was the view of him that his rich aunt Miss Crawley took when she first made him her heir. But she cut him off with twenty pounds when he married Becky; she would have shrugged her shoulders at an affair with "an opera-girl", but she was too good a citizen of Vanity Fair to tolerate his marriage with a woman who had neither wealth nor birth. She had indeed credited him with a more thorough-going wickedness than he really possessed; he did not mind ruining a tradesman by running up bills he had no means of paying; he felt no compunction about having shot Captain Marker in a duel over a charge of cheating at cards; these were things "every fellow did". But he gradually redeems himself in the reader's eyes by his devotion to Becky and later to his son, little Rawdon, and in the end by a fundamental decency which would not let him live on Becky's "presents" from the Marquis of Steyne.

William Dobbin is the third of our officers. The name itself suggests something of his quality. He was an honest plodding fellow, quite without George Osborne's dashing style or Rawdon's unquestioning assumption that he had the right to live fashionably on nothing a year. But he won high opinions from serious members of his profession for his knowledge of military history; he was respected in the regiment, both by the young officers and the men. He was brave and honest. From the moment he first saw her, he had adored Amelia – but she was engaged to George Osborne, whom he had protected as a small boy at school and ever since advised – not with much effect – as a confidential older friend. He had no hope, she had no eyes for anyone but the dashing George; of Dobbin, she had a poor opinion. "He lisped – he was very plain and homely-looking; and exceedingly awkward and ungainly." He trod on ladies' dresses and waltzed abominably. He could not hold a candle to George. But it was Dobbin who bought Amelia's piano at the sale of her father's effects, who sent it to her and let George take the credit; it was Dobbin who persuaded George to stand to his engagement and who arranged all the details of the wedding; it was Dobbin who settled Amelia's affairs after George's death. He was the first of a long line of unselfish self-sacrificing Victorian – heroes? but, no, Dobbin could never be exactly a hero. He was too plain and quite without style. But he was perhaps a first model for Henry Esmond and Colonel Newcome, who had Dobbin's unselfish devotion but combined it with style.

A Perfect Grand Seigneur

VICTORIAN ENGLAND was a long way from the Provence of the troubadours but in the 1840s the ghost of courtly love still walked in Bayswater and the Inns of Court. It hides behind the pedestal on which Victorians of the upper classes liked to put their mothers, their lost loves, the unattainable women of their dreams. Dobbin would never have adored Amelia if he had not been a secret but ungainly priest at the shrine of courtly love. Thackeray himself writes of Mrs Pendennis, the mother of another hero of his, as though she hardly set foot on earth. He speaks of her "tranquil beauty, her natural sweetness and kindness, and that simplicity and dignity which perfect purity and innocence are sure to bestow upon a handsome woman". But he is unhesitatingly realistic about the first woman her son falls in love with. She would listen while the boy talked of passion and poetry, occasionally throwing up her fine eyes and exclaiming "Oh, 'tis beautiful!" but then returning to "her own simple thoughts about the turned gown or the hashed mutton". But then *she* was not exactly a lady.

Young Pendennis was rescued from that scrape but he was a troubadour, a perpetual lover, and was soon in trouble again. "Though we have seen him fall in love with a fool," wrote Thackeray, "it was as a Goddess that he considered her." There were three more goddesses before he finally settled down. It can hardly be doubted that Thackeray felt that something of this troubadour element was necessary to "the character of a perfect gentleman". It was certainly there in Colonel Newcome.

Colonel Newcome, as a young man, had fallen head over heels in love with Léonore, the daughter of a French emigré of noble blood. Both families objected strongly; she gave in to her papa and dutifully married the Comte de Florac, but both for Thomas Newcome and for Léonore there was a life-long sadness.

Thus Colonel Newcome fulfilled the first requirement of a gentleman under the code of courtly love. He was a lover, faithful at heart all his life to one unattainable lady. And he was brave; when we first meet him, he is just back from India on his first leave after thirty years' absence, a lieutenant-colonel and a Companion of the Order of the Bath, famous throughout India for courage in battle. He was clean of speech, like Chaucer's knight and the true lover praised by the troubadours; we first meet him in a public house where songs are being sung, sentimental and patriotic at first, but when a drunken old reprobate started "one of the most outrageous songs in his repertoire", the Colonel sprang to his feet and marched out, with some stinging remarks to everyone present. " 'Never mind the change, Sir! Curse the change!' says the Colonel to the amazed waiter. 'Keep it till you see me in this place again; which will be never, by George, never!' "

The Colonel's mother had died when he was born. His father had married again and had married money, and the colonel-to-be had grown up in an atmosphere of wealth, but it was an extremely *serious* household – that is to say, evangelical. Thomas incurred the displeasure of his stepmother by some mild dissipation, by a desire to go into the army, and finally by his attachment to Léonore – a Papist! He went away to India, and had little beyond his pay; his two half-brothers inherited all their mother's wealth and became bankers.

The Colonel was rather an odd figure when he came back from India. His clothes were thirty years out of date and his simplicity about the ways of Vanity Fair added to the effect of oddity. His younger brothers, the twin bankers, by contrast, were as much at home in Vanity Fair as fish in water. They were very respectable. Sir Brian, the elder, was more; he was a baronet and a member of Parliament, and his wife was an earl's daughter; he lived in Park Lane and gave fashionable parties. He had purchased a long pedigree with his coat of arms. The younger, Mr Hobson Newcome, lived in Bryanston Square, a less fashionable part of London, and gave parties to which intellectual celebrities were invited instead of lords and ladies. He had another house outside London and it was his affectation to look and talk like a country gentleman. *His* wife – as they were both fond of saying – had no pretensions to the aristocracy. But in fact both these rich and influential bankers were hopelessly lacking in a quality which their half-brother instinctively commanded. Lady Anne Newcome, Sir Brian's wife, recognized it at once. She said to her daughter:

Your uncle is adorable. I have never seen a more perfect grand Seigneur . . .

Thackeray himself comments:

Where did he learn those fine manners which all of us who know him admired in him? He had a natural simplicity, an habitual practice of kind and generous thoughts; a pure mind and therefore above hypocrisy and affectation – perhaps those French people with whom he had been intimate in early life had imparted to him some of the traditional graces of their *vieille cour* – certainly his half brothers had inherited none such.

But, as Major Pendennis, high priest of *Vanity Fair*, remarked: "He don't seem to know much of the world . . ."

And when the Indian bank of which he had become a director ran into difficulties, the Colonel, in his simple way, looked on anyone who sold his shares as a deserter in the face of the enemy. Indeed, he felt it his duty to buy more. It was true; he knew very little of the world.

But everyone loved Thomas Newcome and no one had much affection for his half-brothers.

Heart and Style

MISS AUSTEN had one great advantage over Thackeray; she sat at home until her work was finished before she took it to the publisher. She did not have a messenger waiting at the door while she scribbled the last page that would make just the right length for this fortnight's instalment. There is no question that *Emma* and *Persuasion* are finished works of art as nothing of Thackeray's is. On the other hand, his range is much wider; he knows far more of the world; he knows more about women than she knew about men. He knew a great deal about the kind of life lived by young men with chambers in one of the Inns of Court, young men whose allowance is never quite enough, who are glad of an invitation to dinner with a banker or a tallow-merchant in Russell Square and who go on afterwards, perhaps to a reception in Mayfair, perhaps to a sing-song in a tavern, young men who are glad to earn a guinea or two for an article or a sketch. He knows how people live on nothing a year. He understands the background of violence, how a hasty word spoken after an evening's drinking might lead to a meeting at dawn, death for one, flight and a life-time of misery for the other.

Thackeray is admirable also at the trifling indications which enable the true-born Englishman to place a man exactly:

. . . the curious difference of manners among us, which, though not visible to foreigners, is instantly understood by English people. Brave, clever, tall, slim, dark, and sentimental-looking, Tibbits passed muster in a foreign salon . . . and cut us fellows out; whereas we English knew instantly that the man was not well-bred, by a thousand little signs not to be understood by the foreigner . . .

And how sharp an eye this shows, describing a young man recognising a rival when he arrives to dinner at the house of some rich host:

. . . that exceedingly impertinent and amusing demi-nod of recognition which is practised in England only and only to perfection by University men – and which seems to say: "Confound you – what do you do here?"

Colonel Newcome's son Clive understood these points very well and engagingly set about explaining to his adored father the essence of social distinction. The Colonel was just back from India and had taken his son out for the day from Greyfriars. Clive was talking about the families of his father's twin half-brothers.

". . . Aunt Hobson, she's very kind, you know, and all that," he explained confidingly, "but I don't think she's what you call *comme il faut*."

His father gravely asked for a little more information, and the boy replied that it was hard to be exact:

"only one can't help seeing the difference . . . there are some men gentlemen and some not. There's Jones now, the fifth form master, every man sees he's a gentleman, though he wears ever so old clothes; and there's Mr Brown who oils his hair, and wears rings, and white chokers – my eyes! such white chokers! – and yet we call him the handsome snob! And so about Aunt Hobson, she's very handsome and she's very finely dressed only somehow she's not – she's not the ticket, you see."

He goes on to explain that his other aunt, Lady Anne Newcome, *is* the ticket. She is different, more natural. Then he added with a laugh:

"And do you know, I often think that as good a lady as Aunt Anne herself, is old Aunt Honeyman at Brighton . . . she is not proud, and she is not vain, and she never says an unkind word behind anyone's back, and she does a deal of kindness to the poor without seeming to crow over them, you know; and she is not a bit ashamed of letting lodgings, or being poor herself . . ."

Young Clive is talking partly about style, that quality his father had and his banker half-brothers had not, but also about heart. What Thackeray really admires is the man with both. But if he has to choose, he comes down unflinchingly on the side of heart. Towards the end of *Vanity Fair* he records his verdict on Dobbin, in spite of his awkwardness, his lisp and his large hands and feet.

. . . this poor lady had never met a gentleman in her life until this present moment. Perhaps these are rarer personages than some of us think for. Which of us can point out many such in his circle – men whose aims are generous, whose truth is constant, and not only constant in its kind but elevated in its degree; whose want of meanness makes them simple: who can look the world honestly in the face with an equal manly sympathy for the great and the small? We all know a hundred whose coats are very well made and a score who have excellent manners . . . but of gentlemen how many?

If he were to make up a list, Thackeray goes on, Dobbin would be one of the first he wrote down. Becky knew it. Becky was no angel, any more than the wife of Bath, but she knew a gentleman when she saw one and in that last outburst of "contemptuous kindness" to Amelia had said:

"You must have a husband, you fool; and one of the best gentlemen I ever saw has offered you a hundred times, and you have rejected him, you silly, heartless, ungrateful little creature!"

But dear little Amelia had already written begging him to come back.

9
THE VOICE OF THE MOB

A Deep Confused Clamour

TO TURN FROM Thackeray to Dickens is at once to be conscious of greater stature. Thackeray is incomparably more accurate as a social observer but, as Chesterton remarked, Dickens was not so much a man as a mob, and "a deep confused clamour of comradeship and insurrection fills all his narrative". Like a mob, he never thought anything through in rational terms; like a mob, he loved, hated, pitied, laughed, often with a gusto that reason might deplore. He was an elemental force. He was immensely popular and must be taken into account by anyone who wishes to understand Victorian England. He illuminates both its usually unstated religion and its attitude to the structure of society. Thackeray tells us something of what the upper classes thought; Dickens tells us what the great mass of his fellow-countrymen felt.

André Maurois, in a short book intended to explain Dickens to a French audience, has a story to illustrate the extent to which he was felt to be an institution, part of the cosmos, like Parliament and Queen Victoria. When he died, a mother came home and broke the news to her little boy. He drew a deep breath: "And is Father Christmas dead too?" he asked. Maurois went on to relate that, as late as the 1920s, there were music hall performers who would undertake to impersonate any Dickens character the audience cared to name. "Fagin!" the audience would shout, or "Mrs Gamp!" and the versatile artist would plunge his head into a hamper of wigs and bonnets and emerge as a recognisable Fagin and repeat some of his sayings. No French man of letters ever had such an appeal as that, Maurois concluded; Dickens appealed to something very deep in the English spirit.

It is because he was a mob rather than a man that he cannot be left out. And because he is a mob, there are a few general points that have to be kept in mind if his evidence is to be understood.

First of all, he was a story-teller, writing for money, and usually publishing his story as a serial in monthly instalments. There was not much time for revision as the instalments came out. What came bubbling up from the unconscious went down on paper and appeared in print. His first object

was to hold his readers and the plots are melodramatic, often highly improbable. He loved the stage, had wanted to be a professional actor, and
spent enormous energy on amateur acting, both as actor and director. But
his tale, as well as gripping and entertaining, has also a social purpose and an
artistic theme. The social purpose is usually the denunciation of some inhuman institution. In *Oliver Twist*, it is to expose the abuses of the workhouse
system – to which Dickens reverts in *Our Mutual Friend*, the last complete
novel. In *Bleak House*, the target is the legal obfuscation of the Court of
Chancery, the heartbreak and moral ruin that it caused.

The artistic theme usually has a strong moral element too, but it is concerned not with institutions but with human nature. It is the key, in the
musical sense. It gives a unity of atmosphere that smoothes over the coincidences of the plot. In *Little Dorrit*, the theme is prison, the prisons in which
we shut other people and in which we shut ourselves. The corrupting effect
of wealth is the main theme of *Great Expectations* as well as of *Our Mutual
Friend*, in the one worked out against the recurring image of the Essex marshes,
the other against two great symbols – the river, pure and sparkling near its
source, but after London a muddy sewer from which corpses are fished for
pitiful rewards; and the vast mounds of dust, sources of dangerous wealth and
symbols of the futility of saving and scraping.

Dickens, then, is writing to make a living and hold his audience, but
usually with a strong social purpose and an underlying theme that is at the
same time moral and artistic. He feels much more strongly than he thinks
and when a scene is going well he lets his imagination take charge. It is the
same with his characters. He pictures them in the first place in very simple
terms, each standing for a single quality. He may present a minor character
in terms of one physical characteristic or trick of phrase, which pins his
character down on first appearance, fixing it in the reader's memory. But
with a character, as with an episode, the creative imagination may take
charge, the character may assert its autonomy – and then the writer will give
it rein and let it gallop. Some characters never do fill out; Mr Winkle, for
instance, is never anything but a personification of snobbish pretence to
skill in country sports about which he is ignorant. He is a cartoon drawing,
funny but not alive. Mr Pickwick on the other hand becomes a person and
inspires affection. So does Sam Weller and, what is more, Sam's relationships
with other people grow and become alive. His bantering, half-mocking,
wholly affectionate attitude to his father is superb and I believe in his love
affair with Mary, Mr Nupkins' housemaid, more than I do in several more
serious love affairs in Dickens.

The reader then must look at the whole Dickens scene and he will be
aware of "a deep confused clamour", as Chesterton said, but it is not only
"of comradeship and insurrection". He will hear the voices of a great mob
of people, some hardly characters at all but personified vices, like Mr

Pecksniff and Uriah Heep, but others who have come alive and who show qualities they were clearly not meant to have when they first appeared, such as Florence Dombey's little nurse Susan Nipper and Arthur Clennam's old love Flora Finching. From this confused clamour he will pick out certain notes constantly recurring, hatred for pretence, hatred for fine distinctions and red tape, for cruelty and repression; love of openness and honesty, love for the positive, the immediate, the visible; fear of close walls, darkness, loneliness.

Behind the buzz of this immense concourse of voices, there is a strong groundswell of moral conviction. England was supposed to be a Christian country but Dickens was outraged by the stark contrast between Christian professions and the existence of such a place as Tom-all-Alone's. And he hated the hypocrisy of Mrs Snagsby's Mr Chadband and Mrs Weller's Mr Stiggins. His moral values were Christian in origin but had no firm theological or doctrinal basis and degenerated into a sentimental morass at the death of Little Nell, at the sight of a country church, among the mossed old gravestones of a country churchyard. He disliked the Evangelical movement because it was grim and repressive; he pined for the lost innocence of the countryside but could not live without the stimulus of people.

In all this he was representative of many of his fellow-countrymen, at least those of the urban lower middle classes. But it cannot be said that he resembled them altogether in his attitude to the aristocracy. There was a streak of egalitarianism in him, something that disliked the whole idea of an aristocracy; he felt jealous and ill at ease in the presence of an aristocrat. Sir Mulberry Hawk is one of the earliest in his pages and is a caricature. He is altogether in the tradition of the wicked squire in the melodrama of the day, such as *Maria Martin or The Murder in the Red Barn* – the villain who is hissed as soon as he steps on to the stage. Dickens' public was as ready as he to hiss a villain, but most of them liked a lord and were ready to melt into subservience at the sight of a lord in the flesh. Dickens however was instinctively antagonistic to a man born in easy circumstances. But he was determined to work his way up into a class whose privileges he detested and whose values he despised. As to the qualities of a gentleman, Dickens is therefore a muddled, an ambivalent, but on the whole a hostile witness. [21] But he was too honest and too spontaneous an artist to withhold admiration altogether.

A Hostile Witness

No ONE ILLUSTRATES more clearly than Dickens a point I have made before, that the term "gentleman" as a mark of a social class has been used in very different senses by different people. Dickens sometimes means almost anyone not in the lowest ranks of casual labour. His lawyer's clerks are gentlemen; his medical students. At the bachelor party given by Mr Bob Sawyer for Mr Pickwick, a quarrel suddenly develops. One of these grubby and impecunious youths informs another that he is "no gentleman". The challenge is not taken very seriously.

"Sir, a friend of mine shall wait on you in the morning," said Mr Noddy.
  "Sir, I'm much obliged to you for the caution and I'll leave particular directions with the servant to lock up the spoons," replied Mr Gunter.

This is farce of course, but it makes the point that the English were becoming a nation who nearly all believed themselves to be gentlemen and played at the idea of a code of honour. Dickens laughs at the pretence, yet the ideal of a code of conduct proper to a gentleman was so deeply rooted in the English mind that it is sometimes too strong for him. In his hands, the word "gentleman" is sometimes almost meaningless; he is unconscious of the nuances of behaviour that distinguish Mr Elton from Mr Knightley. His heroes are almost classless, although united in hostility to social pretence. Nonetheless, one can be confident that Eugene Wrayburn, when speaking to his friend Mortimer, would have hesitated to call Mr Pickwick a gentleman.

It has been said that Dickens could not draw a gentleman, but it might as truly be said that he could not draw a working-man; the brickmakers in Bleak House, for instance, are a race apart. He is not at home with either. Where he is really at home is in Mrs Snagsby's little drawing-room at six o'clock when it has been prepared by Guster, the charity maid, for Mr Chadband's arrival for tea:

All the furniture is shaken and dusted, the portraits of Mr and Mrs Snagsby are touched up with a wet cloth, the best tea-service is set forth, and there is excellent provision made of dainty new bread, crusty twists, cool fresh butter, thin slices of ham, tongue and German sausage, and delicate little rows of anchovies nestling in parsley; not to mention new-laid eggs, to be brought up warm in a napkin, and hot buttered toast.

This rings true, as neither the fashionable banquets nor the brickmakers' huts do. It is the world of minor shopkeepers, of low-paid clerks, just below the middle of the middle class, the world of the Wilfers, in which he himself had been brought up, from which he hoped to rise, and through the bottom of which he had nearly fallen when he had been set to sticking labels on bottles of shoe-blacking and his father was in prison for debt.

When he sets himself consciously to think about the process of "becoming a gentleman", Dickens is unconvincing. In *Great Expectations*, Pip acquires far too easily and painlessly the polish that leads him to despise his benefactor. Dickens understood the dangers of Pip's transformation well enough. He makes his point, that gentility and wealth may corrupt honest affection, but he does not persuade me that it could really have happened like that.

In this illustration by Phiz Sir Leicester Dedlock seems just the pompous figure Dickens first conceived. It is later in the story that his nobility towards his wife develops. The figure at the piano is Mr Harold Skimpole, said to be drawn from Leigh Hunt and if so a most scathing indictment.

It is just because he is a mob that Dickens clamours to be included among my illustrations. It is just because he is governed by emotion and by the unconscious that his unwilling admiration of a person from a class he dislikes is significant. Nothing is more valuable than the admission of a hostile witness. Let us look then at a character who is undoubtedly a gentleman in the strictest social sense and whom Dickens finds himself, against his intention, allowing to behave like a gentleman in the moral sense too.

Sir Leicester Dedlock stands for much that Dickens dislikes – old county families, privilege, government by a closed circle of well-connected people – and he is introduced in terms not exactly prepossessing:

He is a gentleman of strict conscience, disdainful of all littleness and meanness, and ready, on the shortest notice, to die any death you may please to mention rather than give occasion for the least impeachment of his integrity. He is **an honourable,** obstinate, truthful, high-spirited, intensely prejudiced, perfectly unreasonable man.

His opinions on politics and society are treated as ludicrous. He regards as almost blasphemous any suggestion of change in a system which has provided him with wealth, power and the respect of the world.

When he has nothing else to do, says Dickens, Sir Leicester "can always contemplate his own greatness", and he adds that Sir Leicester "supposes all his dependents to be utterly bereft of individual characters, intentions or opinions . . ." But this is treating him as a dummy and Dickens is too great an artist to go on with it. Sir Leicester comes alive. His actual behaviour to his dependents is not only courteous but considerate. He treats Mrs Rouncewell, his housekeeper at his Lincolnshire house, Chesney Wold, with great respect; she is, nonetheless, a servant and he is shocked that her son should have wished to leave Chesney Wold and make his own way in the world instead of staying on the estate and rising in the course of time to the position of head gamekeeper or butler. He is more than shocked, he is outraged, when Mr Rouncewell, who has made his way very well indeed and become manager of a factory and a man of wealth, is invited to stand for Parliament, where he would actually sit as a fellow-member and an opponent of Sir Leicester.

A mild crisis develops because Mr Rouncewell's son falls in love with a girl who has been promoted from the excellent village school to be trained at Chesney Wold as my lady's maid. Mr Rouncewell has given his children a good education and feels that if his son is to marry her, Rose should leave Chesney Wold and go, at his expense, for two years to the expensive school where his daughters are enjoying advantages he had never had himself. He puts the point to Sir Leicester with great respect, but he is perfectly at ease and states his case fairly and clearly.

Sir Leicester finds the project incomprehensible and distasteful. To educate people out of their station is to open the floodgates to revolution; he refuses to discuss the matter. If the girl chooses to leave her present favourable position, with its great advantages, of course no one will stop her. But there is no point in discussing it with Mr Rouncewell, whose views and his own are altogether at variance. Having made this clear:

"Mr. Rouncewell," says Sir Leicester, with all the nature of a gentleman shining in him, "it is late, and the roads are dark. I hope your time is not so precious but that you will allow my Lady and myself to offer you the hospitality of Chesney Wold, for to-night at least."

Caricature reasserts itself when Sir Leicester is defeated in an election. But he rises to something like greatness as the plot approaches its climax.

Lady Dedlock, who seems to the world so proud, so beautiful and so cold, was engaged, before she met Sir Leicester, to a captain in the army, who was – so everyone believed – washed overboard off a transport in a storm. She bore him an illegitimate daughter but managed to conceal the whole episode and married Sir Leicester. Her secret was discovered, she was threatened and the man threatening her was murdered. She was suspected. She made up her mind that her position was intolerable, and disappeared. She meant to walk until she died of cold, hunger and exhaustion.

It fell to Inspector Bucket to unravel all this to Sir Leicester. He began by a well-judged and perceptive appeal:

"Sir Leicester Dedlock, Baronet, you are a gentleman; and I know what a gentleman is, and what a gentleman is capable of. A gentleman can bear a shock, when it must come, boldly and steadily . . ."

Sir Leicester sat looking at him with an icy face, Mr Bucket, after a little more preparation, mentioned Lady Dedlock.

"I would greatly prefer, officer," Sir Leicester returned, stiffly, "my Lady's name being entirely omitted from this discussion."

But the Inspector convinced him that this was impossible. He listened stonily until the real murderer had been dramatically summoned and arrested. When he was at last alone, he extended his arms to the imaginary presence of her who

. . . has been for years a main fibre of the root of his dignity and pride, but of whom, save for that, he has never had a selfish thought. It is she whom he has loved, admired, honoured, and set up for the world to respect. It is she who, at the core of all the constrained formalities and conventionalities of his life, has been a stock of living tenderness and love, susceptible as nothing else is of being struck with the agony he feels. . . . And even to the point of his sinking to the ground, oblivious of his suffering, he can yet pronounce her name with something like distinctness . . . and in a tone of mourning and compassion rather than reproach.

He suffered a kind of stroke, but he was able to despatch Mr Bucket to search for her with a message of entire forgiveness. He recovered sufficiently to make, with a great effort, and not knowing how long he had to live, a speech to one of his kin and to his housekeeper Mrs Rouncewell, a kind of testament:

"I desire to say and to call you all to witness . . . that I am on unaltered terms with Lady Dedlock. That I assert no cause whatever of complaint against her. That I have ever had the strongest affection for her, and that I retain it undiminished. Say this to herself and to everyone . . . I abridge nothing I have ever bestowed on her . . . I recall no act that I have done for her advantage and happiness."

On this, Dickens comments that his "formal array of words" might at any other time have had something ludicrous in it, but

at this time, it is serious and affecting. His noble earnestness, his fidelity, his gallant shielding of her, his general conquest of his own wrong and his own pride for her sake, are simply honourable, manly and true.

In short, Dickens had, against his own initial intention, portrayed a gentleman.

Wrayburn and Twemlow

THERE ARE two other samples, both in *Our Mutual Friend*. This has perhaps the most complicated plot of all the novels and perhaps the most improbable. But the theme is strong and clear, and gives the novel an artistic unity, while there are some of the most mature characters in Dickens. We are not concerned with the most of the plot, but only with the main theme and my two examples. The unifying theme is the corrupting power of money and it is against this that we see two pairs of lovers. Bella Wilfer has been given, by an eccentric will, the chance of a fortune if she will marry John Harmon, whom she has never seen; she has made up her mind to accept him – just for the money. He is determined to give her up and lose the fortune unless he can win her without the golden bait. Eugene Wrayburn's case is just the reverse; he has no more doubt about Lizzie's honesty, goodness and freedom from mercenary motives than about her beauty – but she is penniless and illiterate, and her father's repulsive calling has been to fish corpses from the river.

Eugene is a briefless barrister dependent on his father's approval; his father means him to marry well and has actually chosen him a young lady. Eugene's social position is more accurately drawn than is usual in Dickens. His father is wealthy and well-connected, has an estate and must be assumed to be of the landed gentry. He has decided their professions for each of his five sons; Eugene has been told to go to the Bar and he has an allowance which would be sufficient to live on if he were careful, which he is not. He was at a public school; he lives in the Temple and dines out in London, like the

Eugene Wrayburn, splendidly a gentleman in outward circumstance, does not behave to his inferior as a gentleman should. Here he is bribing a hopeless alcoholic to tell him where Lizzie has hidden – and contemptuously "fumigating" him with scented pastilles.

young Pendennis and his friends. He is indolent by nature and it is the fashion to be languid and bored; his income is just sufficient to protect him from any absolute necessity of earning his living and he is a victim of one of the diseases of the Victorian gentleman, a corruption of one of Castiglione's graces. It would be rather bad form to be seen to *try*. "When we were at school together," he says to Mortimer Lightwood, "I got up my lessons at the last moment, day by day and bit by bit; now we are out in life together, I get up my lessons in the same way." Lightwood has always admired him; he has style and an attractive personality that cannot be ignored. This is how he appears on one occasion:

. . . a gentleman came coolly sauntering towards them, with a cigar in his mouth, his coat thrown back, and his hands behind him. Something in the careless manner of this person, and in a certain lazily arrogant air with which he approached, holding possession of twice as much pavement as another would have claimed, instantly caught the boy's attention . . .

"Careless" is the word constantly applied to him; he is careless because he has never had to take care, as Dickens had had to take care. He arouses the instant – and volcanic – aversion of Bradley Headstone, partly from a deep-rooted sexual jealousy, instinctive and immediate, but also because Headstone, like Dickens, had had to take a great deal of care.

There was a kind of settled trouble in his face. It was the face belonging to a naturally slow or inattentive intellect that had toiled hard to get what it had won, and that had to hold it now that it was gotten. He always seemed uneasy lest anything should be missing from his mental warehouse . . .

Eugene is an offence to him because of his carelessness and arrogance, because he has so much *without* trying, because he is everything Headstone is not, above all because of Lizzie. When she refuses Headstone, he at once attributes her refusal to Eugene and strikes his clenched fist on a stone wall "with a force that leaves the knuckles raw and bleeding," exclaiming: "I hope that I may never kill him."

The hostility is reciprocated, not because Eugene supposes that Lizzie cares for Headstone but because he finds it intolerable that such a man should be a rival. He treats Headstone from the first encounter with a cruel icy disdain. "There was some secret sure perception between them, which set them against one another in all ways." He deliberately torments him by a scornful imperturbability. It cannot be said that Eugene behaves as a perfect gentleman to Bradley Headstone, who is his social inferior. But, then, even the most polished gentleman does not always behave perfectly to a rival in love. And it must also be admitted that – without that excuse – Eugene treats Mr Riah, the good Jew, with an arrogance, a careless insolence, that is far from Chaucer's *gentillesse*.

But it is his behaviour to Lizzie that is nearest to the true centre of Eugene's character. He is not an habitual womanizer, or a man who glories in his conquests. His interest in Lizzie is aroused by her physical beauty but sustained by her loneliness and patience. When for the first time he drops the affectation of flippant boredom and pleads with her in real earnest he is trying to persuade her to let him pay someone to teach her to read; he genuinely wishes to help her and is perfectly sincere when he says that it will be the first time in his life that he has done anything useful. He wants her to accept this help for her own sake and believes it to be something worth achieving for itself. That does not mean that he does not perceive that it may also help to win her affection. He tells Mortimer that he cannot see the future, that he does not know what he intends, but at this stage he is clearly hoping to set her up in a cottage as his mistress. The moment he has won her agreement to the plan for her education, he turns playfully to her friend the dolls' dress-maker:

> "I think of setting up a doll, Miss Jenny," he said.
> "You had better not," replied the dressmaker.
> "Why not?"
> "You are sure to break it. All you children do."

This surely can refer only to such an intention. But his proposition must have been turned down, for some days later he tells Mortimer:

> "There is no better girl in all this London than Lizzie Hexam. There is no better among my people at home; no better among yours."

Mortimer questions him.

> "Eugene, do you design to capture and desert this girl?"
> "My dear fellow, no."
> "Do you design to marry her?"
> "My dear fellow, no."

He sees the real obstacle to marrying Lizzie. What holds him back is the incompatibility of background, which Dickens never honestly faces. It is not just the attitude of "society" – which here means the dinner-party society of the Podsnaps and Veneerings. Would he not once again be bored? A girl who could not even read! Would she understand his quirks and flippancies? Eugene does perceive at last that he is wronging Lizzie by paying her an attention to which he can foresee no honourable conclusion. He is trying to force himself to a decision – probably an end to the affair – when Headstone's murderous attack falls on him. He marries Lizzie on what he believes to be his death-bed, all the occasional sparks of consciousness that he can summon being directed to thoughts of her. And when he does, after all, recover, he vigorously rejects the idea of emigration:

Eugene's bedside. Eugene has barely parted from Lizzie when he is murderously attacked. As he lies on what he believes to be his death-bed, he begs Lizzie to marry him.

Shall I turn coward to Lizzie and sneak away with her, as if I were ashamed of her!..
I will fight it out to the last gasp, with her and for her, here in the open field.

Noble words and – since she had long before confessed to the dolls' dress-maker that she saw his failings and yet would joyfully die for him – perhaps he was able with her help to overcome his old enemies of lassitude, boredom and depression. Nonetheless, one would like to have peeped at them on an evening when they were alone together twenty years after their marriage.

Eugene is a convincing picture of a gentleman, not indeed of a perfect gentleman, because far from courteous to inferiors, but one born to the part and armed with the demeanour of a gentleman, generous, careless, brave, a man who has both style and heart, a flesh and blood gentleman with failings common among his order.

Mr Twemlow, the second example from *Our Mutual Friend*, is less complex and, like Sir Leicester Dedlock, attracts respect in defiance of his creator's intention. He is introduced as a slightly ridiculous figure, always being asked to dinner because he is first cousin to a lord, useful to the Veneerings to make up their numbers at table and useful to Dickens as a means of making fun of Veneering, a man so recently wealthy that his oldest friends are people he has only just met. This is puzzling to poor Twemlow, and, at first, in a manner typical of Dickens with a minor character, all we know about Twemlow is that he is puzzled by the newness of Veneering's oldest friends. But he begins to come alive when his physical presence is brought before us; he is "grey, dry, polite, susceptible to east wind . . . cheeks drawn in as if he had made a great effort to retire into himself some years ago". And some time later we are not surprised when it is to him that Sophronia Lammle turns for help when she can see no other way out of her difficulty. She is determined to save silly little Georgiana Podsnap from the infamous plot devised by Sophronia's husband. She manages to confide in Twemlow under her breath at a party: "You have the soul of a gentleman, and I know I may trust you." She betrays her husband's plot to him, knowing he will not betray her and that he will do what is needed.

He promises, and Georgiana is saved from marriage to the truly horrible Fledgeby. Poor Twemlow however is placed in great embarrassment when Fledgeby offers to do him a favour. It is mere pretence; Fledgeby has no intention of obliging him in any way, but Twemlow is deeply disturbed at the thought of being beholden to a man whom he has injured, however justly. It is, however, in the last chapter of the novel, when he is once again at the table of Veneering, that this quiet, unassuming, inoffensive, little, poor gentleman comes out very strong. He is asked his opinion of Eugene's marriage to Lizzie Hexam, which everyone else at table has denounced as shocking, while Podsnap has gone so far as to say that his gorge rises at it. He disagrees with the whole vulgar crew:

If this gentleman's feelings of gratitude, of respect, of admiration, and affection, induced him (as I presume they did) to marry this lady . . . I think he is the greater gentleman for the action, and makes her the greater lady. . . . When I use the word gentleman, I use it in the sense in which the degree may be attained by any man. The feelings of a gentleman I hold sacred . . .

And when Podsnap questions his calling Lizzie a lady he puts him down very firmly indeed. "What else would you call her," he asks, "if her husband were present?"

10
A ROMANTIC
REALIST

"A Great Lump out of the Earth"

To TURN from Charles Dickens to Anthony Trollope is to move into an entirely different world. It is in the first place a more modern world. This is partly a matter of dates. Though there were only three years between their births – Dickens 1812, Trollope 1815 – Dickens sprang into fame with *Pickwick* in 1836, while Trollope did not attain even moderate success till *The Warden* in 1855. His most popular period was in the sixties, when Dickens had been a household word for thirty years. But perhaps the sensation of a more familiar world comes as much from the nature of the men.

Trollope did not think highly of Dickens, whom he attacked in *The Warden* as "Mr Popular Sentiment". In temperament and taste they could hardly be further apart. Trollope disliked excess – and Dickens is all excess. In his autobiography, Trollope quotes with pleasure a critic who said that his novels were "just as real as if some giant had hewn a great lump out of the earth and put it under a glass case with all its inhabitants going about their daily business . . ."[22] This was what he aimed at – realism, exactitude, fidelity. He admired industry, common-sense, and honesty – and if those sound like the virtues of a clerk rather than an artist, he would not have demurred. He compared himself to a shoe-maker; he put honest work into his craft and meant to sell the product. When he finished one pair of shoes, he did not hang about for a month admiring them but started a new pair the very next day. Each pair was as good as he could make it.

As an artist, Trollope is not in the same class as Dickens; his emotional range is altogether less. But as a portrayer of the social scene he is more useful, just because he is an honest craftsman, concerned to show things as they are. As a witness, he is instinctively friendly, where Dickens was instinctively hostile, but he is an honest witness who does not bend the evidence. He admires the gentleman and portrays quite a number very successfully. But when he thinks about the *idea* of the gentleman, it seems to me that he does not get it quite right.

Trollope's novels are all about niceties of social position and social behaviour, the interplay of true love with the need for a comfortable income,
about the behaviour proper for a true gentleman and a virtuous young lady.
His feet are firmly on the ground; we know what everyone's estate is worth
and whether he is in debt. His people consult solicitors and write wills.
Parents want their children to make suitable matches; the children frequently want to make matches that are anything but suitable. The distinctions between different layers of society are never far from the minds of his
characters and they are often subtle.

Consider for example the difference between Dr Thorne and Dr Fillgrave.
As medical men, they followed a calling that was only just becoming respectable. But while Dr Fillgrave was in practice in the county town, Dr Thorne
lived in a country village and most of his patients were humble folk. Profes-
sionally, he ranked lower than Dr Fillgrave. But he came of an ancient family;
the Thornes had been squires of Ullathorne since before the Norman
Conquest. It did not cross his mind to doubt that he was a gentleman. Dr
Fillgrave was less sure of himself and he fumed at Dr Thorne's unorthodox
attitude to fees. A physician, thought Dr Fillgrave, "should take his fee without letting his left hand know what his right was doing; it should be taken
without a thought, without a look, without a move of the facial muscles . . .
whereas that fellow Thorne would lug out half-a-crown from his breeches
pocket and give it in exchange for a ten-shilling piece. . . . He had no appreciation of the dignity of a learned profession . . ."

Or consider Mr Walker, a solicitor in the country town of Silverbridge, a
man who moved in very good circles and asked the Rector to his house. He
had to introduce to his friends Mr Toogood, a fellow solicitor from London,
who had come down to Silverbridge to enquire into the mysterious affair
of the cheque that the Reverend Josiah Crawley was supposed to have
stolen. Before Mr Toogood arrived, Mr Walker warned them that he
"wasn't quite – not quite, you know – 'not quite so much of a gentleman as I
am' – Mr Walker would have said had he spoken out freely".

Dr Thorne would have left them to find out for themselves.

The novels are full of this amused irony at pretension. But, as with Miss
Austen, something else is never far from Trollope's mind, a quality not very
different from what Chaucer meant by *gentillesse*. That something else, the
mysterious quality of being a gentleman in the sense that Trollope really
admired, is displayed in a hundred touches, pondered on by many characters,
never narrowly defined. It is not always to be found among the nobly born.
No one had less of it than Lord Mongrober, who thought only of his dinner,
or the horrible Earl de Courcy, who snarled and gnashed his teeth at his
family and his dependents alike and of whom the nearest thing to a good
word ever spoken was the remark of his valet, that at least her ladyship
caught it even worse than he did – and she minded more because *he* could
give his notice.

Doctor Thorne was one of the Thornes of Ullathorne, and knew himself to be a gentleman though he followed the humble profession of a village doctor. He did not hesitate to adopt his brother's illegitimate child – nor to accept responsibility for the woman his murdered brother had seduced.

There is a distinction implicit in the description of John Vavasor, who came of an ancient Cumbrian family but lived a rather idle and self-centred life in London clubs; "he was a man of his word; and he understood well that code of bye-laws which was presumed to constitute the character of a gentleman in his circle . . ." It is implied that something was lacking. He would not cheat at cards or be unnecessarily rude, but he would not put himself out for anyone else. The distinction is made more explicit as the character of Ferdinand Lopez unfolds itself in *The Prime Minister*: "In a sense, he was what is called a gentleman. He knew how to speak, and how to look, how to use a knife and fork, how to dress himself and how to walk. But he had not the faintest notion of the feelings of a gentleman." This is gradually forced on to the unwilling recognition of poor Emily Wharton, who has insisted on marrying him against the advice of all her friends and family. It is shown chiefly in the motives he attributes to other people, which are invariably mean, spiteful or mercenary.

No one has expressed more clearly than Trollope the feeling of Englishmen in the middle of Queen Victoria's reign that to be a gentleman in the truest

Mr Crawley, the perpetual curate of Hogglestock, was struggling to keep his wife and children on £130 a year. He owed money to the butcher and the baker and could not afford new boots, but everyone knew he was a gentleman.

sense was to be initiated into a kind of order, almost a religion, to be possessed of a quality that was enigmatic and indefinable yet immediately apparent to everyone else. Two grooms in an inn-yard were aware of it, talking of Mr Crawley, the perpetual curate of Hogglestock, who was struggling to keep his wife and children on £130 a year. That day Mr Crawley had walked from Hogglestock to Barchester and back, some thirty miles all told. " 'Footed it all the way,' said one. 'And yet he's a gentleman, too,' said the other." Mark Robarts, also a clergyman, but much younger, and rich in comparison, with a good living and a comfortable rectory, overheard them and thought of what they said as he drove home in his smart gig:

It was undoubtedly the fact that Mr Crawley was recognised to be a gentleman by all who knew him, high or low, rich or poor, by those who thought well of him and by those who thought ill. . . . Nobody doubted it; not even they who thought he had stolen the money.

The point is thoughtfully considered by Mary Thorne. She is Dr Thorne's niece. She is almost penniless and she knows that Frank Gresham of Greshamsbury, whom she loves and who wants to marry her, is being told by all his noble relations that it is his duty to marry money and thus redeem the once fine estate impoverished by his father. She was born, she thought, a gentlewoman, and in that case, she was fit to match with any gentleman.

... Then came to her mind the curious questions; what makes a gentleman? What makes a gentlewoman? What is the inner reality, the spiritualized quintessence of that privilege in the world which men call rank ...

And she answered the question. Absolute, intrinsic, acknowledged, individual merit must give it to its possessor, let him be whom, and what, and whence he might.

She thought – it strikes one to-day – of gentility almost as St Paul wished the early Christians to think of baptism. It was to redeem them and to shine in their actions so that the rest of the world recognized them for what they were. But of course it was not so simple and clear-cut as either Mary Thorne or St Paul would have wished. What constituted that absolute intrinsic merit to which Mary attached such importance? We will come back to that point after looking at some examples of men and women whom Trollope regarded as possessing it. But we noticed some time ago that one of the distinguishing marks of a gentleman was behaviour to women. Let us first look at Trollope's view of love and the extent to which the tradition of courtly love has survived.

The Ghost of Courtly Love

TROLLOPE WAS a realist and his aim was to make his people as real as he could. His heroines are never pretty little dolls who tremble and weep in moments of stress. They are girls of fire and humour; they tease the young men they adore and are brave enough to speak their minds with wit and to stand up to any dragon. Nonetheless, there is a strong romantic vein. His heroines of the first class – Mary Thorne, Lucy Roberts, Lily Dale, Grace Crawley, Lucy Morris – love for ever. Only one of them, Lily Dale, when her first love is false, vows herself forever like a Hindu widow to the solitary life of an old maid, but the others too were dedicated to one man and are only saved from the funeral pyre because things come right. Trollope's view of woman's love owes a great deal to the courtly tradition.

There are heroines who did change their mind – but Trollope has to persuade himself that they had unconsciously loved the right man all the time. Alice Vavasor was engaged to John Grey – one of Trollope's ideal gentlemen – but she broke off her engagement because he had no ambition. He was content to live on his country estate near Cambridge, reading quietly in his library and occasionally venturing on a scholarly article for one of the quarterlies – an existence as flat, Alice thought, as the Cambridge landscape. Alice was a radical in politics and something of a feminist – although not to the degree of thinking that women should be barristers or doctors. She ended the engagement; she was not worthy of him, she said; she felt she could not live up to his standards. And she really meant it. She turned to her much more dashing cousin George Vavasor, who was intensely ambitious and meant to get into Parliament. She knew his failings, his passion and inconstancy and violence. She could help *him* and that would be a life worth living.

Alice earned the name of jilt and the strong disapproval of her friends and relations. But – unexpectedly to the reader and very belatedly – she suddenly realized that she did not love George physically and expressed herself with a frankness surprising at that period.

Must she submit to his caresses – lie on his bosom – turn herself warmly to his kisses? "No," she said, "no" – speaking audibly as she walked about the room. But that other one – John Grey – he had come and touched her hand and the fibres of her body had seemed to melt within her at the touch so that she could have fallen at his feet.

She had conceived an ideal distant figure, and since in certain respects John Grey had differed from it she had jilted him. Trollope himself found it hard to understand her behaviour and expected his readers to find it hard to forgive her; she found it very hard to forgive herself.

Emily Wharton made a similar mistake and found it even harder. She had refused Arthur Fletcher more than once; he was her childhood companion, and an ideal match in every way; he was handsome, brave in the hunting-field, a younger son but working hard at the Bar and with prospects in Parliament; she would have £60,000 if she took him; both their families wished it. But she was revolted by the calm assumptions about class of the county folk in Herefordshire among whom she had been brought up, and in the teeth of everyone's advice married Ferdinand Lopez. She felt, when she realized her mistake, absolutely bound to the man she had married; she had done wrong, flying in the face of all her friends, but she must atone for her sin by enduring her misery. She was released from it because he deliberately walked in front of the express train from Euston to Inverness and "in a moment had been knocked to bloody atoms". But Emily felt disgraced. She now realised that she had always loved Arthur Fletcher, but she was determined to refuse him all the same. By all the canons of widowhood, she vowed, she was forbidden to think of love again. "There ought to be nothing left for her but crape and weepers." She was argued out of her determination in the end but it took an unconscionably long time.

Both Alice Vavasor and Emily Wharton were women of intelligence and character, but they had led the sheltered lives of Victorian girls and had constructed an ideal lover without much consciousness of the realities of marriage, rejecting in each case a flesh-and-blood lover, who happened also to be eligible – almost in the spirit of Lydia Languish, who had to have a lover she could elope with. Each awoke late to the reality of a strong physical love – and each was doubly lucky, since her true love was just that "suitable" candidate she had rejected and he was unshakably constant.

The ghost of courtly love still walked. Trollope was not only a realist but a romantic who insisted that there are first loves made in heaven, never to be repeated, even though earthly circumstances had made their fruition impossible. Plantagenet Palliser, Duke of Omnium, often sighed because his Duchess Glencora had once upon a time loved that hopeless scamp and reprobate Burgo FitzGerald. Her relatives stepped in and stopped it; they had married her off to himself. It had been a success; she was a good wife, devoted to his interests and – she *was* very fond of him. But he knew that he had never taken the place of Burgo. Burgo was beautiful as a god or an angel and women loved him (wrote Trollope) because he "seemed to think so little of himself".

In truth it was not so much that he did not think of himself as that he was utterly reckless of tomorrow. Something in Glencora had responded to that recklessness and had died when they were separated. The bloom had gone from her life.

About men Trollope was one degree more prosaic. His heroes are faithful; indeed, fidelity is one of the first qualities of a gentleman. But a young man who is constant at heart may look around. "Young men are such absolute moths!" reflected Trollope, as he recorded Lady Lufton's schemes for marrying her son to Griselda Grantly. And Lord Lufton *did* admire Griselda – who could fail to? – and danced with her and flirted a little, though his heart was set on Lucy Robarts – so brown and small and insignificant in his mother's eyes. Frank Gresham was another splendid young hero, utterly faithful in his heart to Mary Thorne but he flirted with Patience Oriel and even made a halfhearted and almost despairing proposal to the rich Miss Dunstable, very plain and somewhat older than himself. He was lucky; she merely laughed at him, soon wormed out of him the story of his love for Mary, and backed him through thick and thin. Frank Greystoke at heart was pledged to the penniless Lucy Morris – but very nearly lost his head and his feet before the sustained attack of Lizzie Eustace, who was rich and pretty, although he knew her to be almost incapable of telling the truth. Even the faithful Johnny Eames, Lily Dale's unsuccessful suitor – but one could go on for ever. The moths "amuse themselves with the light of the beautiful candle, fluttering about, on and off, in and out of the flame with dazzled eyes, till in a rash moment they rush in too near . . ." Nonetheless, all the best moths are faithful at heart.

Indeed, if a man is not faithful, once he has declared himself, he forfeits the right to be called a gentleman. Mr Moffat, son of a rich manufacturer, engaged himself to Augusta, a daughter of the ancient but impoverished house of Gresham of Greshamsbury, but broke it off when he found a wealthier bride; Frank Gresham, Augusta's brother, felt it incumbent on him to buy a heavy cutting whip and wait for Mr Moffat on the steps of his club, where he fell on him and beat him as unfit to be regarded as a gentleman. And John Eames did the same, rather clumsily and less efficiently, but

Frank Gresham, the young squire of
Greshamsbury, could never lay claim
to perfection, but he stuck to Mary
Thorne in spite of opposition from all
his family, and showed spirit and proper
feeling when he horse-whipped on the
steps of his club the man who had
jilted his sister.

with the same intention, to Adolphus Crosbie when he jilted Lily Dale for
Lady Alexandrina de Courcy. "On my honour, as a gentleman, I cannot
understand it!" old Mr Dale, Lily's uncle, kept saying of Crosbie to his
nephew. That such a man should have sat as a guest at his table! "Treat him
as a rat," was the old squire's conclusion. And Trollope agreed. He had
"degraded himself to the vermin rank of humanity".

Contrast the disgraceful inconstancy of Adolphus Crosbie – who is lured
by the smell of success and high rank and London glitter – with the chivalrous
constancy of John Grey and Arthur Fletcher. John Grey had been actually
engaged to Alice Vavasor before she cast him off. "He is perfect!" she
thought to herself. "Oh, that he were less perfect!" And a modern reader
may well agree with her and find John Grey a little too good to be true. But
he is what Trollope thought a gentleman should be, and in relation to women
he is not very different from Plantagenet Palliser, Duke of Omnium, whom
Trollope in his autobiography declared to be one of his favourite characters.
Of the Duke, his wife Glencora said to her confidant Mrs Finn:

"To him a woman, particularly his own woman, is a thing so fine and so precious
that the winds of heaven should hardly be allowed to blow upon her . . ."

But since Trollope regarded Plantagenet Palliser as "a perfect gentleman" –
and added: "If he be not, then am I unable to describe a gentleman" – he
must be sketched in the round.

The Duke of Omnium

TROLLOPE WROTE in his autobiography that he "lived with" his characters. The novelist, he said, wanted to make them real to his readers and:

They must be with him as he lies down to sleep, and as he wakes from his dreams. He must learn to hate them and to love them. He must argue with them, quarrel with them, forgive them and even submit to them.

And in this, I, for my part, find him successful. I too argue with his characters. I find myself wishing that someone would give Emily Wharton a good shaking, and I reproach Mr Wharton bitterly for giving way so suddenly and letting her marry Ferdinand Lopez without a less perfunctory investigation of the man's finances. He, of all men! A successful barrister who had made his way by hard work in the Equity courts! But his line of battle crumpled in the face of Emily's silent misery. His friends thought he should have held out – but he didn't. There is no accounting, one feels, for the way people behave; that was what he did. One never doubts his right to act unexpectedly. And this seems to me one of the peculiar virtues of Trollope.

Of all the hundreds of characters who throng the novels, Trollope in his *Autobiography* asserts his special and enduring affection for Plantagenet Palliser and his wife Glencora. He says: "Plantagenet Palliser I think to be a very noble gentleman." Yes – no one would argue about that. But was he, as Trollope argues later in the same book, "a *perfect* gentleman"? I would certainly argue that he was not *the* perfect gentleman.

The old Duke of Omnium, whom Plantagenet succeeded as duke, owned half Barsetshire and was one of the richest men in England. But Lady Lufton knew he was "unprincipled", would not meet him if she could avoid it and treated him with distant courtesy if she must.

He first appears in *The Small House at Allington*. This was before he succeeded his uncle as Duke of Omnium, when he was still in the House of
Commons.

He was about twenty-five years of age and was, as yet, unmarried. He did not hunt or
shoot or keep a yacht, and had been heard to say that he had never put a foot upon a
race-course in his life. He dressed very quietly, never changing the colour or form of
his garments; and in society was quiet, reserved and very often silent. He was tall,
slight, and not ill-looking; but more than this cannot be said for his personal appearance – except, indeed, this, that no one could mistake him for other than a
gentleman.

This is not a very enticing picture for a hero – and indeed he was far from
being a hero.

. . . he was very rich, surrounded by all the temptations of luxury and pleasure; and
yet he devoted himself to work with the grinding energy of a young penniless
barrister labouring for a penniless wife. . . . He was an upright, thin, laborious man
. . . whose parts were sufficient to make his education, integrity and industry useful
in the highest degree [to his party].

Not the sort of man, you would say, to excite a romantic passion – and you
would be right. How decorous was the moment when he at last attempted
to reveal to Lady Dumbello the interest he took in her – an interest which
had excited everyone else for so long!

"Griselda," he said – and . . . the word sank softly into her ear like small rain upon
moss, and it sank into no other ear.
"Griselda!"
"Mr. Palliser!" said she; – and merely glanced at him . . .
"May I not call you so?"
"Certainly not."

She rose and asked him to call her carriage. It was just what she had been
waiting for – the moment she had long foreseen when he would forget himself. It was the nearest he ever did come to forgetting himself and she never
had to repeat that one glacial look. After that rebuff he submitted obediently
to an arranged marriage with Lady Glencora – and came to love her dearly.
It was to Lady Glencora that Plantagenet showed that nobility of which
Trollope spoke. She was as different from her husband as anyone could well
be. She was physically very different, small and fair and smiling with very
bright blue eyes, but still more so in character; she was outspoken and enthusiastic; she was warm, impulsive, mischievous. "I do not know," Trollope
remarked on one occasion, "that she was at all points a lady, but had Fate so
willed it, she would have been a thorough gentleman." He makes the point
because she never referred, even when tempted, to the fact that her own

Trollope considered Plantagenet Palliser, later Duke of Omnium, the perfect gentleman. But was he *too* perfect? How decorous was his one lapse from virtue, when he ventured to address the beautiful Lady Dumbello as Griselda!

immense wealth made a contribution to their joint estate that almost equalled the Palliser share. But he might have made it equally well because of her loyalty – to a comrade, to a daughter, to a subordinate.

She was very young when she was forced to marry Plantagenet. And she was in love with Burgo Fitzgerald. Soon after the marriage came a crisis. He was to be at Lady Monk's ball and she tried to avoid going. But Plantagenet insisted; he took her to the ball and left to study blue books. When he came back, Burgo was pressing Glencora to run away with him that very night.

He had a carriage waiting. All three behaved with perfect decorum. " 'Mr Fitzgerald,' said Glencora, 'I left a scarf in your aunt's room. Would you mind getting it for me?'

" 'I will fetch it,' said Mr Palliser" – and there was "a touch of chivalry in his leaving them again together which so far conquered her". But next morning she was rebellious, mutinous, at her naughtiest. She told him that she had never loved him – and she did not think he had ever loved her. She loved only Burgo. Suddenly the icy Plantagenet melted; he told her that he did love her; he put his arm gently about her and promised to take leave of the House of Commons for six months and take her on the Continent. And almost as he said the words there arrived on the doorstep the Duke of St Bungay to offer him the post he had longed for, the summit of his ambition. To be Chancellor of the Exchequer! It was for that he had hoped and toiled. But he refused it. His first duty was to his wife.

That was true nobility. Glencora recognized it and when she was alone tore up into small fragments without reading it a letter she had in her pocket. The thing was settled. But Burgo did not know he was beaten and had made another plan. Lady Monk was to invite Glencora to her house one afternoon and from her house Burgo was to take her to the four o'clock train for Southampton and St Malo. Glencora had promised to see Burgo again, and as soon as the plan was formed he walked boldly to her house in Park Lane, hoping to find her alone and persuade her.

" 'Is Lady Glencora at home?' " he asked, not seeing that in the shadow behind the servant who opened the door stood Plantagenet, on the point of going out. " 'I am not sure,' said Mr Palliser, making his way out, 'the servant will find out for you.' Then he went on his way across Park Lane . . . never once turning back his face. . . . Nor did he return a minute earlier than he would otherwise have done." Surely there was nobility in that.

She sent Burgo away and lived the rest of her life with Plantagenet, a dutiful wife even though she sometimes chose to interpret her duty in a way she knew he did not approve. Often she shocked him; he was deeply shocked when she spoke of one of his political colleagues as that "odious baboon with red bristles". She determined, when he was Prime Minister, to entertain as no Prime Minister's wife had ever done before – and he thought it vulgar. He shrank from her enthusiasms and her animosities alike. "I know an enemy when I see him," said the Duchess, "and as long as I live I'll treat an enemy as an enemy." He was much the finer spirit of the two, too fine indeed and too sensitive for every day life, but their marriage grew, in a depth of shared experience and mutual respect, and he came to be entirely dependent on her.

He was surely, as Trollope thought, a noble gentleman; tender and forgiving to his wife, and in the end to his children, incapable of a mean act, or of trivial spite, but he was lacking nonetheless in something that Castiglione had known the perfect gentleman should have. He had no spontaneity.

Plantagenet was what in the world of the public school was to be called by a variety of opprobrious names; he was a "tug", a "sap" or a "swat", someone who worked hard and was not ashamed to say so. In the ethics of the public school, which were still in the developing stage, it was not the thing to try too hard. There was admiration for brilliance if it seemed to be effortless, even for brilliance as a scholar, but painstaking hard work and long practice, even in an athlete, took all the glitter from achievement.

In the wider world too the skilful amateur was admired, in sport, in politics, in everything. But a man who could beat the professionals at cricket or at billiards must not let it be known that he practised. In politics, an admired figure was the Duke of St Bungay, who did not read Blue Books and did not much believe in legislation, but who "had always been great in council, never giving his advice unasked . . . and cautious at all times to avoid excesses, on this side or on that . . ." He stayed in the background, a maker of prime ministers without aspirations for himself. There was a following too for dazzling phrases, for a touch of unstudied swagger. "When I want to read a novel, I write one," said Disraeli – and there was an element in the Victorian public that admired that kind of insolent showing off, just as it admired Hugh Lonsdale. But there were those, you will remember, who had not thought Hugh Lonsdale quite the thing, nor for that matter Disraeli. Trollope was one of them; he thought that Disraeli's novels "smelt of hair-oil". Trollope had worked hard himself and did not see why he should hide it. He would have been false to himself if his perfect gentleman had not been hard-working.

But Plantagenet could not unbend. Even his closest associates were in awe of him. After Glencora's death, when he ached for the confidence of his children, the best he could do, when his son Lord Silverbridge arrived ten minutes late for dinner and said he was "awfully sorry", was this:

"There is no occasion for awe . . . since sufficiency of dinner is left."

I do not doubt that he said it. I am sure he did; it was just the kind of thing he would say. It was meant to be jocose and forgiving. But it was pompous and crushing and the perfect gentleman would have appeared more spontaneous, more winning. He really loved Silverbridge but could not show it. Colonel Newcome, who also loved his son, would have found a phrase to show it.

11
ALMOST A RELIGION

LET US TRY to construct a picture of a Victorian gentleman with something of that style and spontaneity that Plantagenet Palliser lacked, and consider how he would differ from Sir Philip Sidney, the Elizabethan gentleman.

Some qualities were constant through the centuries. Courage was one of them, shown in the long Victorian peace chiefly in the hunting-field – though it was not the thing for a disappointed lover to ride suicidally, as Arthur Fletcher once did and also Burgo Fitzgerald. But physical courage a gentleman must have, while the confidence to look a man in the face and the courage to make a hard decision were essential ingredients in the Victorian ideal.

Castiglione's courtier had to be able to handle his weapons; he was to be a soldier who happened to be a poet, not a poet who happened to be a soldier. And here there has been a distinct change of emphasis. The Victorian gentleman need not be a soldier, though he should be able to ride and shoot. This was as much because these were expensive rural amusements, which marked him off from the manufacturer and the shopkeeper, as because they indicated courage; they were only a survival from the days when the rank of gentleman meant feudal tenure of land and military service.[23]

As to being a poet, that was distinctly to be deprecated. If a Victorian gentleman had, one day after dinner, expressed a wish to sing verses of his own composition to his own tune and accompany himself on the lute, the mammas in the drawing-room would have rustled disapprovingly and looked anxiously to see who their daughters were talking to. It was desirable to be able to stand by the piano and turn over the pages while an admired young lady sang a popular ballad. But few indeed were musicians or poets as Sidney and his contemporaries had been. It was quite the thing to be philistine.

To be a scholar and a gentleman was a matter for praise, though sometimes remarked with a note of slight surprise, but on the whole the change is in a direction hostile to the intellect and the arts. It is a swing to the country and away from the court. The emphasis is now on character, on avoiding excess, on doing the right thing naturally. In the time of Lord Chesterfield, there had been a great gulf between the polished wit of the court and such a fox-hunting country gentleman as Squire Western. A hundred years later, country gentlemen such as Squire Gresham (Frank's father) or Squire Dale (Lily's uncle) are more polished than Squire Western, but they are also less accomplished than Lord Chesterfield and less learned.

Why was this? Surely it was part of something much wider.[24] Before the French Revolution and the proclamation of equality, Squire Western and his kind had known very well that because of their birth they were quite different from the common people. Therefore a gentleman could be familiar with his servants and talk bawdy to them. But once the great kingdom across the Channel had become a republic where all men were said to be equal, it became more necessary to insist on difference – and the difference must be expressed in some way not easily acquired. It was not enough to be a scholar; scholarship could be learnt at school. It was not enough to be a musician or a linguist. It became necessary to concentrate on something indefinable, what Chesterfield had called the 'je ne sais quoi', which could only be acquired by upbringing from the earliest days in the company of those who already had the qualification.

This need to be distinguished from the people was surely the reason for the growth of prudishness as well. Physical functions were something shared with the great mass of the people, so the privileged few who had to show they were different pretended that they did not exist. Such things must not be mentioned in the presence of ladies – and, since ladies could read, such things must not be mentioned in print. Sometimes a dictionary, which after all existed to *explain* things, found it necessary to refer to some obscene practice or some less honourable part of the human body, and in that case it would use Latin, which it was presumed a lady would not understand, while a gentleman would.

Victorian prudishness was a remnant of the Manichaean heresy, the belief that matter was evil, which in the time of Augustine had spread over the Mediterranean world, almost choking Christianity, and had broken out again in Languedoc in the early Middle Ages. Courtly love was an indirect offshoot; the humdrum companionship and exchange of marriage was to be despised and women were to be admired as though they were disembodied spirits. It was a man-made world and it was men who built up the pretence that women – at least ladies – were fairy-like creatures, almost unconscious of the body, a pretence that Victorian women courageously disproved every day of the year. This remnant of the Manichaean heresy had never quite died, but it was the French Revolution and the fear of equality that brought it to life in the 19th century.

Insistence on a country background again was something that was to

Phineas Finn was far from rich and the son of a country doctor in Ireland. If Plantagenet Palliser was too reserved to be the perfect gentleman, Phineas was too impulsive. But Lady Laura trusted him "as a gentleman" and he kept her secret.

persist in English life until the late 20th century, but which was new since the time of Sidney and Spenser. Then the country was something to be looked at and admired but the court was the place to live. Indeed, it was more recent than that. The one thing Lord Chesterfield and Dr Johnson had in common was a distaste for the country. The squire's younger son might be apprenticed to a cloth-merchant, but he was aware of a difference and, as the shadow of equality grew larger, one way to mark it was a pleasure in country sports – or the affectation of such a pleasure. Mr Winkle pretended to be a sportsman because to be able to ride and shoot was the mark of a gentleman. But that kind of country snobbery did not occur a century earlier.

We are agreed, I hope, that Trollope was wrong in feeling that Plantagenet Palliser could stand as the perfect picture of a gentleman. It is worth looking at Phineas Finn as a contrast. Phineas started with every disadvantage when compared with Plantagenet. He was Irish and a Catholic (though incidentally he never seems to go to Mass nor does he think of his religion when he contemplates marriage with Lady Laura Standish or Violet Effingham). He was the son of a country doctor and by the standards of London society and the House of Commons he hadn't a penny. But he was intelligent and quick-witted, a big fine-looking man, whom most women and some men immediately liked; he was generous, emotional and high-principled. He rode well to hounds and could come to terms with a difficult horse; like Ferdinand Lopez, he knew how to walk and talk and look like a gentleman – but there was a big difference from Lopez because with Phineas the heart was in the right place and he understood how a gentleman felt. Indeed, to behave like a gentleman appears to be his guide to conduct; his Catholicism affects him no more than their religion affects the lapsed Protestants who surround him.

He was more punctilious about honour than most. He resigned on a point of principle because he disagreed with the party when he was in office – and an office where he enjoyed the work as well as the power. He could not be as confident of his own status as a gentleman as, let us say, Frank Gresham; he could not contemptuously refuse a challenge to fight a duel – as John Grey did when challenged by George Vavasor. He had to accept an absurd challenge, meet Lord Chiltern and get a bullet in his shoulder on the sands of Blankenberg.

By origin Phineas Finn was on almost the lowest rung of the ladder of those whom Trollope would call gentlemen. But from the point of view of true *gentillesse*, he ranks higher. Lady Laura Standish had refused him because she had to marry money; she had realised too late what a mistake she had made, and one day she forgot herself and poured out her heart to him, telling him that she loved him still and always had. "You had better go now," she ended, ". . . and forget what has passed between us. I know that you are a gentleman and that you will forget it . . ." She was justified in her trust.

But I do not suggest that Phineas any more than the Duke was the perfect gentleman. If the Duke lacked spontaneity, Phineas had too much. He was too impulsive and responded too readily to the mood of the company where he found himself. He went to Ireland after his first London successes with his mind full of Lady Laura, determined to propose to her when he came back. But in Ireland, his heart warmed again to Mary Flood-Jones, the little Irish girl without a fortune who adored him, and he cannot be said to have behaved to her with perfect integrity. Later, when Lady Laura told him she had decided to marry money, he quickly and conveniently fell in love with Violet Effingham, who had money and beauty as well as wisdom and a kind disposition. But when it was clear that she was going to marry Lord Chiltern, he went back to Mary Flood-Jones. True, once he was committed to Mary, he turned down a proposal from Madam Goesler – who had everything. He would not now betray Mary "and that kept him from being a cad. But it did not quite make him a gentleman", writes an observer with very high standards.[25]

In the ideal that was beginning to emerge, there was an increasing emphasis on solidity and constancy as well as an element of stoicism. It was important not only to bear physical pain without squealing but also to repress all signs of emotion. And this too was very different from the Elizabethans. It was the mark of a cad to be a bad loser but not much less contemptible for a winner to show elation. "I can't bear a fellow who can't take his oats," was a characteristic comment. Far from carving the name of Rosalind on every tree, the lover will now try to conceal his passion as long as he can, and will be most reluctant to discuss his sweetheart with anyone else. And as the century wore on there was an increasing reluctance of a similar kind to open the heart about religion. Love and religion were private areas of the soul, not to be exposed to discussion in the club or the mess – and only very guardedly in the drawing-room.

It is strange that the two most absorbing and universal of human experiences should have been banished from polite conversation. In part it was because they can hardly be discussed without some display of feeling. Thus the tendency to be furtive about religion was part of the wider tendency towards stoicism. And stoicism was admired because it distinguished the aristocrat from the thoughtless and emotional lower classes. The public schools, of which the number increased so rapidly in the Victorian period, encouraged the Spartan ideals for the same deep reasons as the Spartan state. The Spartans were a racial aristocracy, served by a nation of Helots, and they valued the qualities which distinguished them from the Helots. The English were a subtly graded society in process of becoming more democratic, and their leaders therefore laid increasing emphasis on minor aspects of social behaviour which accentuated the grading; they were also the rulers of an empire for which they needed an imperial class of officers who must appear impassive, god-like and impartial in the eyes of the chattering natives.

It was part, then, of the mask of stoicism with which the upper classes were covering their faces not to talk about anything that might rouse emotion. But that is not the whole story. The state religion was on the whole Protestant. The Oxford Movement was a reaction against Protestantism and indifference, but it was a minority movement and the majority claimed a sturdy independence for the individual in his dealings with the Almighty. He needed no help from priest or saint or learned father in his dialogue with eternity. An almost Islamic austerity had spread over the land, and the crucifix was replaced by a plain stylized cross. Men did not care to look on the torn humiliated body that bore witness to human cruelty and divine compassion. Flesh was slightly obscene: and if the Word had been made flesh, the less said about it the better.

On the whole, then, it was better not to think too much about the Sermon on the Mount and the dangerously radical doctrines of the *Magnificat*. You might say in church that the poor were to be blessed and the rich sent empty away, but what was needed for everyday life was something less demanding, a sub-Christian cult, and to concentrate on a standard of behaviour altogether easier and more comfortable, something almost a religion, conduct in fact that was becoming to a gentleman.

It followed as a corollary that a clergyman must be a gentleman. It was

A Master Parson with a Good Living: 1760.
The 18th century was a bad time for the church everywhere,
and no doubt in England it often looked like this.

with horror that Archdeacon Grantly first met Mr Slope, the chaplain to
the new Bishop.[26] "Did you ever see an animal less like a gentleman?" he
almost shouted to his father-in-law. It was partly professional pride, outrage
that the tone of his profession should be lowered, but there was something
else that he shared with many laymen, an active disgust that sacred things
should be talked about or handled by such a man as Mr Slope. It was as
strong a feeling as the horror aroused in the Archdeacon later when he believed, quite wrongly, that his sister-in-law Eleanor was inclined to marry
Mr Slope. The religious distaste and the sexual were akin.

In many respects, the ideal Victorian gentleman at the end of Trollope's
life (that is, in the 1870s) had a good deal in common with two other ideal
figures, the Rajput noble and the Muslim. Both were much admired by
Victorian travellers. We see them of course through Victorian eyes, through
the writings of travellers and administrators. Nonetheless what the Victorians
admired in them tells us a good deal about the Victorians themselves. Some
qualities were essential to all three. Courage was the first. Hospitality,
courtesy and generosity were also important to all, but with a different
emphasis. Hospitality to a guest was one of the most sacred of all obligations
to the Muslim noble; for the Rajput, it was somewhat circumscribed by the
fact that he could not eat with anyone not of his own birth and breeding. An

OPPOSITE Morning Prayer. In the 19th century there was a revival of religion, and in many a household like this a gentleman of moderate means piously read morning prayers to his family while the maids sat in the background, the kettle simmered on the hob and the muffins kept warm on the fender. But Christianity is a demanding religion, and it was sometimes easier to concentrate on being a gentleman.

RIGHT A curate writing a sermon in his lodgings, early in the 20th century. Perhaps he was a brilliant theologian, but he looks as though he would be happier captaining a cricket team!

Englishman did not often give hospitality to strangers, but though in general he regarded hospitality as desirable, in excess it might be vulgar, while improper behaviour on the part of a guest might terminate the host's obligation. Major Pountney, when the guest of the Duke of Omnium, ventured to ask for His Grace's backing as Parliamentary candidate for Silverbridge, which had always been regarded as His Grace's borough.

"I think, sir," said the Duke, "that your proposition is the most unbecoming and the most impertinent that ever was addressed to me." Parliament had recently taken a step to end the influence of the landed aristocracy in elections and the Duke considered himself bound by its views. He was insulted by the suggestion that he would disregard them. Major Pountney was altogether taken aback; he received a stately note that evening suggesting that he should leave Gatherum Castle as soon as he found it convenient – and that if he wished to stay the night he should dine in his own room. Had an Arab or a Pathan chief received from a guest what he conceived to be an insult, one may suppose that he would have avenged it more drastically – but not until the guest had left his protection and was on neutral ground.

Rajput, Arab and Englishman alike admired the gentleman who did not reveal his emotions. In all three cultures, the gentleman would rather be cheated than visibly count the change. All three paid tribute to the man who put duty and honour before natural affection and would rather shoot a son than betray a trust. But there was perhaps a difference of emphasis as to what was meant by honour. If it meant name before the world, then no one could give it higher rank than the Rajput. But if it meant a secret inner integrity, then there is less certainty. Perhaps the Englishman would have laid most stress on that.

It was an area in which the code of a gentleman showed many variations. Must a gentleman tell the truth? Ideally, yes, of course, but Laurence Fitzgibbon, son of an Irish peer and MP for Mayo, took a different view of telling the truth from the Duke's:

In dealing with a tradesman as to his debts, or with a rival as to a lady, or with any man or woman in defence of a lady's character, or in any such matter as that of a duel, Laurence believed that a gentleman was bound to lie, and that he would be no gentleman if he hesitated to do so.

In that respect, his view of the proper conduct of a gentleman was in conflict with the expressed opinion of most Englishmen, but one may guess that the Rajput and the Arab would on the whole have agreed with Laurence.

There would have been a difference of emphasis too about courtesy. Courtesy to guests, to courageous enemies, to noble strangers – on this all three were agreed, but there was much less agreement about courtesy to women or to servants, which the Englishman regarded as of more importance than the other two. Indeed, courtesy to women was much the biggest difference between them.

This was because the morality of the gentleman in England was a cult derived from Christianity. And that was the cause of another difference of emphasis. "Death before dishonour!" was a motto all three would have acclaimed, but the Rajput, in the high period of chivalry when his legends were recorded, often interpreted it in a sense that was suicidal. For him it was dishonour to leave a battle alive unless victorious. If the day was lost, he must turn back to die by the swords of his enemy. No doubt this owed much to a belief in reincarnation. Direct suicide was also honourable in the Japanese military tradition and in the German. In the British army, there was the recurring case of the man irretrievably disgraced who was deliberately left alone with a revolver. But that was not honourable suicide; such an affair would be hushed up. And a British officer did not shoot himself because he had been defeated in battle. For one thing, he knew that he had only to wait; the English always won the last battle. But I suspect that there was also preserved in the British version of a gentleman's morality a memory from the main stream of Christian belief that suicide embodies the ultimate sin of despair.

A PRIVATE TURN-UP, *in the Drawing Room of a Noble Marquis.*

Drawn & Etched. by H. Alken Esq.

London. Published by Jones & Co. July 21. 1821.

The Sporting Gentleman

ABOVE The fashion for "pugilism" among the English aristocracy was perhaps a reaction to the doctrines of equality proclaimed in France. A gentleman would often defend himself with his fists to prove that he did not take shelter behind his rank in society. But prize-fighting was illegal, and "pugs" had to meet in private.

BELOW This is from *Life in London, or The Day and Night Scenes of Jerry Hawthorn and his elegant friend Corinthian Tom*, illustrated by George and Robert Cruikshank (1821). Here the two young men-about-town visit the inn kept by Tom Cribb, the Champion of England.

Drawn & Eng.d by I.R. & G. Cruikshank.

CRIBB'S PARLOUR. *Tom introducing Jerry and Logic to the Champion of England.*

Tom and Jerry "Masquerading it" among the Cadgers in the "Back Slums".

Drawn & Eng.d by I.R & G. Cruickshank.

ABOVE Tom and Jerry "masquerading it" among the cadgers in the "back slums". A taste for low life was part of the Corinthian tradition.

BELOW Another scene from the adventures of Corinthian Tom which shows the obsequious "snip" at work – and how impossible it was for Rose to marry Evan Harrington if he followed the profession of the great Mel.

Drawn & Engraved by I.R & G. Cruickshank.

Jerry in training for a "Swell."

FENCING. *Jerry's admiration of Tom in an "Assault" with M^r O'SHAUNESSY, at the Rooms in St James's St.*

ABOVE Jerry and Tom at a fencing school in St James's Street. This is 1821, but fencing and single-stick were fashionable throughout the century.

BELOW Further evidence of Corinthian Tom's taste for low life. Gin was the cheapest spirit available, and in 1821 a penn'orth was a good strong tot.

BLUE RUIN. *Tom & Bob tasting Thompson's Best.*

ABOVE Thomas Assheton Smith, MP and
MFH, a master of hounds for forty-eight
years and usually his own huntsman. He
was one of the best batsmen in England,
would tackle any man with his fists, and if
pressed would "admit a life-long devotion
to Horace" – presumably acquired at
Eton, where this early portrait by Sir
William Beechey still hangs.

RIGHT The most famous of George
Osbaldeston's many "matches" was his bet
of a thousand guineas that he would ride
two hundred miles in under ten hours,
including all rests and changes. He divided
the distance into fifty heats of four miles
each and used 28 horses, finishing in 8
hours 42 minutes, an average speed of over
22 miles an hour.

Frederick Burnaby by J. G. Tissot:
a heavy swell of 1870. He has the same
languid air of superiority that Thackeray
described in Rawdon Crawley.

Cricket at Eton in 1843. Like hunting, cricket was a bond between
the classes and was almost a religion. Only a gentleman had leisure
to be *taught* cricket. He was expected to be a more polished batsman
than a countryman who had learned to take a swipe on the village green.

"A very gallant gentleman." This was the epitaph for Captain Oates
which in 1913 everyone felt was exactly right. J. G. Dollman's painting
is subtitled ". . . who willingly walked to his death in a blizzard
to try and save his comrades beset by hardship".

12
FACTORIES FOR GENTLEMEN

A Peculiar Institution . . .

BEING A GENTLEMAN had then, by the second half of the 19th century, become almost a religion. But it was not quite a religion, which implies worship, a sense of awe, a tap-root to the supernatural. It was the very fact that it did not require any dangerous commitment to the eternal that made the cult of the gentleman so useful as a social device. It was a code of conduct that fitted a man for society without causing embarrassment. It could easily be combined with an outward Christianity that was not deeply felt. It might even, although not so comfortably, be combined with a deeper Christianity.

In Elizabethan times, when wealth was growing and there was vigorous movement up and down the social ladder, Harrison had thought, you will remember,[27] that there was some need for definition and had explained that the term might be applied not only to landowners but to those who had read in universities and followed the learned professions, to "captains in the wars", to anyone who had distinguished himself by public service. The Victorian was also an age of vigorous social movement and the same need for definition arose. It was made sharper by the threat of proclaimed equality from across the Channel. In Harrison's time, men who felt they might venture on this change of status applied to the heralds for a coat of arms, and in the 19th century some followed their example – but by no means all. That criterion was already felt to be artificial. No one in Trollope asks whether a man bears arms.

There is a good deal of tolerance up to a point for a man of humble birth who is not openly offensive in manners, if he is backed by someone of high standing. Lord Silverbridge, son of the Duke of Omnium, puts up Major Tifto, who is really no more than a horse-coper and trainer of race-horses, for the Beargarden Club and he is elected – and is treated as a member so long as his behaviour is kept within bounds. But he disgraces himself and is ejected. There is a real need for some definition of what makes a gentleman. And, by the end of the century, it had come to be felt that a kind of first sketch of a definition had been made when it was known that a man had been "at a public school".

It was only a preliminary indication of what might be expected. He might not have been there very long; he might have been asked to leave. In *Dr Thorne*, no one thinks Sir Louis Scatcherd, Bart., a gentleman; he had been at Eton long enough only to learn how to spend money and was sent away for getting tipsy twice in a week; his short career at Cambridge in "a fast, slang" set, did him no good either. Again, as between schools, there was a wide spectrum of excellence, social, moral and academic.

Here of course there was a parallel with military titles; there was all the difference in the world between Captain Rawdon Crawley of the Life Guards and a captain in an obscure regiment of infantry of the line; as much again between a regular captain in even the most obscure line regiment and some of the doubtful majors and captains of the race-course and the billiard-saloon, whose rank, if it had any justification at all, came from a year in some now disbanded body of Fencibles or Volunteers.

To have been at a public school pointed – as a bare minimum – to parents who could spend money on education and thought it worth spending. Education, however, in the sense in which it would have been understood in a French lycée, was only a part of what these schools aimed at providing. They did not explicitly set out to provide a definition, a distinguishing mark, for those who were to be classed as gentlemen. But they did, all of them, though in varying degrees, deliberately try to encourage and develop the qualities that *made* a gentleman. Throughout the century the demand grew for this peculiar English institution, for boarding-schools that would not merely prepare for examinations but "build character" as well.[28]

There were two reasons for this growing demand, not only the need for a definition, a new social marker, but also the need for a much larger ruling class, a class to provide army officers, colonial civil servants, judges, school-masters, members of Parliament, magistrates, leaders of society. That is why the emphasis was on manners, on responsibility, on character, rather than on scholarship.

To the nine generally classed as public schools at the beginning of the century were added a long list of new schools and also of ancient grammar schools, formerly drawing pupils from a provincial countryside but now from all parts of the kingdom. By 1914, the number who might on various grounds claim the title had risen to nearly three hundred.

All of them, old and new alike, had by then been influenced by Arnold's headmastership of Rugby. He was not long at Rugby, only 13 years, from 1828 to 1841, but so vigorous was his personality that his favourite pupils and assistant masters formed a band of disciples who remembered him all their lives. His influence spread throughout the kingdom and was still spreading at the end of the century.

Arnold would most emphatically have contradicted the view that being a gentleman was in any way an alternative to being a Christian. His religion came first in his life and it was the strength of his convictions that gave him so strong a hold on those he encountered. He believed that the society in which he lived was at best half Christian and that the upper classes had failed to do their duty by the poor. It was necessary, he felt, to persuade an aristocracy by birth to justify itself by merit and responsibility; his personal vocation was to create a chosen band who would undertake this task. His declared aims were to instil, first, religious and moral principles; second, "gentlemanly conduct"; finally, intellectual ability. It was his constant hope to "sophronize" his pupils – to make them wise – a word coined by himself from the Greek and preferred to the Latin "civilize" because he meant more than making them fit to live in a state. Although he was a gifted orator and a tireless preacher, he was convinced that the change of heart he hoped for was most likely to come if he trusted senior boys to act as his apostles and missionaries. And it was one of the secrets of his achievement that, in spite of his deep sense of the wickedness of the world in general, and of boys in particular, he did delegate power. He trusted his masters; he trusted senior boys to rule their juniors.

The most famous picture of Rugby in Arnold's time is of course *Tom Brown's Schooldays*, written by a former pupil, Thomas Hughes, in 1856, 14 years after Arnold's death. Before Tom went to Rugby, his father, a Berkshire squire, mused on his reasons for sending the boy. "I don't care a straw for Greek particles or the digamma. . . . If he'll only turn out a brave, helpful, truth-telling Englishman and a gentleman and a Christian, that's all I want," thought the Squire. What he hoped for was not very different from what Arnold aimed at giving, although Arnold put Christian first and gentleman second. But for both the intellectual came last. Tom himself, asked what he wanted to take away from Rugby, replied:

I want to be A 1 at cricket and football and all the other games and to make my hands keep my head against any fellow, lout or gentleman. I want to get into the Sixth before I leave and to please the Doctor and I want to carry away just as much Latin and Greek as will take me through Oxford respectably . . .

Then, on reflection, he added: "I want to leave behind me the name of a fellow who never bullied a little boy or turned his back on a big one."

Tom was at this time about sixteen and supposed to be a typical public schoolboy. He was a lively games-playing extrovert, and as a character he has some degree of autonomy. He is not merely a mouthpiece for the author. His world is divided into "louts" and "gentlemen", and "getting into the Sixth" meant exercising responsibility as a prefect. He says nothing about Christianity, having a feeling that such matters are not to be talked about. He is being questioned by George Arthur, a fair slight delicate boy, who has

ABOVE This figure of knightly purity forms the initial letter in a chapter of *Tom Brown's School-days*, published in 1857. It introduces a chapter on the ethics of cribbing. The first of Tennyson's *Idylls of the King* had been published in 1842.

RIGHT Tom's little friend Arthur nearly died. Here he is convalescent and ventures to talk to Tom about "serious" things.

just been ill with "fever and supposed to be on the point of death – a danger real enough in the schools of the period. Arthur, on the strength of his escape, does venture to speak to Tom about religion – and here, one feels, it *is* the author who is speaking. The evangelical strain in Arnold was strong among his chosen band, but in the public school tradition much less lasting than other contributions; Arnold was better in the long run at making good public school boys than at making good Christians. It was after all much easier. By the end of the century, although a nostalgic reference to the school chapel was obligatory in a public school novel, it was skill at games and striking the right note, getting on well with others, "character" in short, that counted among the boys. There was a kind of extrovert self-sufficiency, based on internal integrity, on confidence in himself, that made a boy already respected at sixteen and which would make it easy for him to exercise

ABOVE Roasting a fag. Tom was roasted until he fainted from the pain, but he would not say who had done it. Public schools were brutal places but they were supposed to make a boy self-reliant.

BELOW In the end, Tom and his friend East got the better of Flashman, the bully, who never dared to touch them again.

Tom Brown comes back as an old boy to reverence the tomb of Dr Arnold. It was Dr Arnold's "personal vocation" to instil in his pupils, first, "religious and moral principles", second "gentlemanly conduct", and finally intellectual ability. His disciples carried his influence into all the schools of England.

authority in his last year. But Arnold, though he had made the ideal public schoolboy a little more like the ideal gentleman, though to good manners he had added training for responsible leadership and a touch of Chaucerian *gentillesse*, had failed to make him necessarily Christian. In H. A. Vachell's *The Hill, A Romance of Friendship*, a story about Harrow, written in 1905, there is a boy known as "the Caterpillar" who is regarded by his house as the authority on "good form", what is done and what is not done. "One doesn't pretend to be a Christian," he remarks, "but as a gentleman one accepts a bit of bad luck without gnashing one's teeth."

Arthur was a year younger than Tom and Tom had protected him against bullies. He was marked by his delicacy and feminine good looks as the kind of boy who would probably either be bullied or become a bigger boy's "favourite" (there were coarser terms). He was lucky to find in Tom a protector near his own age, deliberately chosen, according to Hughes, by "the Doctor". A later generation might be surprised at official encouragement of such a friendship – but the Victorians of this period were not disturbed by male friendship, which they would have defended by referring to Plato, and which was in fact almost always what is generally called Platonic. It was a strange feature of the Victorian achievement that it owed so much to men who had postponed marriage for so long that they had come to prefer the society of boys or young men to that of women and who lived in a close, affectionate friendship that remained Platonic with their pupils in school and university or with the young men in their regiments.

Some of the new schools showed in the charters or constitutions drawn up by their founders that they were meant to fill a particular need. Wellington charged reduced fees for the sons of army officers and sent a high proportion of its boys to the army; Cheltenham was not very different. Marlborough made similar provision for the sons of clergymen. The most explicit of all in

Speech day at Harrow. Graded sartorial propriety that would have pleased the Caterpillar.

Blundell's was once a grammar school where the sons of West Country squires shared a bench with the sons of farmers. Like other local grammar schools, such as Uppingham, Oundle and Sedbergh, it became a national public school in the 19th century to meet the need for gentlemen to rule the empire. Most of them followed the Rugby tradition.

its purpose was Kipling's school, the United Services College at Westward Ho!, which was virtually a joint stock company of military officers, who clubbed together to start a school which would get their sons through the entrance examination for Sandhurst without the high fees demanded by crammers. It merged later with Haileybury.

Blundell's at Tiverton in Devon has been drawn in *Lorna Doone*; it was a local grammar school of repute to which in the 17th century squires' sons came from up to a hundred miles away to sit beside farmers' sons from up to ten. Sedbergh in the North was another grammar school of this kind. Such schools might have pious founders who went back to Henry VIII or Edward VI. They went through great ups and downs according to the reputation of the master, dropping in a bad period perhaps to no more than a dozen boys or so, and then, with a new master, attracting boys from much further away and sending a good quota to Oxford or Cambridge. Oundle, Uppingham, Repton belonged to the same category. But sooner or later, an apostle arrived, a new headmaster who had been a pupil of Arnold's or the pupil of a pupil. He would reform and concentrate and improve, and the provincial grammar school would blossom into a national public school.

The Owners of Their Faces

THE WHOLLY NEW schools and the upgraded grammar schools alike accepted the aims of Squire Brown, of Tom and of Dr Arnold. Each of the three – parent, boy and headmaster – had put his aims in a slightly different order and the schools too varied in their emphasis, but most agreed in putting purely intellectual achievement low in the scale. "Character" was what counted and it was developed by team games and by hardship. Cold baths, cold dormitories, runs in the rain, plain food, helped to build "character". A boy must learn his place in a graded society; he was kept in his place by a host of unwritten laws. To part your hair in the middle or put your hands in your pockets in the first year might mean a beating, but year by year the growing boy acquired the right to do just what he would take good care his juniors should not do. In the end, the new boy who had once cleaned boots and cut bread-and-butter for a lordly prefect had himself a fag who performed these offices for *him*. As a rule, only one full meal a day was provided, but there would be "commons" of bread and cheese or bread and butter which would keep body and soul from parting company – and it was good for the character to learn that if all your pocket-money was spent by half term, there would be no more jam or eggs or sausages before the holidays.

I have pointed out in another book that the system was very like Plato's ideal education for those who were to be guardians of the state and its future rulers. They were to be "swift of foot" and "high-spirited" as well as being trained to think; they must practise manly exercises and keep their bodies strong and healthy, living on simple food and sleeping hard. They must believe themselves to be quite different from the ordinary people of the state whom they would rule – gentlemen, not louts – while to ensure that they were just and impartial rulers they must have no property of their own and must forget their parents.

Of course the English public schools did not go quite so far as this. Compromise was an essential part of being English. Home influence was important in Arnold's eyes and this was one of his reasons for concentrating on an upper middle class of squires and clergymen and army officers. He persuaded a duchess to send her son to Eton instead of Rugby and would have sympathized with another headmaster, who argued against the admission of boys from the lower middle classes, on the grounds that whatever improvements might be achieved at school such boys would be "contaminated" in the holidays by a home where they would pick up "mean habits and vulgar tricks" and find "little of that honourable love of truth" which headmasters sought to instil.

But to accept the "contamination" argument meant that the school was not carrying out the plain intention of its pious founders. Accordingly, a new school was sometimes started to educate boys of the classes for whom the old school had been intended. Charterhouse and Tonbridge are examples. It was all part of the process of accentuating class difference which was so marked in the century and a half after the French Revolution.

In spite of Arnold's belief that a love of truth was to be found only in the manors of squires and in country rectories, a distrust of the home grew among schoolmasters. It was expressed facetiously by a reverend schoolmaster in the phrase: "parents are the last people who ought to be allowed to have children", and more and more parents seemed also to be of the same opinion, sending their sons away to preparatory schools at eight years old and to public schools at thirteen or fourteen. At the schools themselves, there was a growing tendency to discourage associations with the home. Christian names came to be regarded as effeminate; mothers and sisters were to be mentioned as little as possible and, at the best, guardedly and in Latin. "My mater", little boys of eight were told to say, if they mentioned her at all. "Don't talk about home or your mother or sisters" was Tom Brown's advice to Arthur on his first day at Rugby, and the tradition lasted at least a hundred years.

The process aimed above all at *hardening*. The public schools were meant to produce a ruling class, and there was a wide-spread view that great empires of the past had fallen because the ruling classes had grown luxurious and effeminate. G. O. Trevelyan, the nephew and biographer of Macaulay, wrote in 1864 of the decay of Rome when Mark Anthony and his followers became half-Egyptian, but went on exultantly that with the British in India "precisely the opposite result has taken place. The earliest settlers were in-dolent, dissipated, grasping, almost Orientals in their way of life. . . . But each generation of their successors is more simple, more hardy, more Christian than the last". And this, he frequently implied, was due to the Arnold tradition. And a house-master, hearing of a boy who had had two hot baths in a week, told him sternly: "That is the kind of thing that brought down the Roman empire."

Hardiness, self-composure, coolness in the face of pain and danger, con-fidence in one's own decisions – these were qualities required by the imperial class which a growing empire demanded. But the public schools claimed to teach more – something which it had hardly been necessary to teach to gentleman by birth in Elizabethan times. A boy learned to do as he was told without question; later, he learned to take it for granted that he would be obeyed. He learned to punish and to encourage. He learned in short to rule. That was one reason for the growing number of public schools; quite simply, more rulers were needed. Another was that since the upper classes were being constantly reinforced in numbers by the recently wealthy, it was advisable to make sure that in the next generation as many as possible of the recruits should be trained to the standards of the veterans.

The qualities of a ruler were required in Parliament, in the management

ABOVE Eton boys buying buttonholes for the Fourth of June.
Elegance was held in esteem at Eton, less so at
schools in the Rugby tradition.
BELOW But even at Eton, elegance was not everything!

The Lower School at Eton:
public schools were
ancient, uncomfortable
and ill-equipped, and this
was generally considered
desirable because they
were meant to form
character rather than
intellect – and in any case
no equipment was needed
to study Plato.

BELOW Tuck-box, 1875.
Schools usually provided
one meal a day,
supplemented by
"commons" of bread and
perhaps cheese. Anything
beyond that had to be
bought or came from
home – and that too was
good for character, as it
taught a boy to value a
good home, to look after
his money and to choose
his friends.

of business, in the administration of an estate as well as in the armed forces and the church and overseas. It was a matter of ensuring that the establishment – a word not then used in that sense – should be of the highest quality.

The public school world was linked with "the establishment" – that is, with the rulers of Victorian England – through the parents, through the universities, and through the church. Preferment in the church was in the hands of the Prime Minister, and the headmaster of a public school might be promoted to bishop or even archbishop or appointed on retirement to a comfortable living with not very onerous duties. Hardly anyone who had attained a place within the establishment questioned the principle that society should be organized as a pyramid, with increasing rewards of wealth and privilege as a man rose from stage to stage and at the same time incurred an increasing burden of responsibility. But the system would only work if high standards were maintained. Vigilance must therefore never be relaxed, and while success was rewarded, failures must be eliminated.

In all this, the school was a microcosm of society. Arnold was ruthless about expelling a boy whom he judged unlikely to be "sophronized". Nor had he any doubts about the efficacy of punishment to reform. Hughes records a scene when Arnold is discussing with a prefect the case of a bully. The headmaster says that if he knew of the case officially he would have to expel the boy publicly. But he thinks there is some good in him, so he will

" I believe this letter is for you, Stacey, because it was given me by a loafer at the Three Fishers, who must have mistaken me for you ! " said Wharton. " I believe it's from some disgraceful bookmaker. Do you claim the letter under that description ? " Stacey's lips set in a bitter line. Many eyes in the Rag were on him—breathlessly.

As late as 1935, there was enthusiasm for school stories about schools rather *like* public schools; everyone wanted to have been at one. This is Harry Wharton of Greyfriars, who appeared weekly in *The Magnet*. Billy Bunter is in the background.

leave it to the prefect, who will call a house levy. "There's nothing for it but a good sound thrashing before the whole house . . . severe physical pain is the only way to deal with such a case." Years later, Hughes continues – after a short defensive digression showing that he expects criticism – the culprit sought out the prefect in question and thanked him for the thrashing; it had been an act of kindness which had been the turning-point in his character. On this, too, Victorian society as a whole was unflinching. Punishment was necessary as a deterrent and it should be severe. In youth, at least, it might perhaps reform, but that would be a bonus. Deterrence came first.

It was part of the ruthlessness in pursuit of excellence that, in certain chosen bodies such as the Royal Navy and the Brigade of Guards, there was no excuse for failure. It made no difference whose fault it was; if a boat coming alongside scratched the paint, it was the midshipman commanding the boat who was punished, even though he had given the right order. Eighteen of the best for the midshipman, though it was the coxswain's fault.

The public schools, then, set out to polish recruits for the imperial class, to keep up the standards of the ruling class as a whole and thus to strengthen its hold on the country. It must deserve to rule and it would not rule long if it did not. It must consist of men with a sense of responsibility for those they ruled, accustomed to administering justice, hard with their own order as with others. The school also provided a focus for the loyalty of the new rich – who in the third generation could send their sons to their own schools.

He was not an entirely new type of ruler whom the public schools sought to produce. What they did was to produce more of the kind. He has been sketched, not in the kindest of spirits, and no doubt in a moment of exaspera-tion at some lack of response from the noble young man he loved, by Shake-speare in Sonnet XCIV.

> They that have power to hurt and will do none,
>   That do not do the thing they most do show,
> Who, moving others, are themselves as stone,
>   Unmoved, cold and to temptation slow;
> They rightly do inherit heaven's graces
>   And husband nature's riches from expense;
> They are the lords and owners of their faces,
>   Others but stewards of their excellence.

A beast, in short, but a just beast. Many an imperial pro-consul must have looked just like that to an Indian or Egyptian suppliant.[29] And perhaps even in England those of Her Majesty's subjects whom Tom Brown distinguished as "louts" felt a similar irritation at the imperturbability, the mask of cold indifference, which had often been so expensively acquired.

13
EVAN HARRINGTON

IT IS THE BUSINESS of the novel to portray the human spirit at odds with circumstance – true love, for instance, contending with parental obstinacy or social convention, families divided by the impersonal malignity of war or perhaps a man tormented by his own temperament or upbringing. But it may incidentally say a great deal about social attitudes. There is one novel which more than any other of the mid-Victorian period concentrates the adverse forces in the one question: "What makes a gentleman?" and which puts in one scale good manners, courage, a noble generosity, accomplishments and education, an attractive person – and in the other, birth in a status thought to be degrading. It is like one of those South African novels about a man with "coloured" ancestry who can "pass for white"; he looks "white", no one guesses, but his brother is unmistakably black, so that if their relationship is exposed he will have to give up his profession, leave his home and perhaps face prosecution for marrying the wrong wife.

Evan Harrington is a comedy. George Meredith insists on that more than once. But there is bitterness behind the laughter, partly because Meredith himself had experienced the same kind of humiliation as his hero, and partly because he and his hero alike are secretly half on the side of the effortlessly well-born who sneer at them.

The tale begins with "the great Mel", Melchizedec Harrington, a tailor of Lymport, but a tailor who kept horses, who had affairs of gallantry with high-born ladies, who dined with the squires of the countryside, who had once, in the course of an escapade at Bath with some young gentlemen of good family, been addressed as "my lord", had accepted the title, and had kept up the joke for three days, passing as a marquis, no less. No one had such manners, such a presence, such wit as the great Mel. He had held a commission in the militia dragoons during the Napoleonic wars and there were those who said his father was a real marquis. But he was a tailor, his name was over the shop-door in Lymport, and he was too wise, too honest, ever to deny it when challenged. The squires asked him to dinner because he was such good company but they did not ask his wife.

It adds much to the interest of *Evan Harrington* to know that George Meredith's grandfather was also called Melchizedec. He too was a tailor. He had a naval outfitter's shop in Portsmouth. He too consorted with the gentry of the neighbourhood; he too kept horses and hunted and he was known as "the Count" because of an adventure at Bath very like the great Mel's.

In the story, Melchizedec Harrington's three daughters, all strikingly beautiful, are brought up "above their station" and marry accordingly, the youngest, Louisa, doing best in the eyes of the world by marrying a Portuguese

Melchizedec Harrington, "the great Mel", was a tailor. But he had held a commission in the Militia Dragoons; he kept horses, hunted had affairs with ladies of rank, dined with squires (though his wife was not invited) and was known as "the Marquis". Here he lies in state.

count, who is a Minister in the service of the Portuguese crown. She is on friendly, even affectionate, terms with duchesses and ambassadors and does everything to conceal the fact that her father is a tailor. That this should be known would be to her the collapse of her whole elaborate structure, a disaster comparable to that facing the South African with a black brother.

The countess had asked her younger brother Evan to stay with her in Lisbon when he left school, and he too had mingled with the Portuguese nobility and the diplomatic corps, and so charming were his manners and appearance that he had been invited to fill a temporary post as secretary in the British embassy. There he met Rose Jocelyn, niece of the ambassador; they rode and danced and talked and laughed together.

Evan came back to England with his sister the countess as guests of the Jocelyns in a ship of the Royal Navy. He was met by the news of his father's death. His three sisters all found reasons making it impossible to go to the funeral. Evan was too generous to disregard his mother's summons. But it was a severe shock to learn that his father had died five thousands pounds in debt and that his mother, a formidable woman, saw no honourable course open to Evan but buckling down to work in the tailor's shop and paying off his father's debts. In her view, they were in trouble enough already from aping the gentry. But Evan had been brought up as though he was to go into the army or the diplomatic service. To become a tailor meant giving up all that was pleasant in life; above all it meant giving up thoughts of Rose.

Hateful though such a course appeared, it was also hateful that his father should be called a rogue for not paying his debts. Evan steeled himself for the sacrifice. He even allowed his mother to have his name painted over the shop. He started for London to learn something of the trade. But his sister, the Portuguese countess, swooped; she intercepted him at an inn on the way. She was going to visit the Jocelyns at Beckley Court and Evan was included in the invitation; surely he could spare a few days? It meant that he would see Rose again and stay in the same house with her. A last glimpse of heaven! He fell. He went to Beckley Court.

There is no need to follow the ebb and flow of events at Beckley Court. The countess was wholly committed to getting Evan some lucrative but gentlemanly post and marrying him to Rose. Everyone at Beckley Court accepted him as a charming and well-brought up young man of independent though insufficient means. He and Rose were soon in love. Evan, being a gentleman by nature, would have liked to tell Rose and her mother Lady Jocelyn the whole truth. But the countess was determined to keep her father's tailordom dark; she intercepted a letter, she even forged a letter. The plot becomes tortuous and slightly farcical; there are no less than two eccentric wills, by means of which Evan becomes the owner of Beckley Court, which he nobly renounces – whereupon a crusty old bachelor settles a thousand a year on him and all ends happily. All this is rather absurd. You may say that here is all the machinery of a Christmas pantomime, the fairies and trap-doors only lightly disguised. And you would be right about the machinery. Nor is Meredith's prose style immediately appealing; it is often crabbed and allusive; it demands close attention and the reader must work in order to appreciate the sudden felicity. But the characters are real and their feelings strong, and the social scene is sketched with a scornful if envious accuracy. Lady Jocelyn is drawn with marked economy of line; practical, sensible, decisive but kind, hating pretence, only half accepting the standards of those who surround her, amused by the airs of the countess. And Rose, by the side of Amelia Osborne or Little Dorritt, is a girl of flesh and blood, a girl who ought to be whipped – thinks one of her aunts – something of a tomboy, teasing the young men whom she treats as friends and calls by their Christian names, impulsive, courageous and as honest as her mother.

For our purpose, however, the interest lies in the assumptions on which everyone acts. Everyone at Beckley Court, including the servants, accepts it as unquestioned dogma that there is something contemptible about being a tailor. When the rumours began, Rose asked her maid one night, when she was undressing her, what was the nickname people gave to tailors. "I told her they were called snips," said Polly. "And I saw her saying it in the glass . . . and Miss Rose, she seemed as if she couldn't forget how ugly it had made her look. She covered her face with her hands and shuddered." Evan had been called the son of a snip when he first went to school and so perhaps had Meredith. Were tailors looked down on more than other tradesmen? Yes, they were. So the servants at Beckley thought, so nursery rhyme and proverbs had it. It took nine tailors to make a man, and:

> Four-and-twenty tailors went to kill a snail
> The best man among them durst not touch her tail . . .

Perhaps it was the obsequious act of kneeling before a customer who insisted on having trousers that were "perfect triumphs of the art" – as Mr Sponge's were. "Many were the trials and the easings and the alterings ere he got a pair to his mind" – and to kneel before someone like Mr Sponge, patting and adjusting – no wonder Rose shuddered at the picture.

Evan Harrington came out as a serial in 1860. Arnold of Rugby had died in 1842; he might never have lived from the evidence of this story. The manufacture of gentlemen at public schools had not yet got under way. Yet in some ways it is a surprise to find that the novel is so early. Although the scenery and costumes are mid-Victorian, the people appear to belong to a later generation. Perhaps it is Meredith's obsession with his own case, but England has become far more caste-like than it had been in the time of Shakespeare and Dekker, when the younger son of the squire might be apprenticed to a merchant. Wholesale trade may be forgiven after a generation or two; Rose's grandmother had had some connexion with manufacturing

The great Mel had died deep in debt; was Evan to take on the tailor's shop and pay off his father's debts? His mother said yes, his sister, the Countess, said no – and pleaded with him (above) to keep his birth a secret and to marry Rose.

ABOVE Evan Harrington, son of the great Mel, was brought up as a gentleman and no one would know that he was the son of a "snip". He went to Portugal to stay with his sister who had married a Portuguese Count; he hobnobbed with duchesses, he met Rose, the niece of the British ambassador . . .

RIGHT Old Tom Cogglesby had once loved Rose's mother – but it was impossible! Now he was a rich bachelor and he plays the pantomime fairy; the debts are paid, the shop is sold, Evan has a handsome allowance and a diplomatic appointment, he marries Rose. *Evan Harrington* is a comedy – though a bitter one, for Meredith's grandfather was a tailor and his name was Melchizedec. It was first published with the subtitle "He would be a Gentleman".

and had brought money to the family. Brewers will just pass if rich enough –
but to sell anything over a counter, to kneel at a man's feet and admire his
trousers – that could not be tolerated. At Beckley Court, Evan's bearing and
character had been "so thoroughly accepted as those of a gentleman, and
one of their own rank", that Lady Jocelyn and her husband had not a word
to say to each other on that score when the news broke. But he could not go
on being a tailor and marry a Jocelyn.

Lady Jocelyn and Rose were both regarded as radical by the aunts and
would both have said that they despised rank and social convention and
looked for "true worth". Yet even Rose, when Evan, to shield his sister,
nobly confessed to a mean trick he had not committed, could not banish a
moment of horrid doubt. Might there not be something in it after all? Might
not the stain of birth show itself in conduct? Evan himself "never took
republican ground in opposition to those who insulted him . . . nor compared
the fineness of his instincts with the behaviour of titled gentlemen". He
thought it natural that Rose should despise a snip, just as Othello in his
heart of hearts found it surprising that Desdemona should prefer him to the
curled darlings of her race and was therefore the more ready to listen to
Iago's poison. Othello knew colour prejudice was a poison but was himself
infected. Evan despised class prejudice but he too was infected – and Meredith
remarks ironically of the countess, who was the worst snob of all, that she
was after all a heroine fighting class prejudice with great success, because
she, "issuing out of tailordom", had become a countess and had contrived
that a duke should adore her sister while the daughter of Beckley Court
adored her brother. But she fought, he adds characteristically and with a
double irony, by accepting altogether the standards of her enemy.

Taken at the most superficial level, *Evan Harrington* is a snob's orgy. And
personally I have little doubt that Rose's aunts were representative of their
class and period. But, in spite of the unanimity of prejudice at Beckley and in
spite of the conflict within both Meredith and Evan, the distinction between
"behaving like a gentleman" and being born in easy circumstances was
never more sharply drawn; Evan at every point is more of a gentleman than
his rival Lord Laxley or Rose's brother or the loutish young squire George
Uploft. Rose's maid Polly is well aware of that. The wife of Bath's principle
is once again established:

> Christ wills we claim of him our gentillesse
> Not of our elders for their old richesse.

14

CHRISTIAN AND GENTLEMAN

A Heart-Piercing Fact

WHY DID THE ENGLISH establish as a moral code this strange sub-Christian cult of "behaving like a gentleman", a word which in other countries acquired no such moral significance?

The short answer is that the official religion of England was Christianity and that Christianity demands a standard of conduct altogether too exacting for ordinary mortals if it is taken simply as a moral code. It demands devotion. Who can turn the other cheek and give away his coat from a naked sense of duty? It is a creed of perfection from which everyone falls short. It only becomes bearable if there are means to assure an offender of forgiveness and provide him with divine comfort. And for a long time now it had been hard for an Englishman to be confident of forgiveness and divine comfort in the positive and personal sense which he had enjoyed before the Reformation.

In the 18th century, there had crept over the English church something like the film called a cataract which obscures the vision of old people. Many of the clergy were worldly and had no true vocation; the parson was often the younger brother of the squire, with more interest in field sports than in religion, and sometimes he paid a harmless drudge to read morning and evening service. The sacraments were often scantily or perfunctorily administered; and without sacraments, without a living faith, the morning and evening services became dreary and repetitious. Religion – in the sense of personal contact with divine and eternal energy – had been at a low ebb. As the century drew to a close, there was, no doubt, some continuation of pious habits; there were, no doubt, some devoted parish priests, but for the layman it was not easy to find in the established church a means of grace that would satisfy the human heart.

To-day, in the late 20th century, many people vaguely suppose that their Victorian great-grandfathers enjoyed an enviable certainty about their beliefs and principles. But this was by no means the case with many of the more thoughtful and sensitive Victorians. Their reaction against the Age of Reason was intensified by dissatisfaction at growing materialism and by the impossibility of reconciling a literal reading of *Genesis* with the findings of science; this combination drove some to atheism or agnosticism and tormented many others with doubts and difficulties. At another level of sophistication, the widespread human demand for something simple and direct that would satisfy the emotions led to further schisms, notably of the Methodists. Meanwhile, within the Established Church, dissatisfaction with laxity, with torpor and with indifference resulted in two very different currents of reform, the Evangelical and Tractarian movements. Methodists, Evangelicals and Tractarians alike tried to take Christianity seriously and made severe demands on the conduct of their followers. But there were men who needed a code of behaviour that was less exacting and involved no commitment to a doctrine; and for them it was enough to be a gentleman.

It happens that one leader of the Tractarians, the first among them in intellectual force, Cardinal Newman, has left among his writings a discussion of the difference between a gentleman and a Christian. I have asserted more than once that for the Victorians the gentleman provided an ethical code that was a substitute for Christianity. At the same time, it derived from Christianity many of its finer points. Nothing more clearly illuminates both the debt and the difference than this discussion. But it has to be set against the background of Newman's thought and development as described in his famous *Apologia Pro Vita Sua*. This was published in 1864, twelve years after his discourses on *The Idea of a University*, which contains his thoughts on what makes a gentleman, and nearly twenty years after his conversion to Rome. The earlier work was written when he was Rector of a new Catholic University in Ireland and, in distinguishing the gentleman from the Christian, he assumed that his hearers would know what he meant by a Christian. But for the world at large, this is best explained in the *Apologia*.[30]

The point at which Newman's statement of belief logically begins is expressed in one sentence:

If I am asked why I believe in a God, I answer that it is because I believe in myself, for I feel it impossible to believe in my own existence (and of that I am quite sure) without believing also in the existence of Him, who lives as a Personal, All-seeing, All-judging Being in my conscience.

But that essential belief must be read in the light of a second which must be quoted at some length to give its full effect.

To consider the world in its length and breadth, its various history, the many races of man, their starts, their fortunes, their mutual alienation, their conflicts; and then their ways, habits, governments, forms of worship; their enterprises, their aimless courses, their random achievements and acquirements, the impotent conclusion of long-standing facts, the tokens so faint and broken, of a superintending design, the blind evolution of what turn out to be great powers or truths, the progress of things,

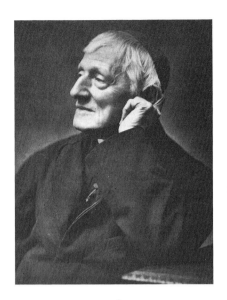

John Henry, Cardinal Newman, saw with
piercing clarity that "it is well to be a
gentleman, to have a cultivated intellect,
a noble and courteous bearing", but that
holiness was something quite different.
Nonetheless, his view of the gentleman
left something out . . .

as if from unreasoning elements, not towards final causes, the greatness and littleness
of man, his far-reaching aims, his short duration, the curtain hung over his futurity,
the disappointments of life, the defeat of good, the success of evil, physical pain,
mental anguish, the prevalence and intensity of sin, the pervading idolatries, the
corruptions, the dreary hopeless irreligion, that condition of the whole race, so
fearfully yet exactly described in the Apostle's words, "having no hope and without
God in the world" – all this is a vision to dizzy and appal; and inflicts upon the
mind the sense of a profound mystery, which is absolutely beyond human solution.

There is no shallow Victorian optimism here! And in the face of "this
heart-piercing, reason-bewildering fact", he can only conclude that the
human race is "out of joint with the purposes of its Creator", and thus the
doctrine of original sin "becomes to me almost as certain as that the world
exists and as the existence of God". And is it not then a probability, indeed
almost a certainty, that "the blessed and loving will of God" should "inter-
fere in this anarchical condition of things by extraordinary means?" Hence
the Incarnation of the Divine Word in human form and the foundation of a
Church that after a long debate defines the truth and continues on earth
the Presence of the Incarnate Word.

That, in an extremely compressed form, was Newman's lifelong belief. It
was also an essential part of his belief that "the exterior world, physical and
historical, was but the outward manifestation of realities greater than itself",
from which followed the Sacramental system, really the expression in religious
terms of the same truth – "the doctrine that material phenomena are both
the types and the instruments of real things unseen . . ." It was this that from
his earliest days made him regard himself as a Catholic; he argued that this
was the teaching of the early Church and he found it in the teaching of the
great Anglican divines of the 17th century. For nearly twenty years he

taught that the Anglican was a part of the Catholic church, a part which had held fast to the true doctrine of the Apostles and the early Fathers. But he believed it was in desperate need of reform.

It is no part of my argument here to follow Newman through the distress which it caused him to find he could not continue in his opinion that the Anglican church was truly Catholic. He was astonished at the uproar caused throughout England by his famous Tract 90, in which he tried to show that the Thirty-Nine Articles – clearly a document drawn up as a compromise and meant to enfold as wide a variety of opinion as possible – could be interpreted in a Catholic sense. He had said in this Tract that "the Church of Rome . . . alone, amid all the errors and evils of her practical system, has given free scope to the feelings of awe, mystery, tenderness, reverence, devotedness, and other feelings which may be especially called Catholic". The uproar convinced him that "the English Church showed itself intrinsically and radically alien from Catholic principles. Men of Catholic views were too truly but a party in our church". At about the same time, he suddenly perceived that many of the arguments which in the 5th century put him firmly on the side of the Catholic Church against various schismatics applied equally to the Anglicans in the 19th. He was received into the Catholic Church in 1845. But he "retained a firm belief that grace was to be found in the Anglican church".

In all the controversy about Newman, there is a note which has nothing to do with theology, a note of irritation at "extremism", at being asked to take religion seriously. "Puseyite" became an almost meaningless term of abuse; the Earl of Scamperdale called Mr Sponge a "Puseyite pig-jobber" for riding into his hounds, although there is no more evidence that he ever went to church than that he ever sold a pig. What is to the point is that the whole story of Newman's life illustrates his total commitment, whether as Anglican or Roman, to an eternal, supernatural, reality and his belief that this was the essence of Christianity.

The Considerate Infidel

THE OCCASION for the *Apologia* was Charles Kingsley's statement that the Catholic clergy in general, and Newman in particular, had little regard for the truth. Kingsley was hopelessly outclassed in the controversy that followed – intellectually he was not in the same street as Newman. But he is far more representative of most of his countrymen. He was Rector for most of his life of Eversley in Hampshire and belonged to the school of "muscular Christianity" – the phrase is Disraeli's – but in Kingsley's case "boisterous" would perhaps be the better adjective. He was not at Rugby but in spirit he was a Rugbeian of the pure Arnold school. He wrote an Ode to the North East Wind:

> 'Tis the hard grey weather
> Breeds hard Englishmen.

and in a verse letter to Thomas Hughes (the author of *Tom Brown*) he wrote:

> What we can we will be
> Honest Englishmen
> Do the work that's nearest
> Though it's dull at whiles
> Helping, when we meet them,
> Lame dogs over stiles.

It is perhaps not quite fair to quote that, because he did achieve moments of poetry in songs and ballads, such as *The Sands of Dee*. Nor is G. M. Young's summary dismissal of Kingsley in his *Victorian England* altogether fair:

Kingsley . . . relieved many souls of their burden by communicating his own delight in the body, in the ardours of exploration, sport and sex. . . . Unluckily the world is not entirely peopled by young country gentlemen newly married to chastely passionate brides, and it is perhaps rash to identify the self-contentment which comes of a vigorous body and an assured income with the glorious liberty of the children of God.

This was hard on a man who had in his youth written *Alton Locke*, a novel strongly imbued with sympathy for the Chartist movement and for the poverty of the manual labourer. But Kingsley became reactionary as he grew older and vehemently supported the severity of Governor Eyre's punitive measures after the black rebellion in Jamaica of 1865. All in all, he was a representative of what Newman called "sound Church-of-Englandism or orthodox Protestantism". And it is interesting to note that in his controversy with Newman he does not appeal to their common Christianity but to the fact that they are both "gentlemen". "The course you demand of me is the only course fit for a gentleman," he writes, and again (after an apology in which he virtually says: "If that is what he says he means, I suppose I must take his word for it"), "I have done as much as one English gentleman can do for another . . ."

Newman's opinion of the gentleman is part of his vision of a University, which must aim at imparting a *liberal* education. Newman, incidentally, hated liberalism in religion, which he regarded as mere laxity; in education, he meant something quite different. The subject matter of all knowledge is the Creation and therefore, since all subjects are the acts and work of one Creator, all are linked. Students cannot study them all, but by living together in a university with others who between them are studying a wide range of subjects, they learn "to respect, to consult, to aid each other". And thus "a habit of mind is formed that lasts through life, of which the attributes are freedom, equitableness, calmness, moderation and wisdom".

Charles Kingsley, the exponent of what Disraeli called "muscular Christianity", a fine hearty country parson, the representative of most of his countrymen in his sturdy convictions about the excellence of the English and all their ways.

It is common, he goes on, to speak of "the liberal arts and studies and of a liberal education as the especial characteristic and property of a university and of a gentleman . . ."; and he goes on that "The true definition of what is liberal is that it is what is done for its own sake". There may be a material end as well, but that is distinguishable and secondary. The true physician, he would have said, acquires his knowledge of the body from pure love of knowledge; he uses it to heal the sick and is still a true physician. But the earning of money is another kind of skill altogether and when the physician makes out his bills he is no longer a physician but an accountant. This of course is the teaching of Plato.

This liberal or gentleman's education becomes "an acquired illumination; it is a habit, a personal possession, and an inward endowment". But even in this high sense, education makes "not the Christian, not the Catholic, but the gentleman". And here he must be quoted at rather more length:

It is well to be a gentleman, it is well to have a cultivated intellect, a delicate taste, a candid, equitable dispassionate mind, a noble and courteous bearing in the conduct of life; these are the connatural qualities of a large knowledge; they are the objects of a University; I am advocating . . . I shall insist, upon them; but they are no guarantee for sanctity or even for conscientiousness; they may attach to the man of the world, the profligate, the heartless. Quarry the granite rock with razors, or moor the vessel with a thread of silk; then may you hope with such keen and delicate instruments as human knowledge and human reason to contend against those giants, the passion and the pride of man.

The Church, on the other hand, is engaged in that very warfare with giants, aims at regenerating the very depths of the heart. He comes back to the gentleman, a hundred pages later, in a passage which you may find vaguely and rather incongruously familiar, because by some strange quirk of some forgotten oculist or optician it became for a hundred years the standard text used for testing the eye's ability to read small print:

It is almost a definition of a gentleman to say he is one who never inflicts pain . . . he is mainly occupied in removing the obstacles which hinder the free and unembarrassed action of those about him. . . . The true gentleman . . . carefully avoids whatever may cause a jar or jolt in the minds of those with whom he is cast . . . his great concern being to make everyone at their ease and at home. . . . He is tender towards the bashful, gentle towards the distant, and merciful towards the absurd . . . seldom prominent in conversation and never wearisome . . . he makes light of favours while he does them and seems to be receiving when he is conferring. He observes the maxim of the ancient sage, that we should conduct ourselves towards our enemy as if he were one day to be our friend. . . . He is patient, forbearing and refined on philosophical principles . . . he is too clear-headed to be unjust. . . . If he be an unbeliever, he will be too profound and large-minded to ridicule religion . . . too wise to be a fanatic in his infidelity, he is the friend of religious toleration. . . . Such are some of the lineaments of the ethical character which the cultivated intellect will form apart from religious principle. They are seen within the Church and without it. The possessor may be a St Francis de Sales or a Gibbon . . .

It is clear that Newman takes a high view of the gentleman's character. He does not even mention the meaning attached to the term by Sir Walter Elliott – a man of property and birth. Nor could his definition be stretched to cover the Squire Osbaldeston or the earl of Lonsdale. He says nothing about courage and the martial virtues, nothing of the stoic qualities admired by Tom Brown and his friends. Chaucer, on the other hand, would have agreed that Newman's gentleman understood what was meant by *gentillesse*. But to Chaucer *gentillesse* had been the gift of Christ and it would hardly have occurred to him that there could be an unbeliever who displayed it. Newman's gentleman owes a great deal to the Christian ethic; he is a considerate and kindly infidel, tolerant, modest, forbearing. Chesterfield would have recognized him; he understands the *bienséances*. He was far from representative of the gentleman as most Englishmen pictured him, but he did stand for one important element in the ideal of the gentleman as it emerged towards the end of the century. Newman himself embodied it. No one could doubt that he was himself a gentleman as well as a Christian.

15
THROUGH POLISH EYES

The Chance Missed

TOWARDS THE END of the 19th century, there were several writers who combined wide popularity with serious purpose and literary skill. But H. G. Wells and G. B. Shaw were reformers rather than observers: both looked forward to a utopian world in which social differences would disappear. Shaw is concerned not so much to describe the social order as to stand it on its head. Wells is most successful in science fiction or when he keeps strictly to the background of the lower middle class, as in *Mr Polly*. Neither really suits my purpose.

Thomas Hardy is a poet, an artist of greater stature than either. But for him tiny man is the helpless plaything of the gods, his small ambitions are set against the eternal silence of the stars and the infinite distances of space. He is not at his best in describing social distinction, although in Gabriel Oak he did picture a shepherd whose behaviour to Bathsheba was altogether knightly.

Rudyard Kipling is another matter. His whole life, and much of his writing, was affected by his boyhood at one of those factories for gentlemen, and at one avowedly intended to produce officers for the army. He was altogether a writer, irretrievably wedded to the inkpot, too short-sighted to play even football, but he admired and envied the Captain of Football and Head of the School who becomes the perfect subaltern and the youngest major in the army – a figure he has drawn with the loving realism of an advertisement for evening dress in George Cottar of *The Brushwood Boy*. The effect of his upbringing on Kipling and his art is a long and complicated question – on which I have already written a book. That is perhaps sufficient reason for not calling him in evidence here. I prefer to turn to the picture of one man, a man of stature, a tragic figure, whose tragedy grew directly from the fact that in the centre of his being, in all that made him a man, he was of that special kind we have been discussing, a gentleman, jealous about his reputation in the eyes of men, jealous about his integrity in his own eyes, and jealous about his responsibility for those who had mysteriously and unaccountably been entrusted to his care.

It is a picture of an Englishman, but not seen through English eyes. Joseph Conrad's family were "noble" in the European sense, small land-owners in Poland; his father had suffered exile for protesting against the Russian occupation of Poland. The boy was brought up by an uncle on the plains of Poland – in the heart of the great European land mass – and there ·fell in love, romantically and for ever, with a Far Princess – life at sea, a life of duty and adventure, a life which he eventually realised under a British flag. He retired from the sea after twenty years and spent the rest of his life writing novels, among which *Lord Jim* is one of the highest achievements.

They are passionate and mysterious novels like no others in English. They are filled with a sense of brooding immensity, an immensity of sea or sky or tropical forest, and of an immensity in time too, against which human figures appear tiny and momentary yet supremely important. No one else has expressed so vividly in fiction one aspect of what a French spiritual writer[31] calls "the sacrament of the present moment". The first mate of a tramp steamer in the Indian Ocean may be coming off duty at the end of his watch, a moment prosaic enough and to most of those concerned a matter of dull routine. But to Conrad the vastness of the ocean and the liquid depths of light in the sky are charged with an intensity of feeling that can never be repeated. That moment will never come again and it is a moment in which he is conscious of eternity. It was at just such a moment that the first great crisis of Jim's life occurred.

Jim's place in this book is as a specimen of the genus "gentleman", but Conrad did not see him as a type, rather as a unique and enigmatic individual. Nor did Conrad in the least idealize those who in common speech are called gentlemen by social position. There is a passage in Flaubert, a writer Conrad much admired, describing a gathering of French provincial nobility in the first half of the century.

In their unconcerned looks was the calm of passions daily satiated, and through all their gentleness of manner pierced that peculiar brutality, the result of a command of half-easy things, in which force is exercised and vanity amused – the management of thoroughbred horses and the society of loose women.[32]

With that clearly in mind, Conrad wrote of an Englishman:

He was tall, well set up, good-looking and healthy; and his clear pale face had under its commonplace refinement that slight tinge of overbearing brutality which is given by the possession of only partly difficult accomplishments; by excelling in games or in the art of making money; by the easy mastery over animals and over needy men.[33]

No, Jim was not that kind of gentleman. Yet it is an essential part of his story that he was "one of us", a phrase used of him several times by Marlow, who is pictured as telling Jim's story to a group of men, relaxed, after dinner on a tropical night. Marlow himself was a sea captain and at least one of his hearers seems to have been another; the phrase might mean "a fellow sea-man". It can also be given the class meaning that it does usually suggest on an English tongue. But it is part of the irony of the whole tale that it carries both these meanings and more too. Marlow is aware of a bond with Jim which he can express only in this ambiguous phrase, but the fact is that he and Jim alike belong to a natural aristocracy concerned with honour and fidelity and with responsibility for those entrusted to their care.

Jim was the son of an English country parson. He came from a background with a moral code, although again it is stated ironically:

Jim's father possessed such certain knowledge of the Unknowable as made for the righteousness of people in cottages without disturbing the ease of mind of those whom an unerring Providence enables to live in mansions.

But Jim, brought up far from the sea in an "abode of piety and peace", fell in love, like Conrad himself, with the idea of life at sea. He dreamed of adventure, of a chance to prove himself a man. The chance came and he failed.

He ought not to have been in a ship like the *Patna*. He had been chief mate in a good ship, but a falling spar had broken his leg in a storm and he had been put into hospital in the first port they called at. When he was well, his ship had gone, and after hanging about a little, waiting for a good berth, he decided he must take whatever he could and signed on as chief mate of the *Patna*.

The *Patna* was owned by a Chinese merchant determined to make as much out of her as he could before she went to the scrap-yard. She was to carry Muslim pilgrims on their way to Mecca, eight hundred of them, Arabs, Javanese, Malayans; the crew were lascars, and of the five white officers only Jim belonged to that brotherhood that Marlow had recognized. The captain was a "renegade New South Wales German", a repulsive figure, "with a purple nose and a red moustache", "the incarnation of everything vile and base that lurks in the world we love"; he was perhaps all that the poor old *Patna* could now expect, and the same might be said of the Chief Engineer, an alcoholic Scot. The others were little better and the ship was "eaten up with rust worse than a condemned water-tank". They were a truly horrible gang on the floating corpse of a ship, and Jim had no business to be in that company.

Night fell.

The thin gold shaving of the moon floating slowly downwards had lost itself on the darkened surface of the waters, and the eternity beyond the sky seemed to come down nearer to the earth, with the augmented glitter of the stars . . .

They were all on deck when the *Patna* hit something. It was perhaps a submerged wreck. There was nothing visible; no one was to blame. There was a sharp shock but she lifted and rode over it. But when Jim went forward, he found there was a big hole in her bows and the sea pouring in to fill the fore-peak, a compartment shut off from the rest of the ship only by a thin rusty bulkhead. That bulkhead was already bulging and as Jim stood by it he saw a great flake of rust peel off "as big as the palm of my hand". It could only be minutes before it gave way and the ship went down.

He was not thinking of himself. He was not afraid of death. He was thinking of all those pilgrims, women with babies, old men, rich and poor, trustfully sleeping, suddenly to be overwhelmed, struggling in the sea. There were only seven boats. And there was nothing to be done. If only there had been time! Time to prepare himself, time to think out a course of action! He stood there, picturing the pilgrims in the sea. The other four so-called officers were frenziedly struggling to get a boat over the side for themselves, cursing Jim for standing aloof. Three of them tumbled in. They shouted to the fourth. They did not know that he was already dead of heart failure. "Jump!" they shouted. And Jim jumped.

He did not know why he jumped. He found himself alone with those men so alien to his being. One of them saw the masthead light go out and they thought the *Patna* had gone down. He thought of swimming back to die with the pilgrims – but rejected the thought. It would do no good and it was the easy way out. He stayed in the boat, savagely hostile, resentful at his companions, at fate, at the chance he had missed, above all at himself.

It was a main shipping route and they were picked up; they were brought back to the port from which they had sailed. And then the news came that the *Patna* had been found, still afloat, without officers, and brought safely to harbour. There was a public enquiry. The others ran away, but Jim would not, though he was offered the chance; he felt himself a bear tied to a stake. He had to fight his course. He was found guilty and sentenced to lose his certificate. It was an end to his career at sea.

It was at the enquiry that Marlow saw him and at once recognised his essential nature.

He came from the right place, he was one of us. He stood there for all the parentage of his kind, for men and women by no means clever or amusing, but whose very existence is based upon honest faith and upon the instinct of courage. . . . I mean that inborn ability to look temptations straight in the face . . . an unthinking and blind stiffness before the outward and inward terrors, before the might of nature and the seductive corruption of men . . .

That was what Marlow saw in him but there was that unaccountable flaw. He had missed his chance. And although he had stuck it out at the enquiry, standing there for all to point at, he could not afterwards bear to be in the presence of anyone who knew what had happened. Anyone, that is, except Marlow. He knew that Marlow understood the bond between them.

He blurted it out once, in his inarticulate way.

"Of course I wouldn't have talked to you about all this if you had not been a gentleman . . . I am – I am – a gentleman too . . .", he stammered and it was the only time that either of them used the word.

He found employment, as a water-clerk, a kind of tout for a ship's chandler, whose duty it was to be first alongside any incoming ship and to lure her captain to the office of his employers. This was in another port, where he hoped the story would not be known. He did it well – superlatively – until someone mentioned the *Patna* in his hearing. And then he was off, looking for a place where they did not know the story. It was the same with the next job and the next.

Paradise

IN THE END Marlow found him a place cut off altogether from the world of white men and big ships, where sooner or later someone came to *know*. Patusan was forty miles up a river in an island of the southern Pacific so remote that no one from the outside ever came there. There was supposed to be a trading-post, but it was long since it had sent any goods out or brought any in.

The story leaves a great deal unsaid; it comes to us, as is Conrad's way, through Marlow's memory and through what other people told Marlow. But it seems there were three centres of power in Patusan; the Raja, the Bugis and the Arabs. The Raja, the nominal ruler, was soaked in opium and reluctant to reach decisions, but liable to sudden and violent impulses; he was surrounded, inevitably, by corrupt and extortionate advisers. The Bugis, a people from the Southern Celebes, traders, fighters, sea-farers, wanderers like the Norsemen in Europe, had settled there long ago under their chief Doramin and formed a stable self-contained community, well able to look after themselves in face of the Raja and the local people, but threatened now by an Arab pirate, who had established himself in a position that seemed impregnable on top of a hill and who "hung over the town like a hawk over a poultry-yard".

There was an old loyalty, the memory of an adventure in which they had been comrades, between Stein, Jim's employer and Doramin, the Chief of the Bugis. Doramin recognized the bond and treated Jim hospitably. But he was not content to live in Doramin's compound and under Doramin's protection. He was in Patusan to establish himself in his own eyes and to make some return to his employer. But no one trusted him and he could do nothing without trust. And then his idea came – a plan for taking the Arab fort. It was altogether successful and the Arab leader fled the country.

From that moment on, Jim became Tuan Jim, Lord Jim. He was credited with supernatural powers; everyone listened to his words; he was the King of

Patusan. When a village had a grievance against the Raja they came to Jim and, very politely and respectfully, he would give the Raja a lecture, telling him the right course for a just and wise ruler. And the Raja would give orders that the matter should be put right. The Raja hated Jim of course, but he feared him; Doramin was his friend; Dain Waris, Doramin's son, about his own age, was his close friend and companion. Everyone trusted him now.

Dain Waris was a natural leader, a gentleman in the Muslim tradition. "A firm glance, an ironic smile, a courteous deliberation of manner seemed to hint at great reserves of intelligence and power." He and Jim together had planned and carried out the operation against the Arabs and that comradeship had cemented an instinctive liking. Dain Waris trusted him and understood him better than anyone, better perhaps than the girl.

For there was a girl. Her mother had been half Dutch and half Malay; her father was a white man who had promised fidelity but had suddenly disappeared, going back to the menacing cosmos from which he had come. She had grown up in Patusan, knowing nowhere else, fearing the unknown world to which her father had suddenly returned. Her mother was dead.

She watched over Jim at night without his knowing; she warned him of plots to murder him. She loved him with an utter absorption, but jealously, remembering her father, afraid that that other world would claim Jim too. As for him, it was a Paradise; he had a friend and a lover, he had power, he believed in the value of his work, everyone trusted him. Only there was that shadow, the knowledge that in the outside world his failure would be remembered.

To that Paradise came a snake. He had stolen a ship, he was a pirate, every man's hand was against him. Brown was a hateful man in every sense of the word, full of hate. He came up the river to Patusan with fourteen armed ruffians because he had heard rumours of a white man who ruled in that country and whom he supposed must be making a good thing of it which he could be forced to share.

He found the place bigger and better organized than he had expected. He got ashore, but was quickly shut up in a stockade with his fourteen men, besieged. Jim was away; but Dain Waris and a strong party of the Bugis went downstream to a narrow place that could be held against reinforcements coming up or against a remnant going down. An assault on the stockade was postponed until Jim's return.

Jim went fearlessly to parley. Brown recognized in him at once the quality that Marlow had seen, but Brown hated it. He knew at once that it was no use expecting Jim to share in piratical extortions. He quickly made up his mind that the best he could hope for was to get his men away in safety. He begged with skill for a fair passage down the river; he understood the nature of the man he was pleading with and he was fortunate in the words he chose. He had had bad luck, he said; everyone was against him. He had jumped outside the circle of respectable people. All he needed was another chance. Had Jim never needed a second chance? He must have done something. Hadn't he jumped himself?

His words went home to Jim's essential decency. He called a council of Doramin and his Bugis and the Raja's people. They all wanted to fight, to wipe out Brown and his men. Jim persuaded them not to. He made a long speech, drawing on all the reserves of trust he had built up, pledging himself that Brown's party would go peacefully away. Doramin accepted his advice; the others followed. They did not like it but they trusted Jim.

He went back and promised Brown free passage to the mouth of the river, where his stolen ship lay waiting for him. He sent a message to Dain Waris, lying in ambush in the narrow place, telling him to let them pass. He gave the messenger his ring, the token of Doramin's old friendship, which he had brought with him when he came, the symbol of loyalty between himself and Doramin's people. Dain Waris took the ring and put it on his finger; he would let them pass. But out of sheer wanton hate, in a spirit of frustrated malice against all mankind, Brown and his pirates crept secretly to the other side of their position and poured in three aimed, murderous volleys. Dain Waris was killed.

The survivors brought his body back to Doramin's compound. He lay there in state with Jim's ring on his finger. Jim put the girl aside. He would not listen to her. He would not fly, nor would he fight; there was nothing left to fight for. He went, unarmed, to Doramin's stockade. He walked up to the body of his dead friend and looked on his face. Then he walked slowly towards Doramin, step by step. "I am come in sorrow," he said. He waited. Doramin, bulky, majestic, tried to rise. Two attendants helped him to stand upright and then, with one of the two flintlock pistols that lay always on his knees, he shot his son's friend through the chest.

A Ghost Laid

THE GIRL was destroyed. The whole structure of peace and confidence that Jim had built was destroyed. Jim himself was destroyed in the eyes of most men, though not, surely, in the eyes of Marlow nor of any who had followed Marlow through the tale. For to anyone who knew as much as that, it must be clear that Jim was a noble creature.

The waste and tragedy of his story sprang indirectly from that first chance missed when he jumped from the *Patna* instead of staying by his ship. But, directly, it was the consequence of his essential decency. He had been given a second chance when Stein sent him to Patusan – and Stein had given him that chance in gratitude to a trader who had given him just such a chance long ago. Doramin had remembered the old debt to Stein of which the ring was the token. And thus Jim had felt that he must complete the circle, do as he had been done by and give Brown a chance. That he utterly failed to plumb the depths of Brown's hate was part of his simplicity – stupidity in the eyes of Brown, who was a man in hell, a man whose nature was hell. But in Jim it was greatness of soul.

Jim was a noble creature, but Sir Walter Elliott would not have called him a gentleman. Nor was he very like Sir Philip Sidney. He did not play the lute or write a ballad to his mistress' eyebrow. He knew nothing of fencing or horsemanship. He had no skill in painting or literature. But he was brave, he was concerned about honour – both honour in the world and his own integrity – he fell in love with a distant dream and followed it, he did not count the change. And certainly it was part of his essential being that he was a leader, that he expected obedience and felt responsibility for those he led.

Marlow had been puzzled by the contrast between Jim's evident quality and his failure in the *Patna*. He confessed that he had sought him out and encouraged his confidences because he hoped for a miracle. He wanted to find that there had been some excuse for that jump and thus to prove to himself that he had been right in what he had instinctively felt about Jim. To prove that would lay a ghost:

... the most obstinate ghost of man's creation, the uneasy doubt uprising like a mist, secret and gnawing like a worm, and more chilling than the certitude of death – the doubt of the sovereign power enthroned in a fixed standard of conduct ...

Marlow does not refer to that ghost again but surely he must by the time he had finished telling Jim's tale have felt that it was laid, that Jim had lived by such a standard. And it was surely the standard of a sub-Christian cult, drawing its ethics from Christianity though deprived of supernatural dimensions. It was very different from the standards of the French nobles pictured by Flaubert, having acquired in Victorian England a powerful additional element. This kind of gentleman accepted responsibility for those who accepted his leadership. It was a development which owed a good deal to Dr Arnold.

16

THE EDWARDIANS

Before the Lights Went Out

THERE IS A NOVEL called *The Edwardians* by Victoria Sackville-West which paints the rich, fashionable set who were friends of Edward VII against the background of a great ducal house, a house that had stood since Tudor times with its stables and gardens, its bakehouses and breweries, its gamekeepers and carpenters, in the midst of its park, with its girdle of encircling farms – self-sufficient, demanding, apparently unchanging and everlasting, yet doomed.

The fast set live for the pleasures of the moment; the servants for the pleasures of the rich. When Sylvia Roehampton, the most fashionable beauty of the fast set, thinks in despair that she would endure any privations for the sake of Sebastian, the young Duke of Chevron, her creator adds in a sardonic parenthesis that "to Sylvia privation meant three instead of fifty thousand a year"; but Miss Wace, the Duchess of Chevron's confidential secretary, earned one hundred and fifty pounds a year and a farm labourer twenty-six. Yet the servants at Chevron do not question the accepted order; on the contrary, they excel their masters in absurd attention to the minutiae of precedence, visiting lady's maids taking rank according to the seniority of their mistresses' titles. They take it for granted that they are there to serve the long elaborate dinners, to help ladies in and out of their gorgeous dresses, to sit up till their mistresses are ready for bed, to call them in the morning with tea and to run baths for them. They think that inequality is as certain as death; they think that Chevron will go on for ever. Wickenden, the head carpenter, whose father and grandfather had been head carpenters before him, is in tears because his son wants to go away and be a motor mechanic.

Never had the few lived in such luxury. "They were eating quails. . . . That particular dish of the Chevron chef was famous; an ortolan within the quail, a truffle within the ortolan, and *pâté de foie gras* within the truffle." Never had there been such peace as drowsed over the lawns of Chevron. Never had the few been so remote from the lives of the many. Even the subtle bond between the lady and her maid had become artificial; there is a tinny note in the voice of the duchess of Chevron – Sebastian's mother – as she talks to Button, her maid, before the mirror.

"Don't pull my hair like that, Button; really I never knew such a clumsy woman; now you have given me a headache for the rest of the evening. . . . Now, Button, haven't you nearly finished? Don't drag my hair back like that, woman. . . . Really, Button, I thought you were supposed to be an expert hairdresser."

It is very different from the days, two hundred years ago, when Millamant shared with her maid Mincing the joke of using her love-letters as curling-papers and finding that poetry set the curl as prose never would.

The mental barriers were higher than they had ever been. This was partly because, since the French Revolution, the whole principle of stratification was threatened and therefore it was necessary to be persuaded that the barriers were not conventional but real. It was partly because the poor really were poor. Their expectation of life was shorter than that of the rich. They were more likely to be diseased. The Edwardians, like the Victorians, had some reason for a feeling which the poet Clough had called "an almost animal sensibility of conscience", and which the historian G. M. Young described as "a super-morality of the nerves and the senses, of bodily repulsion and social alarm".[34]

To read a social history of the Edwardian period [35] is to build a picture of strife and to conjure up visions of impending doom. A third of the urban working-class lived in deep poverty; in the country, where hours of work

Evening promenade in Hyde Park, 1890. Never had society been more sharply divided than in the last years of Queen Victoria and the reign of King Edward.

The earl of Albemarle's partridge shoot, 1912. The house party takes luncheon. A morning walking up the partridges on the stubble is hard work, and one mustn't take the risk of going hungry or being uncomfortable . . .

might stretch in summer eighteen hours from dawn to dusk, food was of the simplest and poorest; no one ever bought butcher's meat; two-thirds of the weekly wage went on bread and it was impossible to save. The threat of illness or unemployment hung as a dark threat over the labouring classes. There was no old age pension until 1909, when it was five shillings a week for a man over seventy, 2s 6d for a woman. Fear of the workhouse made old age a thing of terror. To an observer who studied tables of wages and compared them with the cost of inescapable necessities, the poverty would have seemed a recipe for revolution. From 1906 onwards, it is true, steps were taken to lessen the contrast between rich and poor, to soften the starkness of the Victorian belief that poverty could best be discouraged by treating it as a crime. But history suggests that such steps sometimes trigger the explosion. The country was rent by strikes; there were radical attacks on the House of Lords; Ireland seemed on the point of civil war; suffragettes chained themselves to the grill of the Ladies' Gallery in the House of Commons and one threw herself in front of the King's horse in the Derby – a double sacrilege, against royalty and against sport! The German General Staff judged that the country was so deeply divided that England would not go to war.

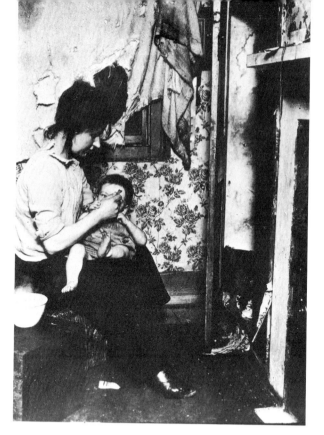

LEFT But the poor really were poor.
BELOW Yet in the country everyone came to the Meet to see the hounds and watch the hunt move off.

Yet in 1914 England suddenly became one. The Irish dropped their quarrels and came to the colours, the whole sprawling Empire was united. That surge of national purpose revealed a deep underlying unity that had many causes; there can be no single explanation. It is not the purpose of this book to analyze the many strands that held together a fabric so deeply divided by class, by race and by culture. One strand alone concerns us – and it was a bond not only in Britain, but in India and Africa and to a lesser extent in the white dominions too. Britain in 1914 was half way to being a democracy, but effective power was still in the hands of a ruling class. That class was not a closed caste but a body to whose ranks there was continual recruitment, for which purpose expensive training establishments had evolved. And the name for that ruling class carried moral overtones and stood for certain standards of behaviour. The paradox lay in the fact that

Raymond Asquith stands in the centre of his platoon. Scholar of Winchester and Balliol, with Firsts in Classics and Law, winner of Craven, Ireland, Derby and Eldon Scholarships, a Fellow of All Souls, he was captain of his college football eleven; he played rugger and rowed. He was killed in action in the Battle of the Somme on 15 September 1916. He may stand for all that lost generation of brilliant young men who led their soldiers against the machine-guns in the Great War.

while the rank had little point if it included everyone, almost everyone thought that it might one day include himself or at least his son, and almost everyone admired the ideal of conduct.

Until about 1910, nine-tenths of the population took it for granted that there must be a governing class. The poorest were often dazzled by the glitter of riches; no one was more popular than Hugh Lonsdale, the most glossy and spendthrift of aristocrats. On the other hand, in the middle classes, there was an illusion of "progress"; not only were national wealth, comfort and morals improving but also they themselves would rise in the social scale and their children would rise further.

In short, almost everyone admired the qualities which he believed a gentleman possessed; among the more intelligent and ambitious, almost everyone could picture himself as a gentleman and suppose that this was something that he, or at least his son, might become. This, surely, was something that drew people together.

These are generalisations. The justification for them is to be found in the popular fiction and drama of the Edwardian period.

The Lordly Hero

POPULAR NOVELS and plays almost always centred on a hero who was born into comfortable circumstances and had no regular occupation. Of all these stories, *The Prisoner of Zenda* is one of the best and is in several respects characteristic. First published in 1894, it was a favourite of my boyhood; it has gone into many editions and is still in print; it has been the basis for a long succession of films. But who today would dare to start an adventure story in terms at all like its opening passage?

"I wonder when in the world you're going to do anything, Rudolf?" said my brother's wife.

"My dear Rose," I answered, laying down my egg-spoon, "why in the world should I do anything? My position is a comfortable one. I have an income nearly sufficient for my wants (no one's income is ever quite sufficient, you know), I enjoy an enviable social position: I am brother to Lord Burlesdon, and brother-in-law to that charming lady, his countess. Behold, it is enough!"

We know, after that short paragraph, that Rudolf Rassendyll is an earl's brother and does nothing for his living; we learn as the story develops that he rides, shoots and fences with distinction, that he is a tall, handsome, well-set-up young man at whom women look with pleasure, that he speaks German as readily as English, is fluent in French and can get by in Italian and Spanish, that he has dignity of carriage and yet a lightness of touch, that in short he would have held his own with Castiglione's courtiers at Urbino. But there is more than accomplishment, charm and good manners; he kept his word and he always played fair. He would not shoot the wicked Rupert

"Rudolf – Flavia – always!" Rudolf Rassendyll was the younger brother of an earl, a brilliant swordsman, a fine horseman, the lordly hero – and too much a gentleman to take advantage of the situation and marry the woman he adored. *The Prisoner of Zenda* first appeared in 1895. This is George Alexander playing Rudolf in a stage adaptation the following year.

Rudolf and Flavia – but she was Queen of Ruritania and he was only a pretender, in the king's place for a day. Sentimental no doubt, but he was the last of the troubadours and many a boy dozed off to sleep in a fantasy that he was playing such a part as Rudolf's. (An illustration by Charles Dana Gibson.)

of Hentzau when he had him at an advantage, but would only kill him in fair fight. "I had but to raise my revolver and I sent him to his account with all his sins on his head. He did not so much as know I was there. I did nothing – why I hardly know to this day . . ." But *we* know. Apart from the fact that Rupert will be needed again for the sequel, we know that it would not be the act of a gentleman.

Above all, Rudolf is a gentleman about Princess Flavia. On the strength of an hereditary likeness, he has temporarily taken the place of his distant cousin and has been crowned King of Ruritania. The real King has been kidnapped, and it is the hero's duty to rescue him and then gracefully disappear. The real King is to marry Princess Flavia; everyone wants it to happen. She had known her duty and had acquiesced. Then, suddenly, she found she was in love; duty had become pleasure. When she discovered that the man she loved was not the King, she fainted in his arms and "with a great cry of pain I gathered her to me.. . . . I laid her softly on the ground, and stood up, looking at her, cursing heaven that young Rupert's sword had spared me for this sharper pang". They met once again and he vowed that "no touch save of your lips will ever be on mine". But they knew that they must part. Honour bound them and they said good-bye to all hope of happiness.

All this is very different from James Bond. No scruple ever holds him back from taking any advantage that comes his way, and he usually slips into bed with the fascinating young woman who has shared his adventures. He wears silk shirts and drives fast cars but he does not behave like a gentleman. But the Edwardian hero had to be a gentleman, both in social position and in behaviour. And the tradition of courtly love hung in the air, though with a difference. The troubadours sang the praises of a lady they had no serious intention of attaining; their love is an unreal convention and it is public. Rudolf and his lady really do love each other but they believe that love is not the only thing in the world – heresy to the troubadours – and they must renounce it in the name of honour; above all it must be kept secret. But she is his queen; he is her knight; their love is for ever, they are reverent, almost religious, about it. They owe a great deal to the troubadours.

The Prisoner of Zenda is only one of many stories in which the lordly hero is prevented by some often obscure point of honour from "taking an unfair advantage" and winning the heroine. If he has rescued her from some peril, he must not say he loves her in case she feels bound in gratitude to reward him by surrender. If she is rich and he is poor, again his lips are sealed; he must not betray his love or she will take pity on him. Seldom indeed did it occur to the hero of this kind of romance that the girl might actually want him.

Something in the same tradition, although greatly inferior, is *The Scarlet Pimpernel*. It was published in 1905 and was immensely popular. When I went to the London Library, to refresh my memory of this boyhood favourite, the copy I obtained, dated 1934, was the sixty-fourth edition. This too has been the basis of many films; it was dramatized and taken on tour all over England. Again the hero is most emphatically an amateur; a baronet, one of the richest men in England, a friend of the Prince Regent, Sir Percy Blakeney does his best to appear an idle fop. No one guesses that he is the master-mind behind the League of the Scarlet Pimpernel, which organises miraculous escapes from the guillotine for French aristocrats. There is a variation from the usual pattern, because he is already married to the heroine, but they are estranged, and when we first see them together, only one observer notices "the curious look of intense longing, of deep and hopeless passion with which

Shy, decorous, a little unhappy, they try to think of something
to say. This is 1922, and courtly love is not quite dead. He thinks
she is fragile, precious and unreal: she has been told she must
not give away her feelings.

the inane and flippant Sir Percy followed the retreating figure of his brilliant
wife''. As a boy of ten, I did not understand this estrangement – but I took it
for granted. Heroes were always in a state of deep and hopeless passion
which they must conceal. It remains mysterious on re-reading; two minutes
frank conversation could have ended the misunderstanding. But Sir Percy is
just as I remembered him: the courtier, polite, careless, beautifully dressed,
accomplished in all the *bienséances*, unfailingly chivalrous and considerate
to a wife who adds enormously to his difficulties by behaving, once she un-
ravels his disguise and falls in love with him, like a love-sick hen. It is a
thoroughly silly book but it makes my two points; Sir Percy is the kind of
hero who could only be popular among readers who admired the characteristics they expected their rulers to display, and these include the sentimental Edwardian version of courtly love.

Another writer of the period, Ian Hay, the pseudonym of Ian Hay Beith,
a master at a Scottish public school who took to novel-writing, follows the
tradition with variations. His heroes are Rugbeian rather than Etonian; they
are upper-middle-class, the sons of army officers or parsons, strong muscular
men who have to make their way in life. The hero of *A Knight on Wheels*, for
example, plays Rugby football and is tongue-tied in the presence of women.
He is a hard worker, fascinated by the new world of motor-cars; he invents a

new kind of brake, with the help of which he saves the life of his lady-love. But of course, in saving her, he is badly hurt himself; of course she nurses him and of course he cannot take advantage of the position to breathe a word of his love. And – equally of course – when, about two years later, he does bring himself to the point, she decides that she must sacrifice herself and him, turning him firmly and irretrievably down because she must look after her selfish and cantankerous father.

It should be added that the hero, in a boy-and-girl friendship with the girl who was eventually to be the one love of his life, had talked a great deal about knights who vowed themselves to the service of their ladies. She had volunteered at the age of nine to be his lady; she usually had to make a good deal of the running. It was courtly love – diluted with Tennyson, but still courtly love.

There were many others of the school. Stanley J. Weyman, Henry Seton Merriman, Maurice Hewlett, Jeffery Farnol, A. E. W. Mason, F. Marion Crawford – romances of gallant swordsmen, scrupulous in love and war. None of their heroes takes the view of Castiglione's Pallavicino, that women are "like unripe apples"; their views on women are much more like Don

It was a graded society – and hats told you something.
The elegant grey topper and the formal black silk set you
apart from the bourgeois felt and the plebeian tweed,
the official kepi and the schoolboy's coloured cap.

Quixote's than like Sancho Panza's.

The tradition continued well into the 1930s. With John Buchan, again, the inspiration is Arnold and Rugby rather than Castiglione; endurance and patience are part of the kind of courage he admires. Dick Hannay is a workaday Scot with a profession, but his friends are extremely well-connected and Sandy Arbuthnot is a true successor to Rudolf Rassendyll – a Border chieftain with a gift for disguise and an almost miraculous knowledge of strange places, ready at a moment's notice to leave the grouse and the curlew for Istanbul or Samarkand. With Sapper, the heroes have been brutalized by the First World War, but they are all of independent means and each has a faithful man-servant. In Dornford Yates, the school reached its sentimental nadir, but the ingredients of the recipe are the same. The hero does not work, has a Rolls-Royce and a faithful manservant; the enemy are cads and bounders and usually foreigners. And the women, unless wicked, are dainty and remote.

But there are interesting variations in the last of the gentlemen amateurs, Lord Peter Wimsey. He is a duke's son, he has been a soldier – of the wry unhappy breed who survived World War I – he is a brilliant cricketer, a scholar, a collector of books and manuscripts, a connoisseur of wines and brandies with one of the best palates in Europe – and his faithful batman has been trained in forensic chemistry and photography. So far he is broadly according to the tradition, although better educated than most. But he is no ruthless bloodhound and when a murderer whom he has brought to book is to be hanged, Wimsey is awake all night in an agony of self-examination. And his love is no distant princess but a not very beautiful though highly intelligent young woman of the professional upper middle classes, a writer of detective stories. In other words, Wimsey is not a man's picture of what he would like to be but a particular woman's picture of the man she would like as her lover. The English still loved a lord but he had to be a rather different *kind* of lord.

The creator of Lord Peter died in 1957. Since then, detectives have been professionals, either policemen or private eyes.

17
OVER HALF
THE GLOBE

OF COURSE it is rubbish to suppose that any one class or group has a monopoly of any virtue. No one was more riotously aware of this than G. K.
Chesterton. Yet it was Chesterton who, in the first quarter of this century,
wrote than "when a navvy wishes to praise a man, it comes readily to his
tongue to say that he has behaved like a gentleman". He went on to say, with
equal truth:

The oligarchic character of the modern English commonwealth does not rest, like
many oligarchies, on the cruelty of the rich to the poor. It does not even rest on the
kindness of the rich to the poor. It rests on the perennial and unfailing kindness of
the poor to the rich.[36]

And in the course of an election in Warwickshire in 1905, an old woman
warned a young candidate: "We don't like to hear the gentlemen becalling
each other." She wanted, poor dear, to go on believing that both the candidates were gentlemen in every sense.[37]

It was a high ideal and one that almost everyone accepted. In 1913, news
reached England that the bodies had been found of Captain Scott's party,
who had died on their way back from the South Pole. They had reached the
Pole to find that a Norwegian party under Amundsen had been there before
them. Their journals and papers told the story of their journey through un-
imaginable cold, of their fading hopes as blizzard after blizzard slowed them
down, of their growing weakness and sickness, and of the heroic end of
Captain Oates. His feet were badly frostbitten and he knew that he was
holding back his three companions, who without him would have a better
chance of reaching the next depot, where they would find food. To give them
that chance, he walked out into a blizzard and was never seen again. The
news of the whole adventure, and in particular of the death of Oates, swept
over England in a wave of emotion. "A very gallant gentleman" was the
verdict pronounced on him and eventually inscribed on his memorial. I
remember being told about it as a small boy; I remember the words. That
was how a gentleman should behave.

The Commandant of the Maharaja's troops, Kashmir, 1880. This officer may stand for hundreds of others who all over the world commanded local troops with whom they often romantically identified themselves, and in whom they inspired devoted fidelity.

The name, the ideal, spread over all the world. For more than a hundred years, the English gentleman had presented the world with a picture that was admired and respected even when it was envied or disliked. At the worst hour of British fortunes in India, after the disastrous retreat from Kabul of 1844, a scribbled promise to pay, with the signature of a British officer who lay, dirty and infested with lice, in an Afghan jail, was good for cash in silver in the bazaar. In the Spanish-speaking countries of the New World, not only did *hora ingles* mean "punctual", but *palabra ingles* meant "true".

ABOVE "Our Joint Magistrate." A print by Captain Atkinson from a book of pictures and sketches, *Curry and Rice*. This young man, selected by family influence for the Honourable East India Company's Civil Service and trained at Haileybury, does not seem to have met with the approval of the artist! Note the hunting crop, the dog, the cigar – a sporting character.

BELOW "Our Pack of Hounds." Wherever the English went they tried, as well as they could, to imitate the life of a country gentleman in England. Here we have the station "bobbery pack", consisting of every kind of dog owned by anyone who would lend it. Another print from *Curry and Rice*, first published in 1854.

In the 1920s, a friend of mine who looked very much as a Frenchman would wish a British officer to look, was passing through Paris and, being out of change, was less generous than was expected to a railway porter. The porter spat out at him a fusillade of filthy argot which no foreigner could be expected to understand. But my friend had just finished a course with the French army and had learned some barrack-room French; he replied in kind. The porter reeled. "Vous portez un monocle mais vous n'êtes pas gentleman!" he gasped.

The tradition spread to India, to Africa, to the South China Seas. A man who in Plato's phrase was both high-spirited and philosophical, or in other words had survived an English schooling and had avoided disgrace at a university, might find himself at the age of thirty in charge of a million people or an area of five thousand square miles, where he administered justice, kept the peace, and in general played the squire, exercising – ideally – the virtues proper to a ruler, courage, justice and mercy, listening to every petitioner, standing up for his people against higher authority, chastising and rewarding like a father, addressed as "father and mother" – and sometimes deserving the title. Of course, the district officer might be idle or cynical or simply unimaginative and unsympathetic, but there were enough who approached the ideal to make it what people expected.

At the beginning of this century, one-fifth of the inhabitants of the globe were British subjects, while the Royal Navy policed the seas of the world. Throughout this vast empire, the rulers, everywhere a tiny minority among the ruled, were men who modelled themselves on the tradition of the English gentleman. There is a compliment, often quoted but it cannot be escaped, paid to this imperial class from an unlikely source, an American philosopher of Spanish origin: "Never since the heroic days of Greece has the world had such a sweet, just, boyish master," wrote George Santayana. And it was because there was some truth in that sentence that so little force was necessary to keep the peace over so wide an area and that the rulers and the ruled so often had respect for each other.

During the Second World War, Pandit Jawaharlal Nehru was held in custody because his activities were obstructing the war with Japan. But his wife was seriously ill and it was decided that he should be released temporarily in order to see her. The District Magistrate of Allahabad was instructed by the government to meet him at the railway station, where he would arrive under police escort; he was to release him, first however obtaining his written undertaking to make no public speeches while he was at liberty. The District Magistrate, a friend of mine, explained this to Pandit Nehru as sympathetically as he could – but he was offended. Although he had had no intention of making speeches it grated on his feelings to give a written undertaking. But if he didn't mean to make any speeches, did it really matter? Yes, it did; at such a time, it was an unfeeling gesture. My

British Columbia: a couple at the dining-table in the 1890s. British Columbia was one of the most uncompromisingly British of the Queen's possessions beyond the seas. The lady is perhaps thinking of home. But it is going rather far to allow a dog on the dining-room table!

friend had his instructions and no authority to vary them; it was the middle of the night. To and fro they paced on the station platform, arguing about it, but Pandit-ji would not yield. Suddenly my friend had an inspiration. "What about a gentleman's agreement between you and me?" "Yes, of course!" At once, all was smiles and handshakes; he was released and the government accepted the modification of their orders.

Nor is the word forgotten. Another friend of mine, Minoo Masani, was before the independence of India a member of the Indian National Congress; he and I used to glower at each other from opposite benches in the Legislative Assembly, but made friends over cups of coffee when the debates were over. He was usually sharply critical of the Viceroy's government. But after independence he found himself increasingly in disagreement with the new rulers of India. Eventually, he left the Congress Party and went into open opposition. He was by profession an adviser to one of the largest businesses in India; after a time, his employers told him that he must either leave the firm or give up criticizing the government. "But I used to oppose the British and you raised no objection." "Ah, but *they* were gentlemen. These people are politicians."

It was not only the Indian Civil Service but its indirect posterity, the Sudan Civil Service and the Colonial Service, which were built on the fundamental concept of men picked for skill in what Plato called the philosophical

ABOVE A British officer in India in 1870. The British, like other ruling races, felt the need for an imperturbable formality in the presence of those they ruled. This man is having his socks rolled on – a custom still known among the older civil officers even in the 1920s. Or perhaps his attendant is cracking the joints of his toes, the final rite of massage which every bearer understood.

BELOW The Governor with his wife and daughter, Private Secretary and ADC in one of many hundreds of British possessions scattered over half the globe. Perhaps the Governor was picked for his brains and the ADC for his good looks!

ABOVE Major Lewin with some Kuki chiefs. The Kuki, with the Chins and the Lushai, are a group of tribes on the north-east borders of India, between Burma and Assam. British officers usually liked them and went among them with just the serene confidence Major Lewin shows – but did not try to change their habits so long as they kept the peace. They were faithful in support of the British during the Japanese invasion.

BELOW Perhaps the subalterns of the battalion, carefully informal with their beloved dogs, and the one "spin" of the station, out for the cold weather to stay with her married sister, in formal riding clothes, gazing remotely into the distance from her pedestal.

Big game in Somaliland, 1890. The spirit
of the troubadours sent lonely men to
the ends of the earth to prove their worth
by planting the flag or shooting elephants.
Hard on the elephants, of course.

and high-spirited principles – although the two younger services put less
emphasis on the philosophical. All three embodied the idea of disinterested
rule as guardians on behalf of those ruled. They expressed the ideal in a
purer form than the squires had done, because the squires drew their rents
direct from their farms. But it was the squires who had worked out – except
as regards poachers – the ideal of "the forbearing use of power", which
according to Samuel Smiles "is one of the surest attributes of the true
gentleman".

The idea of the gentleman had spread to America too. In Virginia, in the
17th century, as in Kenya in the 20th, there were men who tried to create in
an alien land the life of an English squire, with his wide acres of grass, his
woods and fields and streams. Like the English squire, the Virginian admired
a country life, days spent with horses and hounds, with gun and rod – and,
as in England, there should be a library in the great house. Like the English
squire, the Virginian admired courage, courtesy and justice. He had a pic-

Even the most aloof of empire-builders must relax sometimes! Here, under a baobab tree outside the club at Belgaum, not far from Goa, there is little to disturb the bearded hero. Chairs with foot-rests like this were common in India, and were usually furnished with a convenient attachment near the right hand for a tumbler.

ture of the conduct proper to a gentleman that was at first just like the Englishman's. But it was inevitable that differences should develop. In the American South, men had to rely on themselves, rather than on the King's officers, to execute justice. It became a point of honour to avenge a death and the blood feud became an institution, something quite alien to English soil.[38]

That was one difference. Again, the memory of the Red Indian lived on in the names of every creek and mountain; he haunted the countryside. There were black slaves not only in the fields but in the house, waiting at table, cleaning and ironing and cooking; there were poor whites too. Altogether the Virginian had to consider a more diversified society than the English and he was bound to look on the world in ways that insensibly grew apart from the English squire's.

Meanwhile, in New England, another kind of gentleman was developing, just as in England there were gentlemen in the Inns of Court who never saw horse or hound. When the first thirteen states agreed to the Declaration of

Independence, ideals were proclaimed that were in conflict with the un-spoken assumptions of English society and also of Virginian, both of which accepted stratification and hierarchy. It was inevitable, then, that in spite of a common language and a common basis of law, the concept of the gentleman should diverge from the English. And since in the United States it developed in opposition to the declared principles of the Constitution, it has, to an English observer, the air of an exotic growth, not quite in its native soil. The concept constantly reappears in American life and letters but with a subtlety that a foreigner would be bold to feel he altogether understood. Yet among readers of *The New Yorker*, in such a club as the Century, one can sense something of the tradition of the gentleman quite distinct from the Virginian pattern, as well as from the English.

Before withdrawing on tip-toe from the presence of so arcane a mystery, I cannot resist one American quotation:

To ignore, to disdain, to overlook, are the essence of a gentleman. . . . Often most provokingly so, for the things ignored may be of the deepest moral consequence. But in the very midst of our indignation with the gentleman, we have a consciousness that his preposterous inertia and negativeness in the actual emergency is somehow or other allied with his general superiority. It is not only that the gentleman ignores considerations relative to conduct, sordid suspicions, fears and calculations, which the vulgarian is fated to entertain; it is that he is silent when the vulgarian talks; that he gives nothing but results when the vulgarian is profuse of reasons; that he does not explain or apologise; that he uses one sentence instead of twenty; and that, in a word, there is an amount of interstitial thinking, so to call it, which it is quite impossible to get him to perform, but which is nearly all that the vulgarian performs at all. All this suppression of the secondary leaves the mind clear for higher flights if they should choose to come. But even if they never came, what thoughts there were would still manifest the aristocratic type and wear the well-bred form.[39]

So strong is the family resemblance in style and thinking between the novelist and the psychologist that you would hardly guess that this was by William James, not Henry. How beguiling on the lips of either is the phrase "in a word" to introduce a complicated thought! Neither brother can be called representative of the United States, but that note of exasperation surely confirms the view that in American soil the gentleman is an exotic if sometimes a cherished growth.

18
A HIGH IDEAL

Coarseness and Sensitivity

LOOK UP THE WORD "gentleman" in the Shorter Oxford Dictionary and you will find the original meaning of a man entitled to bear arms, some later variants of social usage, and also "a man of chivalrous instincts and fine feelings", with an example of this use in Middle English. It is with this that we have been mainly concerned – but there are several subdivisions of this meaning too. There was a broad difference between the kind of gentleman Arnold tried to make – who was a ruler – and the kind envisaged by Newman – who might be a recluse in a library. Fortunately, each ideal had some influence on the other, but they were distinct.

Let us look back over the journey we have come. We have seen the kind of gentleman admired by Castiglione and Chesterfield, whose aim was to be pleasing to his equals. But this model fell short of Chaucer's, which included courtesy to the weak. Jane Austen's gentlemen, like Castiglione's, must have elegance and good taste, but she lays more emphasis than Castiglione on modesty and reserve, and adds something peculiarly English, a solidity or staying-power, which Mr Knightley has and the flashy young Willoughbys and Frank Churchills have not. Surtees adds a hatred of pretence. Thackeray's best gentlemen, Dobbin and Newcome, both incidentally the sons of merchants, return to the Chaucerian ideal of kindness to the weak. Dickens, to whom wealth and position are almost always corrupting, pays an unwilling tribute to the magnanimity of Sir Lester Dedlock and the integrity of Mr Twemlow, but does not add to the concept. It is with Trollope that the idea of essential integrity becomes central. And it is in Trollope that we perceive that there is a split in the Victorian ideal, between Newman's version and Arnold's.

I cannot agree with Trollope's view that Plantagenet Palliser was his finest gentleman. Plantagenet had no lightness of touch; he was sometimes a prig; he did not put other people at their ease. Several other candidates occur to me. There is Mr Septimus Harding, the Warden, saintly, scholarly, gentle and unworldly, yet in the last resort unflinching in his renunciation of his post as Warden, even in the teeth of his formidable son-in-law the Arch-deacon. There is the very different figure of Frank Gresham, no saint certainly, not even a major figure in Trollope's world, but a young squire, a ruler of men, with the solid qualities of his kind, with constancy and courage and integrity. Or one might take Dr Thorne, who is quite undisturbed by the contrast between his humble profession and his ancient family – or the eccentric Earl de Guest, who is so complete in himself that it never occurs to him to consider how he appears to anyone else. There is surely a fundamental difference between such gentlemen as these, men of integrity who live *in* the world, and such unworldly figures as Mr Harding and Mr Crawley, the perpetual curate of Hogglestock.

Mr Harding was a gentleman in Newman's sense. When he died, all Barchester mourned; "that city never knew a sweeter gentleman or a better Christian." And yet – trying to picture the ideal – does not some degree of leadership, of responsibility for others, enter in? That is the Arnold version. There is the officer to be taken into account as well as the scholar and the Christian. A soldier is not made a gentleman by fighting; an officer is made a gentleman by his duty to put the safety and comfort of the men under his command before his own. And surely it is not learning, but some element of responsibility for disinterested decision, that ennobles, or ought to ennoble, the men who follow "learned professions".

Newman had pictured a gentleman who was not a Christian but a man of taste and learning, considerate for others and seeking always to make others feel at home. Newman's theology was clear; he knew what he meant by a Christian. He meant a man who believed that the Word of God became flesh and lived among men. He thought a man could be a gentleman without that belief. But many Victorian Englishmen, indeed most, were much less clear what Christianity meant and believed rather vaguely that its main message lay in ethical standards, which no one could quite live up to. They were often inclined to talk and write as though to be a gentleman and to be a Christian were the same thing.

This confusion becomes marked in an anthology of definitions, comments and quotations by the Rev Dr Smythe-Palmer, called *The Ideal of a Gentleman*, and published in 1892.[40] In the early pages, self-sufficiency and integrity are the hall-mark of the gentleman; Palmer quotes in his introduction, and again in his text, the saying of John Locke that the gentleman does not think meanly of himself, nor does he think meanly of others. But as the book develops the identification of the gentleman and the Christian grows closer, until a few pages before the end we find this:

The man or woman nurtured, trained on the teaching of the New Testament alone, shall be at a loss in no good society. . . . The lowest saint, the humblest follower of Jesus, shall shine in the highest human society that this or any other land can produce.

And again:

Lord Baddlesmere walked slowly up to Tom and laid his hand on his shoulder.
"There was never but one *perfect* gentleman since the world began," he said
solemnly "and He was the Son of God."

Both these quotations come from forgotten novels of the late 19th century.
Both forget that the word has some social connotation and both ignore a
distinction made by Johnson a century earlier:

BOSWELL: A man may debauch his friend's wife very genteelly; he may cheat at
          cards genteelly.
HICKEY: I do not think *that* is genteel.
BOSWELL: Sir, it may not be like a gentleman but it may be genteel.
JOHNSON: You are meaning two different things. One means exterior grace; the
          other honour.[41]

R. L. Stevenson has made Boswell's point in *The Master of Ballantrae*, when
(as Chesterton put it) he "proved with a pen of steel that the Devil is a
gentleman but is nonetheless the Devil". The Master of Ballantrae had
exterior grace, he had unfailing elegance, but he was cruel and quite without
scruple. Chesterton – whom no one would call elegant – called him a gentleman, although neither Newman nor Arnold would have agreed. But Newman was right to distinguish the gentleman from the Christian, and Arnold
added to the concept something vital. After Arnold, the word is most often
taken to mean not only some degree of exterior grace, not only some degree
of honour in the world's eyes, integrity in one's own and consideration for
others, but also some element of leadership, of responsibility for others, even
if it takes only the form of vicarious advice..

To be a gentleman was a sub-Christian cult, that is to say, a code of conduct
and behaviour derived from the ethics, not from the theology, of Christianity.
But it was a code without a theology and a code can never rise to the height
of a religion. A religion, above all Christianity, is concerned with the individual soul, not with classes and kinds of people. It was that *one* woman
taken in adultery who was forgiven. It was that *one* spendthrift son whose
father put a ring on his finger, not all spendthrifts; some of them are to be
found in the third circle of Dante's hell. A code must be applied fairly, to
everyone whose act falls within a certain definition, and its justice must
sometimes be harsh to the individual. There has to be a certain coarseness
about its operation, and justice inevitably coarsens a little the man who
judges as well as the man who is judged.

The truest of all Christians, the little poor man of Assisi, had no second
coat and nowhere to lay his head; he was a pilgrim and a stranger on earth
and it was nothing to him that his behaviour, if everyone adopted it, would
make civil society impossible. The gentleman, on the other hand – the kind
of gentleman Arnold tried to make – lives in the world and has a part to play

General Sir Albert Williams and the Hon William Lambton, at Sandown Park Races in 1910. After the Kaiser's War, the confident sense of god-given superiority felt by men like these began to evaporate.

in society; indeed, he has usually to exercise some degree of rule over others, distinguishing one line of action from another, perhaps prescribing a course of medical treatment, promoting one man and passing another by. All decisions demand a certain coarseness, a certain toughness. After weighing the possibilities, one line of action, for which there may be something to be said, must be rejected, in favour of another, for which there is more.

In England, and indeed in many societies which have developed a specialised ruling class, there has been a system of training which was meant to instil this element of toughness. Those with whom the treatment was successful acquired a varnish, a crust, apparently impassive, a firmness in holding to the action decided upon, beneath which an inner sensitivity might be preserved. But there were casualties; some rebelled against the system, some were coarsened and became set in ways that made them progressively coarser; some, on the other hand, were too fine.

Ashley

EVERYONE will remember some casualties. For myself I recall one in particular, a man sensitive, imaginative and modest, too modest to question the assumptions of the society and family into which he was born, but betrayed in the end by those very assumptions. No life can ever be said to be wasted but in his life there was waste and unhappiness, just because he was so entirely a gentleman in the sense of being considerate to others and because he lacked that edge of hardness and decision, that realistic vision of himself, that might have enabled him to cut out a new career when it became clear that being a gentleman was not enough. I shall call him Ashley, although that was not his name.

Ashley came of a family with a strong naval tradition. "Three admirals in a row!" he used to say. But the row ended in the third generation with Ashley's grandfather. His father could not get into the Navy because of his eyesight, went to Coopers' Hill and spent his life building roads and bridges in Madras. Ashley was born in the 1880s in Madras, where his mother died in his infancy. He was sent to England, where he was brought up by unmarried aunts in the house of his grandfather, "the old admiral". The old admiral was a remote figure, the aunts indulgent. There was a pony, there was a gamekeeper. There were woods round Petersfield, there were chalk streams with trout; Hampshire was still a rural county. It was a happy childhood, with trees to climb, thrushes' nests to find, things to discover about crops and thatching, hedging and the use of a bill-hook and setting snares.

But of course the system decreed the preparatory school and the beginning of that process of toughening and smoothing that would fix a mask on the face. Twice he ran away from school, to be discovered in a gipsy camp eating a gipsy meal. To him the gipsies seemed to enjoy a more reasonable kind of life than his own, but he had to go back to the class-room and the football field, to blackboard and Latin grammar. He went up for Osborne and the Royal Navy, but like his father was failed for eyesight. Everyone then took it for granted that he would go into the army and he went to Wellington. By now, he was sufficiently hardened to get by without much persecution; his eyes made ball-games difficult but he was big and strong and neat with his hands in everything he did. He was modest by nature and did not think highly of his achievements at school, and indeed they were moderate; he got by. He kept quiet about his holiday skills. There was no need for anyone to kick the side out of young Ashley. He did not run away from Wellington. He was not an active rebel but he did prefer to be left alone.

His father died in Madras while Ashley was still at school and by the time he came to leave he knew that he had a private income sufficient for him to live comfortably in the mess of a good infantry regiment. The old admiral had died too, and the aunts had never been a powerful force. Suddenly he realized that he was his own master; there was no need to spend the rest of his life under discipline. Once again he displayed the initiative that had led to his escapade with the gipsies.

Instead of becoming a regular he joined the Regular Army Reserve, which meant that he must spend two months or so with his regiment every year, most of it in camp, leaving him at least nine months of every year enjoying himself on leave. He acquired a ten-ton yawl, not very fast or very smart, but a good seaworthy boat that he could sail by himself if need be. He looked after her himself; he was an excellent carpenter. Mooring fees were nothing in those Edwardian days, and it made a pleasant way of life for the early summer to potter round the Solent, usually with a friend, in and out of Wootton Creek and Yarmouth and the Beaulieu River. Then there would be camp with his regiment, and after that he would move into his winter quarters in a farmhouse on the borders of Devon and Somerset.

There he would have a bedroom and a sitting-room and stabling for two horses with quarters for a groom. He was clever at finding a hunter with some known defect so that he could get it cheap. One was blind in one eye – and that, he used to say, was splendid as long as you remembered that you had to do all the looking on the near side for both horse and rider. They were not horses for a fast day with the Quorn or the Pytcheley but in Poor Man's Country, as he called it, they were good for two days hunting a week. Sometimes he would be up before dawn to wait in a hide for wild duck or geese; sometimes he would have a day walking after snipe. He learned a great deal about the habits of pike and how a monster could be lured out of his dark hiding place and brought to the farmhouse table. In the spring, his delicate little trout-rod would come out, his line and casts and flies would be checked, and there would be days after the brown trout that dart so quickly in the broken waters of moorland streams. Or there might be an evening in the estuary when the sea-trout were running and the light fading from a clear sky. He made all kinds of friends, from all levels of society, from the Deputy Lieutenant of the county to the earth stopper; he knew the huntsman and the gamekeeper; he listened well and stored away in his mind a great deal of knowledge about the habits of red deer, fox, otter and badger. He began to write articles and stories about Poor Man's Country for *The Field* and *Country Life*.

Ashley was shy with ladies but one day, riding back from hunting, he found himself talking about the kind of life he lived to someone whose enthusiasms were strangely like his own. The friendship developed quickly – but before they could be married the system from which he had run away to the gipsies closed in on him, in the form of her father's lawyers. There must be a marriage settlement – the future must be neatly tied up in parcels. One of the parcels was a trust for the children's education. When the tying-up was finished, there was not so much to live on as had been expected. But no one suggested any serious change in Ashley's kind of life; the reign of George V was just beginning and it was still quite usual for a young man to have no profession. Ashley and his bride settled in a cottage on the Dart and continued to live a country life.

The War of 1914 came and Ashley's regiment was soon in France. He led his men into action with the bayonet. "Come on, you buggers," he said. And they followed him cheering. That was at the Marne, before the deadly horror of trench warfare had settled down to its long stalemate. Men still cheered. He did not often talk about the war afterwards but when he did speak an impression somehow seeped through of an element of release; there was the clear call to duty; there were no doubts or uncertainties. It was satisfying to command a company, to know every man in it and to know just what everyone had to do within that one clear limited field of active service. The men liked him.

It did not last long. He was gassed in one of the earliest attacks with gas, and after that he was not again passed fit for front line duties. He ended the war as a Group-Captain in command of a training camp where newly-joined Air Force cadets did their basic training. He was offered a regular commission, dropping two ranks to Major, but refused. He still wanted independence.

Of course you will have guessed. His capital had shrunk and what was left he put into a farm, a smallish farm with a lot of rough land, where at least a self-sufficient country life was possible. But he had bad luck; a circular saw whipped a big log off the trestles and it hit him in the chest, crushing the rib cage and doing further damage to those damaged lungs. He was eighteen months on his back and he had to sell the farm and everything on it at heavy loss.

He wrote some children's books. Two of them at least were still in print forty years later but he had sold them outright for £25 each. He was desperately poor now and he had no profession. He sold his dinner-jacket – the last symbol of the conventions that had hemmed him in, like an avenue of sphinxes, solid as granite yet all fabulous monsters! He went the round from one employer to another, answering advertisements, offering his services. But he was rebuffed; ex-officers were two a penny and he had nothing to sell that anyone wanted. He lost confidence in himself. He told himself he was a failure. When at last he did find a job, it humiliated him. He had to visit farmers, men who were doing real work which he envied, and to report whether they were complying with regulations which to him as well as to them often seemed unnecessary and officious.

When I knew him he had retired from an occupation that in his own eyes had degraded him. He was a defeated man, living in a wooden cottage which he had built entirely with his own hands; a very big man, very gentle, as only a very big man can be, eagerly sensitive to what might hurt the feelings of anyone else, anxious to cause no trouble, not to be a bore, deeply considerate of others, still very knowledgeable about scythes and billhooks and the ways of badgers. But he was conscious of defeat. He had been too much of a gentleman to be a success. He had been incomprehensibly betrayed by the order in which he had been brought up.

End of an Epoch

ASHLEY was out-of-date. After the Kaiser's War, there were still gentlemen and the pattern of behaviour had not been lost altogether, but it was fashionable to refer to it with mockery. Evelyn Waugh set the tone in *Decline and Fall*, which was published in 1928. There he deployed the horrible Captain Grimes, constantly in trouble for offences that in those days were unmentionable, but always getting another job because he was a public-school man. More subtly destructive, there was Paul Pennyfeather. Offered a cheque for £20 to compensate him for the loss of his good name and his profession, Paul made up his mind to refuse it. Twenty pounds at the moment meant something:

"But," said Paul Pennyfeather, "there is my honour. For generations the British bourgeoisie have spoken of themselves as gentlemen, and by that they have meant, among other things, a self-respecting scorn of irregular perquisites. It is the quality that distinguishes the gentleman from both the artist and the aristocrat. Now I am a gentleman; I can't help it: it's born in me. I just can't take that money."

But he did. And that note of rather mannered farce with a sour sting in the tail seems an effective end to an epoch.

There was still, of course, *The Code of the Woosters*, Bertie and Jeeves, Blandings Castle and the Earl of Emsworth, but this was a convention. It was handled with superb comic skill, but no boy ever imagined himself behaving like Bertie Wooster; he was not a hero like Rudolf Rassendyll. The immense volume of P. G. Wodehouse's masterly compositions tells us only that the ideal of the gentleman was remembered with kindly tolerance – but as something funny.

The fact remained that there had been an ideal, an English standard of conduct, a pattern of perfection that was thought proper to a position of responsibility. And it was a standard distinguishable from the Christian, from the Greek and from the Roman, although derivative from all three, sometimes tending more to one and sometimes more to another. It was also to be distinguished from the European Castiglione model, to which Flaubert had added the footnote that privilege without responsibility means brutality.

The English ideal demanded a sensitivity to the feelings of others and yet – even in its finest form – a power of decision, a certain hardness of outer shell, that the Christian would prefer to be without. The gentleman had to live in a world that was often harsh, and he had often to administer justice. Until 1880, an officer in the army might have to order flogging; men were shot for cowardice in the 1914 war. At various points in history it had been found that a gentleman's conscience could stomach things quite indefensible – slavery, the duel, such punishments as transportation for poaching and hanging for petty theft. Even at the best, he must harden his heart to live in comfort with poverty at his door.

It might indeed be argued that the highest ideal of Christian conduct and the gentleman's were altogether opposed, since the Christian saint aimed at peeling away every attribute of his selfhood, while the gentleman's standard always included self-respect and some honour in the world's eyes. But in practice, once duelling went out of fashion, the opposition was not usually very sharp; most men compromised with both codes and never quite came up to either.

By the 20th century, there were still conventions that were not to be admired, together with some absurdities. A gentleman – at any rate in youth – had no qualms about running up long bills with his tailor or wine-merchant, while it was not really defensible, or even very funny, to steal policemen's helmets on the night of the university boat race. As to absurdities, they flourished luxuriantly, minutiae of distinction – secret signals that a man had worshipped at the right temple – evidence, surely, of an unconscious desire to build castles against the encroaching waves of equality. It was once an offence to button the lowest button of the waistcoat or to wear a fountain pen visibly in the outside pocket of a coat. "In my regiment, before the war, you weren't allowed to smoke a Virginian cigarette," someone told me – *lui, qui portait le monocle*. A rash of commemorative millinery had swept the country at the turn of the century – blazers, ties, cricket caps, mufflers, scarves, sweaters with coloured yokes and cuffs – all designed to show your school, your college, your regiment, to distinguish you from the common herd. But as it spread downwards, it generated its own antibody. Soon there were so many school ties that it became more distinguished not to wear one. In 1920, it was only little boys attending expensive prep schools who wore coloured cricket caps with a badge or monogram on the front. By 1950, every primary school in the country was wearing them, and the expensive prep schools wore plain tweed caps. But the aim was still to be distinct.

The cult was in decline. Nonetheless, there was a pattern, an ideal, which continued to operate fitfully, though broken perhaps more often than observed. In the 1960s, when an aged Prime Minister, whose government was tottering, tried to obtain a fresh lease of office by dismissing most of his senior colleagues, someone rather older than myself turned to me and said, in a voice that was puzzled and almost apologetic: "It doesn't seem quite the behaviour of a gentleman." And even more recently the same sentiment was expressed, rather unexpectedly, by Bernard Levin in the columns of *The Times* when a young man went as his father's guest to the dinner of a private club and reported to the press a speech made there in confidence.

Again, it happened quite lately that a friend of mine was escorting Mr Tony Benn to some appointment in connexion with the publication of a book. They hailed a taxi. The driver drew up, but when he recognized his fare he said sourly: "If I'd known who it was, I'd as soon have run you over as let you into my cab." Mr Benn pulled down the little seat in front, opened the communicating window and earnestly preached socialism to him all the way to their destination. Taxi drivers are usually sturdy individualists, and this man was unconvinced by the political gospel. But he was impressed at being treated as a human being whose opinion was important, and he said good-bye with the words: "I hate your principles, but I will say this for you, you are a gent!"

The pattern of behaviour proper for a gentleman was rooted in inequality. It implied differences of rank and fortune in society as well as differences of character and upbringing. It was therefore what today is called *élitist*, a word that is used, always with disapproval, for the exercise of choice, but only in certain fields. It is *élitist*, and therefore wrong, to choose the children who are best at their school work for a better kind of education, but there is nothing *élitist* about choosing those who are best at football for the club team. To me it still seems right, and indeed the essence of any civilized polity, that choice should constantly be exercised and that those who show the possibility of excellence in any skill should be given the opportunity to develop it. We live, no doubt, in an age of experiment and are in the process of evolving a new kind of society. So far however we have not yet seen a society of any size in which there is not inequality of some kind, of esteem, of comfort, or of power – and I am inclined to think it would be very dull if we did. In particular, there has so far always been inequality of power. There have always been rulers, people with more influence than most on the course of events, whether they are members of Parliament or shop-floor stewards, whether they exercise it by force, by persuasion or by manipulation of votes.

In the period which came to an end with World War I, it was more often than not the case that in England leaders were "gentlemen" in the English sense. Not necessarily born into the class, they did nonetheless admire the pattern of behaviour I have been trying to illustrate. They used power with some restraint, and as a rule with courtesy and with generosity. They thought of the public good with some degree of detachment. They admired courage and honesty and truthfulness. They might fall short of what they admired, but they would have been ashamed if it were known that they had betrayed a colleague or a subordinate or been openly discourteous to an inferior. For my part, since I must be ruled by someone, I had rather that it was by men who acknowledged such standards and who tried to rule themselves and others with dignity and good temper. And it was no bad thing that in the time of England's greatness her ruling class did aim at such a pattern.

19 Epilogue:
THE GENTLEMAN
TODAY

I HAVE ARGUED that it was fortunate for England, and indeed for a great part of the world, that during the period of England's pre-eminence in world affairs – between, say, the battles of Waterloo and of the Somme – the ruling class consisted of men whose ideal of conduct was embodied in the complex, and rather odd, notion of the gentleman. There was a good deal of confusion about it, because the same word was used for two quite different things, the standard of conduct demanded of a gentleman and his position in society; and there was uncertainty about how to define either. Cardinal Newman had a very different idea of what made a gentleman from Dr Arnold of Rugby, and the duke of Wellington would have agreed with neither, although the three would have been much more at one as to who was *not* a gentleman.

But in spite of this vagueness and confusion – and in fact to some extent *because* of this vagueness – it can hardly be disputed that the idea played an important part in English social life. No one wanted to be branded as "no gentleman"; a great many people hoped that they, or their sons, would be regarded as gentlemen.

Today that is no longer true. No one can say that in the 1980s the idea of the gentleman is a social force. But does it exist at all? Does it still influence behaviour, however marginally? It influenced the whole life of the man I have called Ashley. But he was an Edwardian and he died in the 1950s. Does it in any way influence his grandsons and their contemporaries? The remark of the taxi driver to Mr Tony Benn suggests that the concept is not altogether forgotten, and I have asked some questions of people I know. There is nothing "scientific" about my enquiry; it is not "weighted" for sex, age or social position. It is only an impression formed on the basis of several other impressions. The fact remains that everyone who has been asked attaches some meaning to the term – as Mr Benn's taxi driver did. And it is usually a favorable meaning.

One of the most significant answers was from Sarah, who is a typist, born

and brought up in the East End of London. Her boy-friend is a suède-head,
a sub-cult of skinhead; he is lavishly tattooed. She is about eighteen. She said
at once that she knew who was a gentleman; it was someone who was polite
to everyone, whether he was talking to someone rich and important or to
someone poor and humble. No, it made no difference whether *he* was rich or
who his parents were; it didn't matter how he talked or where he went to
school. It was simply a matter of being polite to everyone. In fact, her views
were very like those of the wife of Bath, or at any rate of the old woman in her
story, who insisted that anyone who was truly "gentil" must be courteous to
everyone and that it was not a matter of birth.

"That man is gentle who does gentle deeds," she said, and the man
who does not gentle deeds:

> He nis nat gentil, be he duke or erl
> For vileyn's sinful dedis make a cherl.

Sarah did not find it easy to put her thoughts in words, but she was
perfectly clear as to what she thought. And what she thought was supported
by most of those I talked to. The idea of the gentleman as a station in life is
almost dead. That, you will remember, was the sense in which Sir Walter
Elliott of *Persuasion* used the term. "You misled me by the term *gentleman*. I
though you were speaking of some man of property," he said.

I talked to Ashley's grandsons, both of whom agreed that, in Sir Walter
Elliott's sense, the idea was altogether obsolete. But as a standard of conduct,
yes, it survived, it meant something, although you didn't talk about it.
Sarah, they thought, was not far out, though it was more than superficial
politeness; it was a matter of being considerate and trying to enter into other
people's feelings. To be considerate to everyone, not to show off, not to draw
attention to oneself – all these they felt desirable. Both of them thought it
worth mentioning that not showing off was peculiarly English; it is not a
matter to which either the French or the Americans usually attach importance, and in other cultures folk heroes are seldom reticent about their
own achievements. Few Africans admire modesty, nor did Odysseus and
the heroes of Homer.

As I talked about this, I realized that I was trying to dig up something that
of its essence is unspoken. Neither of these men – aged now between thirty
and forty – would dream of saying to themselves, like the unfortunate Paul
Pennyfeather of *Decline and Fall*, "No, that is not the kind of thing I can do
and remain a gentleman". But there are lines of conduct both would auto-
matically reject, such as letting down a friend or failing to support an em-
ployee who had done the wrong thing in good faith. If asked why, they
would probably say that a decent chap just wouldn't do that sort of thing.

I think I know Ashley's grandsons fairly well, although a man of seventy-
five can never be sure how much he knows of anyone forty years younger,

and I have a strong impression that with both of them consideration for other people is something to which they attach high importance, something by which they would judge a new acquaintance, something in which failure would lower them in their own eyes. Perhaps they learned it from their mother, Ashley's daughter.

The wife of one of Ashley's grandsons thought about my question a good deal. She agreed on the whole with Sarah, but she went further; she herself had a very high ideal of the gentleman and knew very few men who quite reached it. Perfect courtesy to everyone came first, but in her view the gentleman never draws attention to himself. He has a quiet self-confidence that does not need to boast. She mentioned Chaucer's knight without any prompting. I asked her about that readiness to accept responsibility for others that I thought I had found in the Victorian gentleman – certainly in the army officer, the squire, the member of Parliament, but also in a different way in those who give disinterested professional advice, doctors, lawyers, clergymen. But while she agreed that her gentleman would not let down a subordinate, it was clear that taking responsibility for someone else was not central to her picture; indeed, to her the very idea of someone having *power* over someone else was distasteful.

She also mentioned a use of the term – chiefly among older people of the professional classes – to describe someone who is polite and considerate but whose station in life would certainly not have suggested the word to Sir Walter Elliott. The milkman or the housepainter or the gardener – "he really is so thoughtful and polite, so *nice*, if you understand me, in every way, that one can only be rather old-fashioned and say that he is a perfect gentleman!"

Another woman of that generation said that the treatment of women was an important part in her picture of a gentleman. A gentleman wouldn't let a girl down on a date, still less would he boast of his conquests. Yes, the idea did still mean something to her – though she believed society ought to be much more equal than it was – and she had, indeed, supported the idea of comprehensive schools until her eldest child was old enough to go to one.

Here there is a point of substance. You will recall that Sancho Panza had ideas about women very different from Don Quixote's, and there has always been a peasant view of women as a cook and a fieldhand as well as a bearer of children that is utterly remote from the troubadour's worship of a distant princess. Both ideas of course are displeasing to the militants of female liberation and both are on the way out. In the 1980s, so many women go out to work that the old tradition of the division of labour in the home is breaking down; there are men in all classes who do the washing up and women who paint ceilings. But I do not believe either tradition is quite dead; the peasant view lingers on in the working-class, and there are faint relics of the troubadours among the professionals. Change has been slower among manual workers and the habit of showing deference to a woman in small matters, such as opening doors and standing up when she enters a room, is rare in what are usually called working-class homes.

But few of those who still follow, however faintly, the troubadours are conscious of "trying to behave like a gentleman" – something which would have been said to many a boy before 1914 but not often today. I must however confess here that a man of, say, thirty-five said to me – with an air not so much wistful as sardonic – "At Charterhouse my housemaster said they could never make a gentleman of me".

I asked Susie what she thought about the idea of the gentleman. Susie is thirteen and at first could hardly believe that I could possibly have written a whole book on so boring a subject. But she agreed that it would mean something if she was told that of two men, similar in age and occupation and income, one was a gentleman and one wasn't. We agreed that they should both be doctors (because her father is a doctor) and she tried to picture them. She named the one who was not a gentleman Sidney; the other was, quite unaccountably, Christoff. At first, she took a view rather like Castiglione's of the difference between them. Sidney would plod through life in a dull, uninspired kind of way, while Christoff would have holidays abroad and look at pictures; he would go to concerts and perhaps play the cello. Would it make any difference to the way they treated their patients? Well, perhaps not as a rule, but there might be times when it would. Suppose that each of them had asked his wife out to lunch at a restaurant and that each found his patients needed more time than he had expected; Christoff would ring up his wife and say he was going to be late and give his patients the care they ought to get; Sidney would hurry over the patients to make his date. So to Susie responsibility for others was an important part of the idea.

It is hardly worth mentioning the widespread use of "gentleman" as a euphemism for "man", and the even stronger convention that "lady" should be used instead of "woman", part of the linguistic inflation which reduces the real value of words, and distasteful because it implies that there is something discreditable in just being a man or a woman. I notice that in universities, where on the whole words are treated with more respect than in the street, doors are labelled "Men" and "Women". In the House of Lords, on the other hand, they are labelled "Peers" and "Peeresses".

There is also a colloquial humorous use of the world. "I say, old man, I'm out of cash. Can you lend me a pound? Oh, thanks, you're a gent." This is half-humorous, because the favour is a trifling one. But in a matter of any consequence, the phrase "a decent chap" has taken the place of "gentleman". "Ought we to insist on that in writing?" "Oh, I don't think we need. Bloggins is a gentleman": that is what a character in Trollope might have said, but to-day it would be: "Oh, I don't think we need. Charles is a decent chap." The use of the first name is merely inflationary; everyone uses first names just as men and women kiss when they meet; it does not imply that the modern speaker knows Charles better than the Trollopian knew Bloggins. But the thought behind the phrase is identical; the "decent chap", like the "gentleman", is someone who has a standard of things done and things not done; he doesn't count the change or stand on the letter of the law. He will frankly acknowledge his error if he is in the wrong. And there is a freemasonry between those who wish to be regarded as decent chaps, just as there was between those who wished to be regarded as gentlemen.

The decent chap is very like the gentleman and the advantage of the phrase is that it doesn't imply that one social class has a monopoly of virtue. That fits Sarah's view that "gentleman" no longer implies social rank. But is that altogether true? A rich and powerful man need not be a gentleman nor is a gentleman always rich and powerful – indeed, he is very likely not to be. But does there not still linger some shadowy association between the two ideas, particularly perhaps among older people and particularly in the country? Or is it rather that there survives some consciousness of an order, independent of wealth, deriving from upbringing and behaviour, obsolescent no doubt but still entitled to respect?

Two friends of ours, not much younger than myself, employ someone who comes two mornings a week to help with the cleaning of the house. She also goes for two mornings to their neighbours, who are much richer. In conversation one morning, the cleaner referred to the rich couple by their first names, and said that she used those names in talking to them. "Of course I wouldn't do it to you," she said. "But, then, you're gentry and they're not."

I was surprised by this story, not so much by the difference in the cleaner's behaviour as by her frank recognition of the reason. How far there is still respect outside their own ranks for those who feel in their bones that they are still gentry is hard to judge. I have little doubt that it does still exist in varying degrees in the country and among older people, or that it is balanced in towns and among younger people by an eagerness to assert equality.

"Put me in a room with two men and I know who's the gentleman and who isn't," said a mother not long thirty. "But I can't define it or draw a line. It's background and upbringing, isn't it?" Much the same judgement is made unerringly by policemen, who are accurate social barometers, although today they know they must pretend they think all men equal.

There is also the undoubted fact that public schools continue and even grow, the fees being in all cases over £3,500 a year. Why do parents make such a sacrifice of immediate enjoyment? Is it entirely because they think their sons will get a better education than they would in the state system? Perhaps they will say so and think they are telling the whole truth. Or do they half consciously hope that the finished product will have acquired a quality which *they* cannot define, and which *he* will not dare to claim, but which they believe may nonetheless still be a passport to approbation and perhaps success?

Let me sum up. In the 19th century, the idea of the gentleman became almost a religion. This was because Christianity, when deprived of sacramental confession, and when literally interpreted, set a standard of conduct too high for anyone but St Francis of Assisi, while the behaviour proper for a gentleman could be managed more easily. The religion of the gentleman was derivative; it was a sub-Christian cult. Today, when the trend of opinion is anarchic, flowing strongly against formal institutions, formulated creeds, formal distinctions between people, Christianity is the creed of a minority only and the gentleman is hardly mentioned. But such moral force as remains in English society, all that holds it together, is still derived, directly or indirectly, from the central truths of Christianity. The sub-Christian cult survives too. In the strange hotch-potch of modern English behaviour, a practised and discriminating palate can still distinguish a flavour of "the gentleman", diffused through the whole, as the flavour of a few savoury morsels is diffused among all the ingredients of some long-simmering casserole. It is a subtle and unobtrusive flavour, apt to vanish when you concentrate on its analysis, and when what seems to be a true specimen appears, he frequently disguises himself as "a decent chap", one of whose distinguishing marks is that he must never say that he knows in his heart that he is a gentleman.

NOTES ON BOOKS

Writing this book has been an excuse for re-reading old favourites, most of which are pretty well known. No one wants a reading list of books such as *Pickwick Papers* and *Vanity Fair*. Nor is there any point in repeating in the notes the exact particulars of books easily obtained whose authors are given in the text. I have mentioned in the notes only some books which I read specifically for this purpose and which might be difficult to identify.

1 I shall not argue with anyone who finds the plot of *Middlemarch* melodramatic, too complicated and too full of coincidence. But in contrasts of character, in observation of social position, in understanding of jealousy and love and worldliness, it seems to me superb.

2 See W. Alison Phillips, "Gentleman", in *Encyclopaedia Britannica*, 11th edition (Cambridge, 1910–11).

3 I have relied heavily on C. S. Lewis, *The Allegory of Love: A Study in Medieval Tradition* (Oxford, 1936). See also Julian Pitt-Rivers, *The Fate of Shechem or The Politics of Sex* (Cambridge, 1977), and Stephen Runciman, *The Mediaeval Manichee* (Cambridge, 1947). I regard Runciman as relevant because I cannot think it is mere coincidence that the religion of courtly love should have arisen in the south of France at about the same time as the Albigensian heresy with its contempt for marriage. Runciman's is much the best book about the heresy, not excluding E. Le Roy Ladurie, *Montaillou* (London 1978), which is weak on theology.

4 Shelton's translation of *Don Quixote* into Elizabethan English seems just right.

5 Since this book is not meant for specialists but for the general reader, I do not often quote Chaucer in the original. For *The Canterbury Tales*, Nevill Coghill's "translation" is excellent. But it is, as he says, a free translation, aimed at giving the sense and spirit of the original to the modern reader without hindrance. It does not always quite serve my purpose. For example, Coghill points out that "gentil" does not mean gentle, and usually puts in its place some other word, which gives the meaning in that context. This is right for *his* purpose, but wrong for mine. I want to show what "gentil" *does* mean, so I have kept it, in quotation marks. For example, at the end of the Franklin's Tale, the magician says:

> But god forbedë, for his blisful might,
> But-if a clerk coude doon a gentil dedë
> As wel as any of yow, it is no dredë.

Coghill makes this:

> But God forbid in all his blissful might
> That men of learning should not come as near
> To nobleness as any, never fear.

This is readable and gives the sense, but I want to be nearer the original and keep the word "gentil". "It is no dredë" really means "There is no doubt". So I have written:

> And even a clerk can do a "gentil" deed
> As well as any of you, do me heed.

In *The Parliament of Fowls*, for which there is no Coghill, I have followed the same principle and made my rendering as literal as I can.

6 I have sometimes used a translation by Leonard Eckstein Opdycke (London, 1902), but also the Penguin edition.

7 E. Charnaillard, *Le Chevalier de Méré* (Niort, 1921).

8 Charles-Augustin Sainte-Beuve, *Portraits Littéraires*, III (Paris, 1862); Arthur Tilley, *From Montaigne to Molière* (London, 1908). I have been guided over this by my old friend K. H. Vignoles, to whom I owe many thanks.

9 I have used Dent's Everyman edition of the *Letters*, dated 1929. See also S. M. Brewer, *Design for a Gentleman* (London, 1963).

10 Sir John Vanbrugh, *The Relapse*.

11 Tobias Smollett, *Humphrey Clinker*.

12 To read the six canonical novels of Jane Austen in succession was something I had never done before; that and writing this chapter have been two great pleasures. If anyone wants to find out more about Miss Austen, there is *A Memoir of Jane Austen* by her nephew J. E. Austen-Leigh (London, 1886 – but first published in 1870). Mr Austen-Leigh had the distinction of being Vicar of Bray. More recently, there is David Cecil, *A Portrait of Jane Austen* (London, 1978). Lord David told me that he found Lady Catherine and Mr Collins the only characters in Miss Austen who were exaggerated. Well – yes! – but they are great fun! I am grateful to him for various points.

13 W. M. Thackeray, *The Four Georges* (a series of lectures delivered in 1855–6 and published in 1860).

14 *Sketches and Travels in London* (1869).

15 Raymond Carr, *English Foxhunting: A History* (London, 1976). See also note 17.

16 J. E. Eardley-Wilmot, *Reminiscences of the Late Thomas Assheton Smith : or The Pursuits of an English Country Gentleman* (London, 1960).

17 *Squire Osbaldeston: His Reminiscences* (London, 1926). Osbaldeston is pronounced with the accent on the third syllable to rhyme with Weston. There is an injustice to Osbaldeston in Raymond Carr's excellent book *English Foxhunting* referred to in note 15 above. Some time after Osbaldeston, there was a much inferior sporting character who also liked to be known as "the Squire". This bogus squire was guilty of a piece of foul riding on the racecourse at the expense of a professional jockey, which Carr by a slip has attributed to Osbaldeston, who in my view would never have done it.

18 *Lonsdale: The Authorised Life of Hugh Lowther, Fifth Earl of Lonsdale,* KG, GCVO, by Capt Lionel Dawson, RN (London, 1946). See also Douglas Sutherland, *The Yellow Earl* (London, 1965).

19 The best of Surtees are *Handley Cross, Mr Sponge's Sporting Tour, Mr Romford's Hounds, Ask Mamma, Plain or Ringlets.* Some other books for this chapter are F. J. Harvey-Darton, *From Surtees to Sassoon: Some English Contrasts 1838–1928* (London, 1931); *Hunting Reminiscences* by Nimrod (C. J. Apperley) (London, 1843), which is full of splendid characters; and E. W. Bovill, *The England of Nimrod and Surtees* (Oxford, 1959).

20 This chapter is all Thackeray. *Vanity Fair* is his masterpiece and most of what he has to say on my subject is to be found there, with some in *Pendennis* and *Esmond.* But there are many sidelights on Victorian life in *The Book of Snobs* and *Sketches and Travels in London.*

21 Dickens felt instinctive hostility to anyone who was bored or flippant and it was an affectation among many gentlemen to appear always bored. That is one reason why he is from the start a hostile witness. But his admissions in favour of the gentleman carry the more weight for that. I have concentrated on three who *are* gentlemen – far from perfect, but undeniably gentlemen – and at some length in order to make my point. But one could extend the list. Mr Toots, although far from bright, was a gentleman, and so was Cousin Feenix. They are unwilling tributes by a genius who represents Victorian England more completely than any other man.

There are endless books about Dickens and it is as well to know something about his life. Take your pick of the biographies. André Maurois gives a French view which makes a good introduction. For a sophisticated appreciation of how he looks to critics today, try *Dickens and the Twentieth Century*, a symposium edited by John Gross and Gabriel Pearson (London, 1962).

22 For my part, I do not want to read much about Trollope beyond his own *Autobiography.* But the novels are a lasting source of pleasure and the canonical twelve (six "Barchester" and six "political") should be read at least every ten years.

There is a distinguished article on "The Morality of the Gentleman" in the *Cambridge Review* (Part I 7 May 1976 and Part II 4 June 1976) by Shirley Letwin. Shirley Letwin, who is a philosopher, has constructed from the novels of Trollope a compact and closely reasoned theory of the gentleman's standards and behaviour (which she has since expanded into a book). But her examples are taken entirely from Trollope, with whom she agrees that Plantagenet Palliser is the perfect gentleman. I have argued in the text that he is not, and I feel that Mrs Letwin's construction is too narrowly based. Plato, Chaucer, Castiglione and native English opinion have to be brought into the concept, as well as the Stoic tradition.

23 More than one critic who saw an early draft of this book wanted me to include some comments on the Japanese *samurai.* But I know nothing of Japanese culture, and I think it would take a year's work to fit myself to write even half a page of useful comment on the *samurai.*

24 The books I have consulted include Lytton Strachey, *Eminent Victorians* (London, 1918); G. M. Young, *Victorian England: Portrait of an Age* (Oxford, 1936); Christopher Hollis, *Death of a Gentleman* (London, 1943); and Sir Walter Raleigh, *Laughter from a Cloud* (London, 1923), particularly the lecture "The Two Moralities", which discusses the question: How is it possible to be a Christian and a gentleman? Raleigh was Professor of English Literature at Oxford from 1904, and author of the well-known lines beginning: "I wish I loved the human race..." He does not bring his argument to a satisfactory conclusion. But Harold Nicolson has some comments. See note 40.

25 Shirley Letwin, in the essay referred to in note 22 above.

26 In *Barchester Towers*.

27 See pages 26–7.

28 See J. R. de S. Honey, *Tom Browne's Universe: The Development of the Victorian Public School* (London, 1977); and H. A. Vachell, *The Hill: A Romance of Friendship* (London, 1913 – but written in 1905). This is really the archetypal school story, although specifically Harrovian. See also Ian Hay, *The Lighter Side of School Life* (London, 1914); George Macdonald Fraser and others, *The World of the Public School* (London, 1977); Henry Hart of Sedbergh, *A Victorian Schoolmaster* (London, 1923); and L. E. Jones, *A Victorian Boyhood* (London, 1955).

29 The sonnet was quoted by Lytton Strachey of Cromer in *Eminent Victorians*.

30 Newman's *Apologia* is in paperback, published by Fontana. *The Idea of a University* was first published in 1852. I have quoted from the uniform edition of Longman, Green (1912), Discourse V on "Knowledge its own End" and Discourse VIII on "Knowledge and Religious Duty".

31 Jean-Pierre de Caussade.

32 From *Madame Bovary*, translated by Eleanor Marx-Aveling.

33 From *Tales of Unrest*, "The Return", first published in 1898.

34 G. M. Young, *op cit* (note 24).

35 Such as Donald Read, *Edwardian England* (London, 1972).

36 From *Heretics* (London, 1919).

37 Quoted in G. M. Young, *op cit*.

38 It was *Huckleberry Finn* that fixed in my mind for life a picture of the Southern gentleman as ceremonious in family life but merciless in the blood feud. Extensive reading of William Faulkner strengthened my feeling that he had become altogether different from the English variety, and I am grateful to Mrs Frances Lindley of Harper and Row, Publishers, for confirming that view.

39 Quoted by Sir Walter Raleigh, *op cit* (note 24).

40 A. Smythe-Palmer, DD, *The Ideal of a Gentleman: or A Mirror for Gentlefolk: A Portrayal in Literature from the Earliest Times* (London, 1908). See also Mark Bence-Jones, *The Aristocracy* (London, 1979); Christopher Hollis, *Death of a Gentleman* (London, 1943); Harold Nicolson, *Good Behaviour* (London, 1955); Richard Usborne, *Clubland Heroes* (London, 1953); and Simon Raven, *The English Gentleman* (London, 1961).

41 Boswell's *Life of Johnson*, volume II, page 340, 6 April 1775.

INDEX

Page numbers in italics refer to illustrations

Alken, Henry *31*
Alton Locke 185
Arcadia 57
Arnold, Thomas 162–6
  166, 173, 178, 195, 217,
  218, 219, 227
Asquith, Raymond *200*
Assheton Smith, Thomas
  83, 84–7, *156*
Astrophell 57
Austen, Jane 217
  Emma 74, 75–6, 77, 80
  Mansfield Park 70, 74, 76,
  80
  Northanger Abbey 79, 82
  Persuasion 74, 77, 78, 79,
  80, 108, 228
  Pride and Prejudice 71–4,
  75, 76, 79
  Sense and Sensibility 74, 75,
  77

Barchester Towers 134
Benn, Tony 225–6, 227
Bentinck, Lord George
  90–1
bienséances 62, 66, 187
birth, *see* degree
Blackmore, Richard
  Doddridge, *Lorna Doone*
  168
Blakeney, Sir Percy (*The
  Scarlet Pimpernel*) 11,
  203–4
Bleak House 120, 123–5
Blundell's School 168
Book of Snobs, The 107
Book of the Courtier, The
  50–6, 59, 61, 74
Boswell, James 69, 219
Bouchet, Elisabeth du 62
boxing 82, 96, *153*
Brooke, Mr (*Middlemarch*)
  15–16, 18, 19

Buchan, John 206
Bulstrode, Mr (*Middlemarch*)
  18–19
Burnaby, Frederick *158*
Byam Shaw, John *48*

Caldecott, Randolph *95*
Cambridge University 106,
  107, 162, 168
Can You Forgive Her? 135–6,
  137, 138, 139, 140–4
Canterbury Tales, The 34–5,
  37–49
Capellanus, Andreas, *De
  Arte Honeste Amandi* 28
Casaubon, Mr (*Middlemarch*)
  17–18
Castiglione, Baldesar 50,
  51, 60, 92
  The Book of the Courtier
  50–6, *51*, 59, 61, 74, 217
Cervantes, Miguel de, *Don
  Quixote* 29, *30–1*
Charles v, Emperor *25*
Charterhouse School 106,
  170, 230
Chaucer, Geoffrey 10, 12,
  26, 27, *45*, 50, 217, 228
  The Canterbury Tales 34–5,
  37–49
  The Legend of Good Women
  36
  The Parliament of Fowls
  35–6
  The Romaunt of the Rose 42
Chesterfield, Philip
  Stanhope, 4th earl of *46*,
  62–3, *65*, 77, 92, 145, 146,
  217
Chesterton, G. K. 14, 207,
  219
Chettam, Sir James
  (*Middlemarch*) 15–18, 19,
  27

Christianity 163, 181,
  218–19, 225, 232
  see also Protestant Church
Clovis, King *25*
Coghill, Nevill 36, 37
Confessio Amantis 40
Congreve, William, *The
  Way of the World* 68
Conrad, Joseph, *Lord Jim*
  189–95
Corinthians 81–105, *153–5*
courtesy 40, 55, 152, 228
courtiers 50–6, *53*
courtly love 27–33, 35, 36,
  42–3, 50, 78, 114–15,
  135–8, 145, 203–5
Crawley, Rawdon (*Vanity
  Fair*) *112*, 113–14
cricket 85, 105, *159*
Cruickshank, Mr 92
Cruickshank, George and
  Robert *153–5*

Dante Alighieri 27, 219
Darcy, Mr (*Pride and
  Prejudice*) 71–4
De Arte Honeste Amandi 28
Decline and Fall 224, 228
Dedlock, Sir Leicester (*Bleak
  House*) 123–5, *123*
Defense of Poesie, A 57
Defoe, Daniel, *Moll Flanders*
  69
degree 25–7, *25*, 35, 52, 59,
  69, 75
Description of England 26
Devereux, Robert, earl of
  Essex *58*
Devis, Arthur *66*
Dickens, Charles 119–30,
  217
  Bleak House 120, 123–5
  Great Expectations 120,
  122–3

Little Dorrit 120
Oliver Twist 120
Our Mutual Friend 120,
126–30
Pickwick Papers 82, 120–2
Disraeli, Benjamin 143
Dobbin, William (*Vanity
Fair*) *113*, 114, 118
Doctor Thorne 132, 133, 134,
137, 138, 162
Don Quixote 29, *30–1*, 206,
229
Doré, Gustave *31*
Dudley, Robert, earl of
Leicester *58*
Duke's Children, The 161
Dymoke, Sir Edward *43*

Eardley-Wilmot, Sir John
83
Edwardians, The 196–7
Eliot, George, *Middlemarch*
15–20
Elizabeth I 57, *58*
Elyot, Sir Thomas, *The
Governor* 50–2, *51*
Emma 74, 75–6, 77, 80
Empire, British 208–16
Erdeswyke, Robert 26
Eton College 84–5, 88, *159*,
169, *171*, *172*
Eustace Diamonds, The 137
Evan Harrington 155, 175–80

Faerie Queen, The 56–7
Ferneley, John *86*
feudalism 25, 26, 29
Fielding, Henry, *Tom Jones*
69
Finn, Phineas (*Phineas Finn*)
146–7, *146*
Flaubert, Gustave 189, 224
fox-hunting 83–8, 94, *95*,
99, 192, *199*, 209
Framley Parsonage 137

Galahad, Sir (*Morte
d'Arthur*) *41*
gentillesse 12, 27, 36–7, 49,
55, 61, 67, 71, 74, 77, 82,
127, 187
George, Prince Regent
81–2
Gonzaga, Elisabetta 52
Goosey, Thomas *86*

Governor, The 50–2, *51*
Gower, John, *Confessio
Amantis* 40
gravitas 22
Great Expectations 120,
122–3
Greeks, ancient 21–2
Gresham, Frank (*Doctor
Thorne*) 134, *138*, 218
Grey, John (*Can You Forgive
Her?*) 135–6

Haileybury College 168
Hamlet 59
Handley Cross 98–9
Harding, Septimus (*The
Warden*) 217–18
Hardy, Thomas 188
Harrington, Evan (*Evan
Harrington*) 177–80, *179*
Harrison, William,
Description of England 26,
106, 153, 161
Harrow School 106, 166–7
Hay, Ian, *A Knight on
Wheels* 204–5
Hill, The 166
honnêteté 61, 71
Hope, Anthony, *The Prisoner
of Zenda* 11, 32, 201–3
horse-racing 88, 90
Hughes, Thomas, *Tom
Brown's Schooldays* 163–6,
173–4, 185

Idea of a University, The 182,
185–6
Ideal of a Gentleman, The 218
intellectual attributes 21,
27, 53–4, 57, 77
see also musical ability,
scholarship

James, William 216
Johnson, Dr Samuel *46*, 64,
65, 146, 219

Keats, John 32
Kingsley, Charles 184–6,
186
Alton Locke 185
Kipling, Rudyard 188
Knight on Wheels, A 204–5

Lambton, Hon William *220*

Leconfield, Lord 83
Legend of Good Women, The 36
Levin, Bernard 225
Lewin, Major *213*
Lewis, Clive Staples 28, 29,
33
Lonsdale, Hugh Lowther,
5th earl of 10, 83, 93–8,
93, *97*, 201
Lord Jim 189–95
Loris, Guillaume de, *Roman
de la Rose* 42
Lowther, Hugh Cecil, *see*
Lonsdale, Hugh, 5th earl
of
Lorna Doone 168
Luttrell, Sir Geoffrey *32*

manners 61, 71, 77
Mansfield Park 70, 74, 76, 80
Margaret of Burgundy,
Queen of Navarre 29–32
Maria Martin 121
Marlborough School 167
martial arts 22, 25, 27, 52,
57, 144
Masani, Minoo 211
Master of Ballantrae, The 219
"matches" 88–9, 95, *156*
Maurois, André 119
melodrama 121
Melusina, Petronilla 62
Méré, Chevalier de 61–2,
65, 92
Meredith, George, *Evan
Harrington* 155, 175–80
Methuen, Paul 91
Meynell, Mr 84
Middlemarch 15–20
Midsummer Night's Dream, A
60
Moll Flanders 69
moral qualities 12–13, 19,
21, 37, 40, 52, 55, 64, 71,
86, 135, 144, 195
see also courtesy;
gentillesse; *gravitas*;
honnêteté; stoicism
Morshead, Sir Henry *68*
Mother Hubbard's Tale 57
*Mr Brown's Letters to His
Nephew* 108
Mr Romford's Hounds 83
Mr Sponge's Sporting Tour
99–103

Murder in the Red Barn, The
121
musical ability 54, 57, 144,
230
Musters, Jack 84–5

Nehru, Pandit Jawaharlal
210–11
New Yorker 216
Newcomes, The 106, 115–18
Newman, John Henry,
Cardinal 182–4, 217, 218,
219, 227
The Idea of a University
182, 183, 185–6
Nimrod (C. J. Apperley) 85
Northanger Abbey 79, 82

Oates, Capt. Lawrence
Edward *160*, 207
Orczy, Baroness Emma, *The
Scarlet Pimpernel* 11, 203
Osbaldeston, George 83,
87–92, *89*, *156*
Osborne, George (*Vanity
Fair*) *109*, 110–12, *111*
Our Mutual Friend 120,
126–30
Oxford Movement 148
Oxford University 88, 163,
168, *200*

Palliser, Plantagenet
(*Framley Parsonage*, etc.)
139–43, *141*, 217
Palmer, Lynwood *93*
Panza, Sancho (*Don
Quixote*) 29, 56, 229
Parliament of Fowls, The 35–6
Payne, George 91
Pendennis 115–18
Persuasion 74, 77, 78, 79, 80,
108, 228
Phineas Finn 146–7, 152
physical attributes 21, 52,
54, 169, 201
Pickwick Papers 82, 120–2
Plato 12, 21–2, *51*, 54, 56,
167, 169, 186
Pride and Prejudice 71–2, *75*,
76, 79
Prime Minister, The 133, 136,
139
Prisoner of Zenda, The 11, 32,
201–3, *202*

Protestantism 148, 181
see also Christianity
prudishness 145
public schools 13, *23*,
162–74, 231–2

Rambouillet, marquise de
61
Rassendyll, Rudolf (*The
Prisoner of Zenda*) 11,
32–3, 201–3, *202*, 224
Restoration comedy 68–9
Rivals, The 33
Robinson, W. Howard *97*
Roman de la Rose *42*
Romans 22, 170
Romford, Francis 104
Roumant of the Rose, The *42*
Rowlandson, Thomas *68*
Rugby School 162–6, 169
ruling class 171–3, 200–1
Russell, John *65*

Sackville-West, Victoria,
The Edwardians 196–7
Sainte-Beuve, Charles-
Augustin 60, 61
Salisbury, Moot of 26
Santayana, George 210
Scarlet Pimpernel, The 11, 203
scholarship 54, 64, 144
see also intellectual
attributes
Sedbergh School 168
Sense and Sensibility 74, *75*, 77
Shakespeare, William 32,
59–60, 174
Hamlet 59, 60
*A Midsummer Night's
Dream* 60
Shaw, George Bernard 188
Shaw, John Byam, *see*
Byam Shaw, John
Shepherd's Calendar, The 57
Sheridan, Richard Brinsley,
The Rivals 33
Shrewsbury, earl of 96
Sidney, Sir Philip 57–9, *58*,
144
Sitwell, Sir George 26
Small House at Allington, The
137, 140
Smith, Thomas Assheton, *see*
Assheton Smith, Thomas
Smythe-Palmer, Rev. Dr,

The Ideal of a Gentleman
218–19
snobs 9, 107–8
Spenser, Edmund, *Arcadia*
57
Astrophell 57
A Defense of Poesie 57
The Faerie Queen 56
Mother Hubbard's Tale 57
The Shepherd's Calendar 57
sportsmen 68, 81–105, 146,
153–6, *190*, 209
see also boxing;
Corinthians; cricket;
fox-hunting; horse-
racing; "matches"
Squire 67, 214
Stanhope, Philip 62–7, *65*
statesmanship 56, 170–3
Stevenson, Robert Louis,
The Master of Ballantrae
219
stoicism 147–8, 170
Stratford, Edward, 2nd earl
of Aldborough *46*
Sullivan, John L. 96
Surrey, Henry Howard, earl
of 32
Surtees, Robert Smith 82,
98, 217
Handley Cross 98–9
Mr Sponge's Sporting Tour
99–103

Tennyson, Alfred, 1st baron
32, *164*
Thackeray, William
Makepeace 81–2, 106,
217
The Book of Snobs 107
*Mr Brown's Letters to His
Nephew* 108
The Newcomes 106,
115–18
Pendennis 115
Vanity Fair 107, 108–14,
118
Tom Brown's Schooldays
163–6, *164–6*, 170, 173–4
Tom Jones 69
Trevelyan, G. M. 27
Trevelyan, G. O. 170
Trollope, Anthony 14,
131–43, 217–18
Barchester Towers 134

Can You Forgive Her?
135–6, 137, 138, 139,
140–4
Doctor Thorne 132, 133,
134, 137, 138, 162
The Duke's Children 161
The Eustace Diamonds 137
Framley Parsonage 137
Phineas Finn 146–7, 152
*The Small House at
Allington* 137, 140
The Prime Minister 133,
136, 139
The Warden 131
troubadours 27–32, 74
Twemlow, Mr (*Our Mutual
Friend*) 129–30

United Services College 168

United States of America
214–16
universities 182, 185–6
Urbino, Duke of
(Guidobaldo da
Montefeltro) 52

Vachell, H. A. *The Hill* 166
Vanity Fair 107, 108–14,
118

Waugh, Evelyn, *Decline and
Fall* 224, 228
Way of the World, The 68
Wellington College 167, 221
Wells, Herbert George 188
Westminster School 63–4
Weston, Mr (*Emma*) 95
Wilhelm II, Kaiser 94–5

William the Conqueror 25,
26
Williams, Gen. Sir Albert
220
Wimsey, Lord Peter
(Dorothy L. Sayers'
detective novels) 11, 206
Wodehouse, P. G. 224
women, attitudes to 17–18,
27, 28–33, *28*, 55–6, 67,
147, 152, 203
Wrayburn, Eugene (*Our
Mutual Friend*) 126–9,
126, 129
Wyatt, Sir Thomas 32

Yates, Dornford 206
Young, G. M., *Victorian
England* 185, 197